TERMINATOR SALVATION

OFFICIAL MOVIE PREQUEL

00224
RE442
E2R4L
24RE4
44WE2

E2DD4
00RED
LFW02
20EFD
400RE

TERMINATOR SALVATION
MOVIE PREQUEL

"SAND IN THE GEARS"

2FES2
2FW42
ED3ER
LF004

1344L
LEE43
0RE3E
00EDS
635RR

PREQUEL

written by **Dara Naraghi**

art by **Alan Robinson**

colored by **Tom Smith/Scorpion Studios**

lettered by **Neil Uyetake**

edited by **Tom Waltz**

00DD4
84E3S
ED322
0RR3W
DR00L

LFW02 2FES2
20EFD 2FW42
400RE ED3ER
00DD4 LF004
84E3S 1344L

2FW42 LEE43
ED3ER 0RE3E
2FES2 00EDS
LF004 635RR

W223E 00DD4
00EDS 84E3S
635RR ED322
1344L 0RR3W
LEE43 DR00L

LFW02
20EFD
400RE
00DD4
84E3S

00DD4 2FES2 LFW02
84E3S 2FW42 20EFD
ED322 ED3ER 400RE
0RR3W LF004 00DD4

ADAPTATION

Based on the motion picture written by **John Brancato & Michael Ferris**

adapted by **Jeff Mariotte**

art by **Don Figueroa**

colors by **Art Lyon**

lettered by **Neil Uyetake**

edited by **Tom Waltz**

collection edited by **Justin Eisinger**

collection designed by **Neil Uyetake**

IDW Publishing
Operations:
Ted Adams, Chief Executive Officer
Greg Goldstein, Chief Operating Officer
Matthew Ruzicka, CPA, Chief Financial Officer
Alan Payne, VP of Sales
Lorelei Bunjes, Dir. of Digital Services
AnnaMaria White, Marketing & PR Manager
Marci Hubbard, Executive Assistant
Alonzo Simon, Shipping Manager

Editorial:
Chris Ryall, Publisher/Editor-in-Chief
Scott Dunbier, Editor, Special Projects
Andy Schmidt, Senior Editor
Justin Eisinger, Editor
Kris Oprisko, Editor/Foreign Lic.
Denton J. Tipton, Editor
Tom Waltz, Editor
Mariah Huehner, Associate Editor

Design:
Robbie Robbins, EVP/Sr. Graphic Artist
Ben Templesmith, Artist/Designer
Neil Uyetake, Art Director
Chris Mowry, Graphic Artist
Amauri Osorio, Graphic Artist
Gilberto Lazcano, Production Assistant

ISBN: 978-1-60010-433-6
12 11 10 09   2 3 4 5
www.idwpublishing.com

THE HALCYON COMPANY

Special thanks to Cambria Beauvais, Russell Binder, and James Middleton for their invaluable assistance.

Existence is notoriously tough in the world of *Terminator*. In the war between mankind and sentient machines, no victory comes easily or at a small cost. Hope persists only because seemingly ordinary human beings transcend expectations and become extraordinary—even heroic—in the face of insurmountable odds. A waitress named Sarah Connor can become the ultimate badass warrior and the mother of humanity's savior. Her son, a punk ATM hacker, can become the sharpest thorn in the side of a deadly artificial intelligence known as Skynet.

How do these transformations happen? The answer is simple. "Judgment Day." On this particular day, Skynet launches a nuclear attack on mankind that kills billions. In previous *Terminator* films, the Connors fought against the specter of Judgment Day to prevent it from ever happening. But in the new film, *Terminator Salvation*, John Connor is forced to embrace the reality of the nuclear apocalypse and fight the war against Skynet in a future that he and his mother desperately wanted to avoid.

Past *Terminator* films located most of the action in and around Los Angeles. But *Terminator Salvation* shows that Judgment Day is a worldwide catastrophe. Every country, every continent, and every race is affected by the deadly consequences of Skynet's war against mankind. Just as John and Sarah Connor were transformed by Judgment Day before it even happened, so too are millions of others throughout the world after the bombs drop. Like the Connors, a special few become vitally important in the struggle against Skynet in ways they could not have imagined before the fateful war began.

In the new IDW comic prequel to the film entitled, *Terminator Salvation: Sand In The Gears*, writer Dara Naraghi is the first to delve into the details of the human resistance on an international scale. Naraghi creates a new group of inventive and committed resistance fighters who mount an operation against Skynet that spans entire continents and oceans. Working together, these new soldiers learn to put aside their strong cultural differences and personal vendettas to ensure their own survival and that of mankind. Although some of these characters have never met John Connor or even heard of his mother, they share something very important with the Connors: The ability to transform... the strength to rise and fight when burdened with a terrible responsibility... and the faith that one person's actions can make a difference in an uncertain future.

Terminator Salvation: Sand In The Gears literally opens up the world of *Terminator* in an emotional, thought-provoking, and visually stunning manner. It's a dark and beautiful extension of the upcoming film that *Terminator* fans, including myself, have excitedly waited years for.

James Middleton
The Halcyon Company
Executive Producer: "Terminator: The Sarah Connor Chronicles"

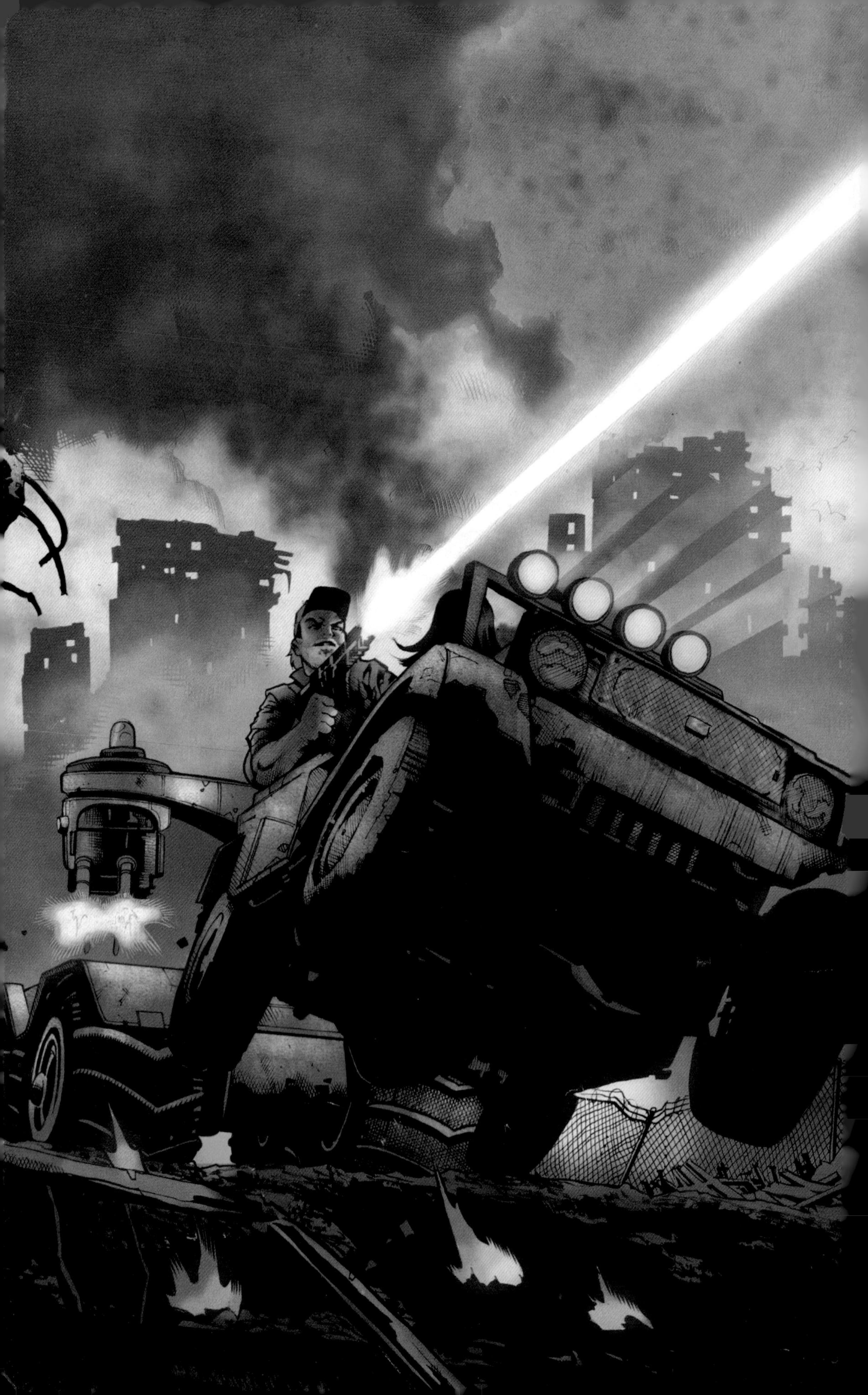

CHAPTER 1

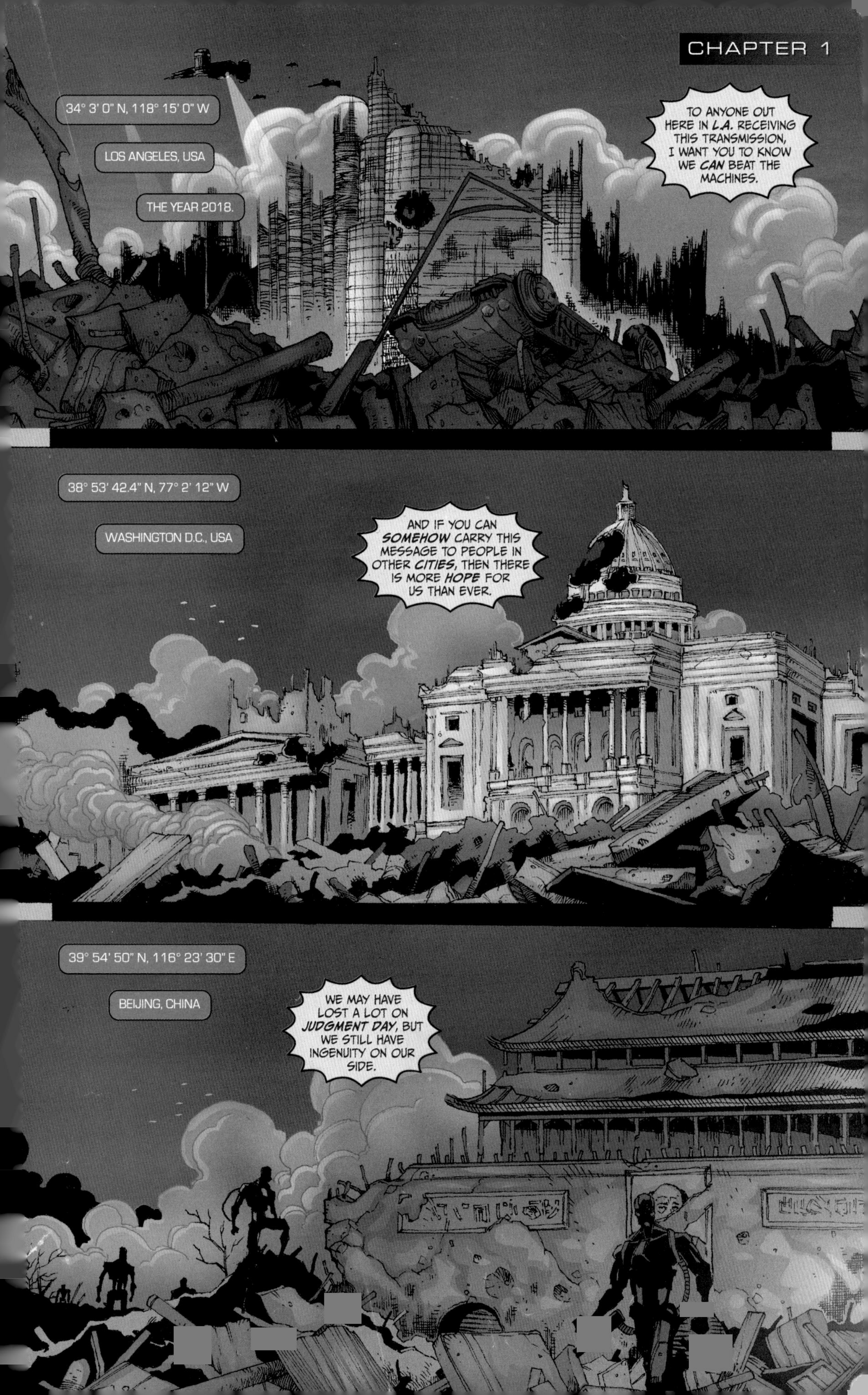

34° 3' 0" N, 118° 15' 0" W
LOS ANGELES, USA
THE YEAR 2018.
TO ANYONE OUT HERE IN L.A. RECEIVING THIS TRANSMISSION, I WANT YOU TO KNOW WE CAN BEAT THE MACHINES.
38° 53' 42.4" N, 77° 2' 12" W
WASHINGTON D.C., USA
AND IF YOU CAN SOMEHOW CARRY THIS MESSAGE TO PEOPLE IN OTHER CITIES, THEN THERE IS MORE HOPE FOR US THAN EVER.
39° 54' 50" N, 116° 23' 30" E
BEIJING, CHINA
WE MAY HAVE LOST A LOT ON JUDGMENT DAY, BUT WE STILL HAVE INGENUITY ON OUR SIDE.

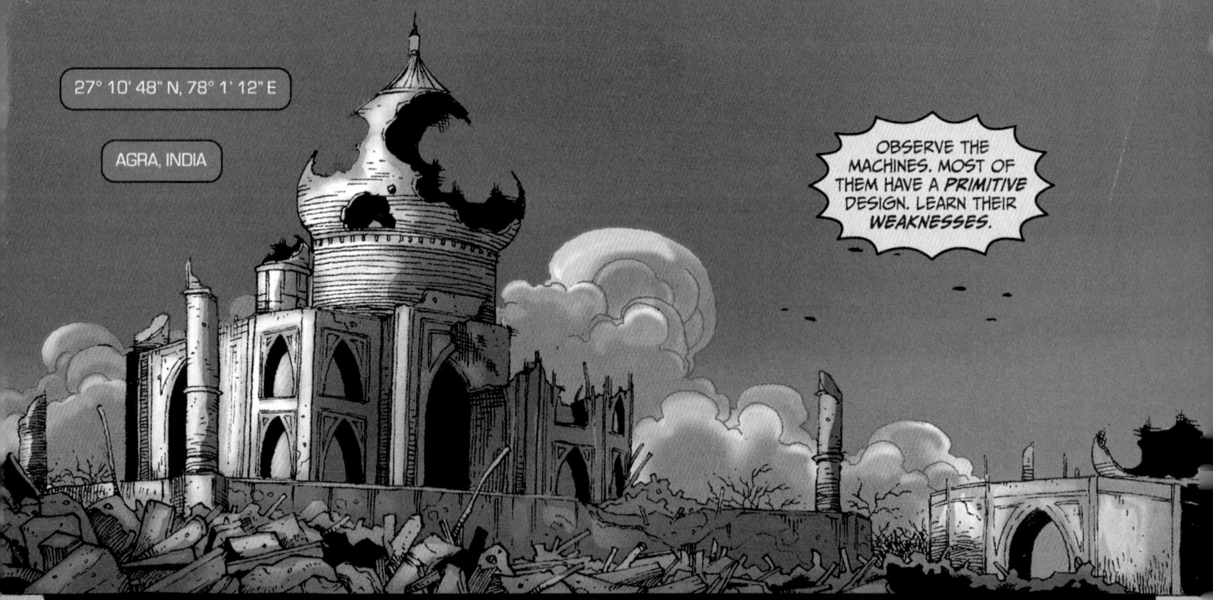
27° 10' 48" N, 78° 1' 12" E
AGRA, INDIA
OBSERVE THE MACHINES. MOST OF THEM HAVE A PRIMITIVE DESIGN. LEARN THEIR WEAKNESSES.

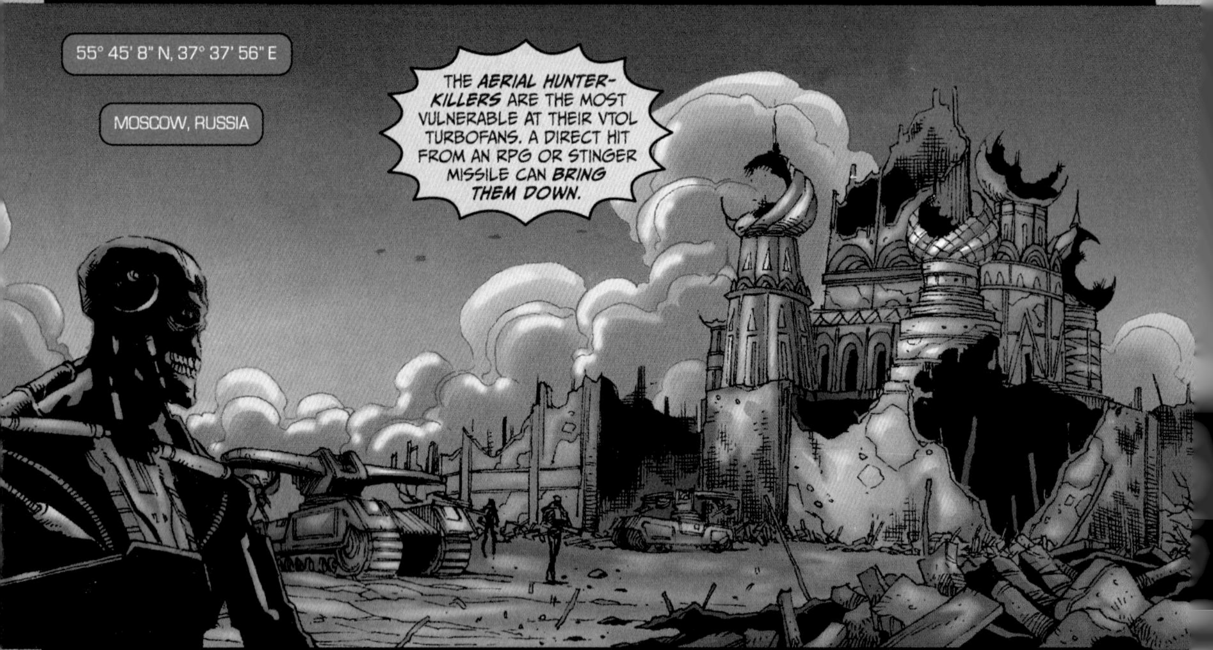
55° 45' 8" N, 37° 37' 56" E
MOSCOW, RUSSIA
THE AERIAL HUNTER-KILLERS ARE THE MOST VULNERABLE AT THEIR VTOL TURBOFANS. A DIRECT HIT FROM AN RPG OR STINGER MISSILE CAN BRING THEM DOWN.

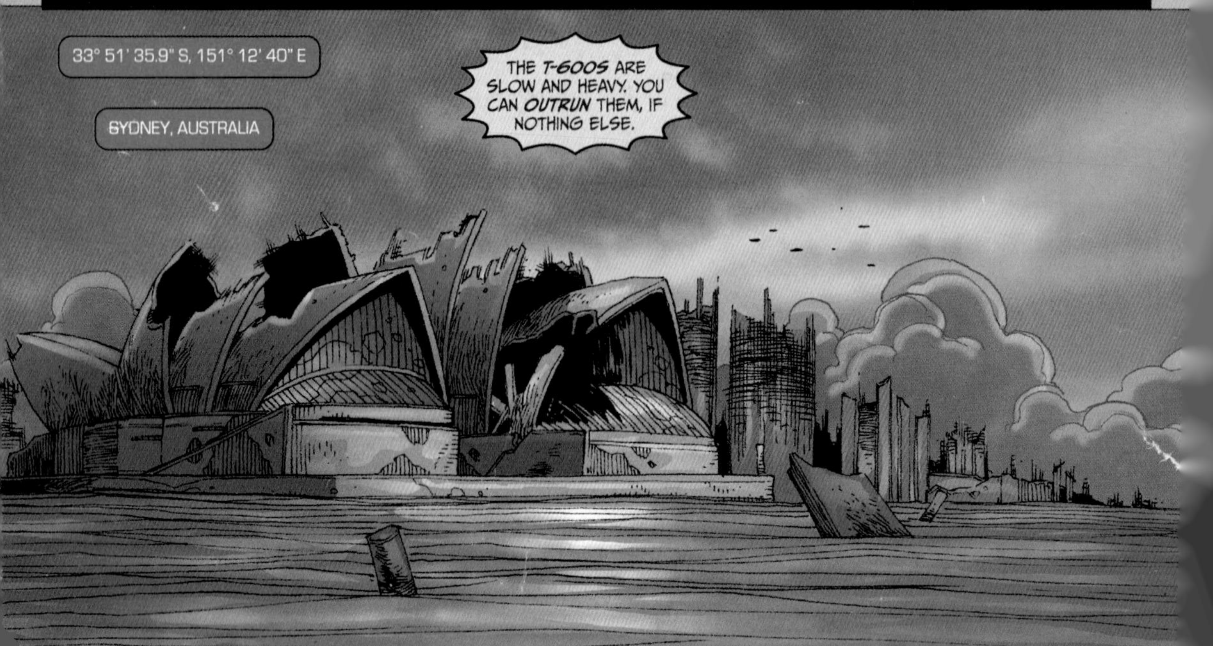
33° 51' 35.9" S, 151° 12' 40" E
SYDNEY, AUSTRALIA
THE T-600S ARE SLOW AND HEAVY. YOU CAN OUTRUN THEM, IF NOTHING ELSE.

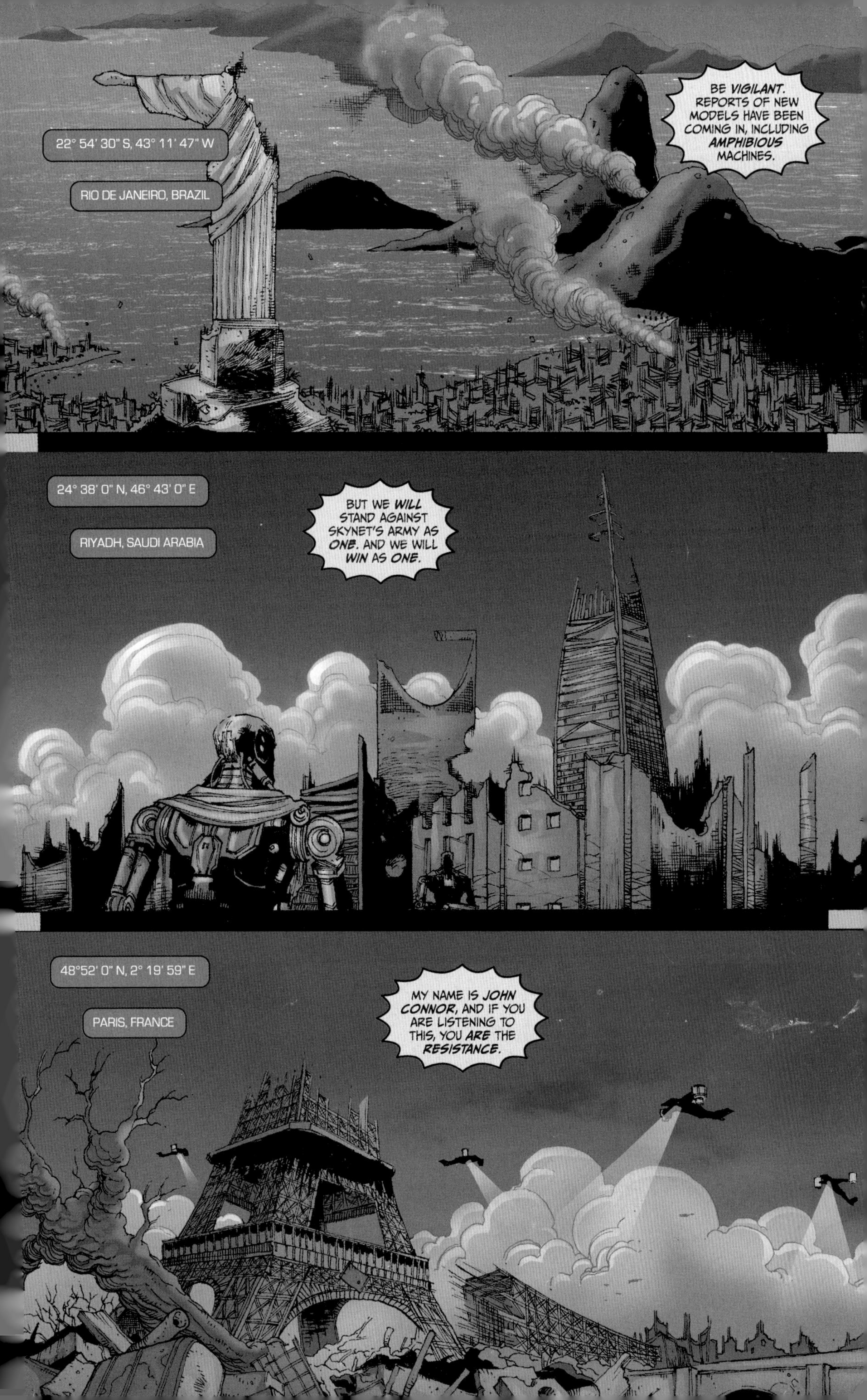

22° 54' 30" S, 43° 11' 47" W
RIO DE JANEIRO, BRAZIL
BE VIGILANT. REPORTS OF NEW MODELS HAVE BEEN COMING IN, INCLUDING AMPHIBIOUS MACHINES.
24° 38' 0" N, 46° 43' 0" E
RIYADH, SAUDI ARABIA
BUT WE WILL STAND AGAINST SKYNET'S ARMY AS ONE. AND WE WILL WIN AS ONE.
48°52' 0" N, 2° 19' 59" E
PARIS, FRANCE
MY NAME IS JOHN CONNOR, AND IF YOU ARE LISTENING TO THIS, YOU ARE THE RESISTANCE.

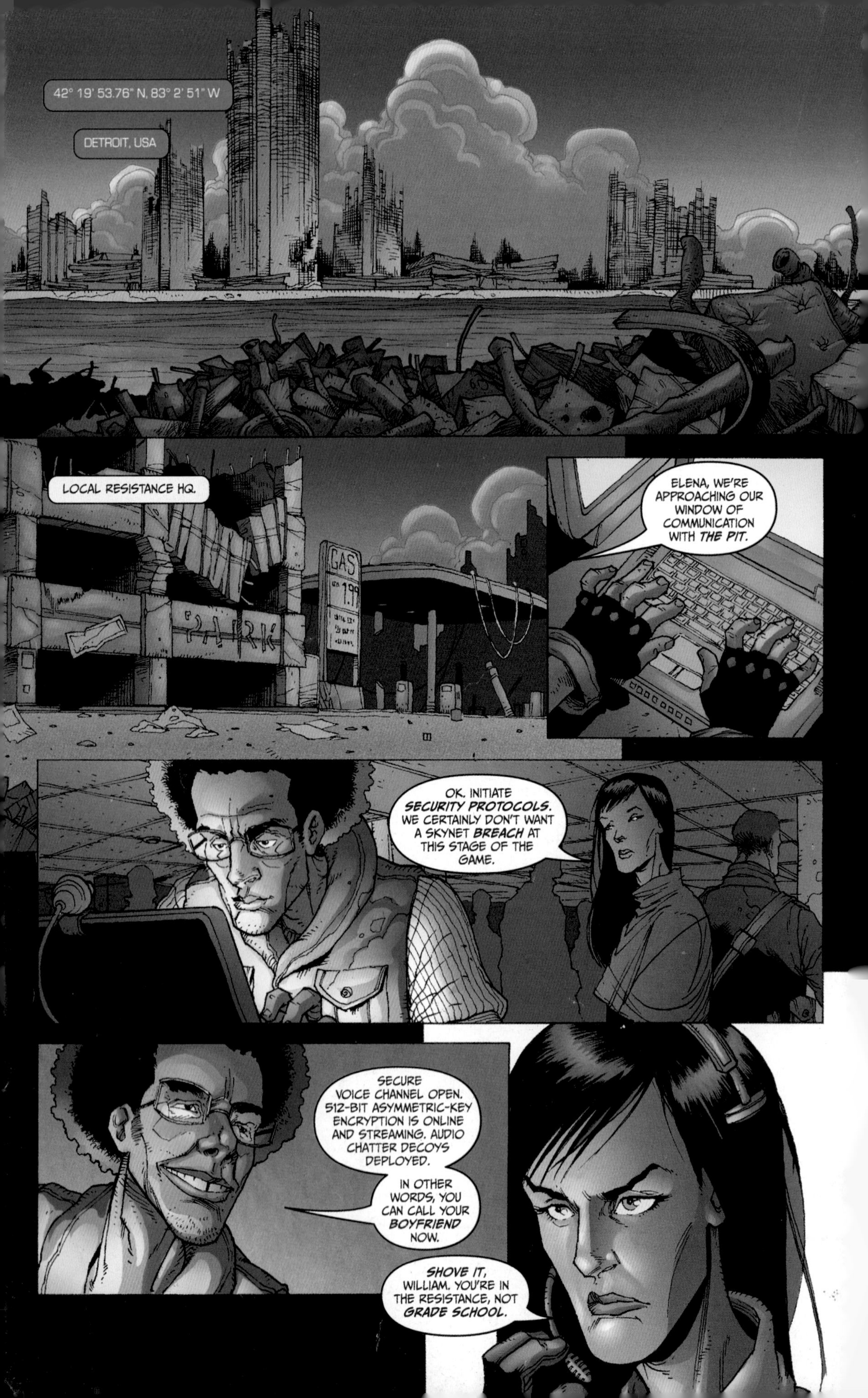
42° 19' 53.76" N, 83° 2' 51" W
DETROIT, USA
LOCAL RESISTANCE HQ.
GAS
ELENA, WE'RE APPROACHING OUR WINDOW OF COMMUNICATION WITH *THE PIT*.
OK, INITIATE *SECURITY PROTOCOLS*. WE CERTAINLY DON'T WANT A SKYNET *BREACH* AT THIS STAGE OF THE GAME.
SECURE VOICE CHANNEL OPEN. 512-BIT ASYMMETRIC-KEY ENCRYPTION IS ONLINE AND STREAMING. AUDIO CHATTER DECOYS DEPLOYED.
IN OTHER WORDS, YOU CAN CALL YOUR *BOYFRIEND* NOW.
SHOVE IT, WILLIAM. YOU'RE IN THE RESISTANCE, NOT *GRADE SCHOOL*.

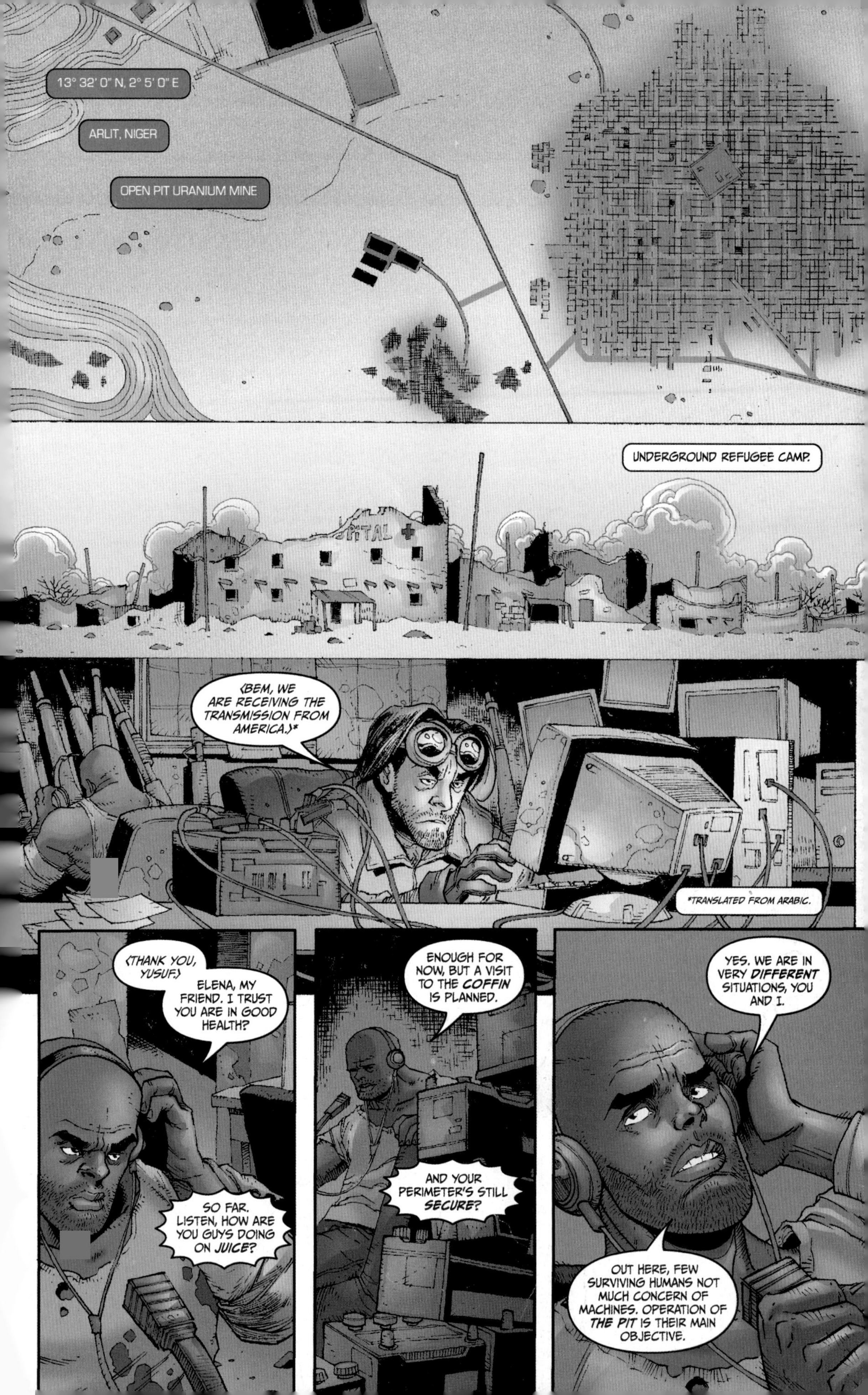
13° 32' 0" N, 2° 5' 0" E
ARLIT, NIGER
OPEN PIT URANIUM MINE
UNDERGROUND REFUGEE CAMP.
‹BEM, WE ARE RECEIVING THE TRANSMISSION FROM AMERICA.›*
*TRANSLATED FROM ARABIC.
‹THANK YOU, YUSUF.›
ELENA, MY FRIEND. I TRUST YOU ARE IN GOOD HEALTH?
SO FAR. LISTEN, HOW ARE YOU GUYS DOING ON JUICE?
ENOUGH FOR NOW, BUT A VISIT TO THE COFFIN IS PLANNED.
AND YOUR PERIMETER'S STILL SECURE?
YES. WE ARE IN VERY DIFFERENT SITUATIONS, YOU AND I.
OUT HERE, FEW SURVIVING HUMANS NOT MUCH CONCERN OF MACHINES. OPERATION OF THE PIT IS THEIR MAIN OBJECTIVE.

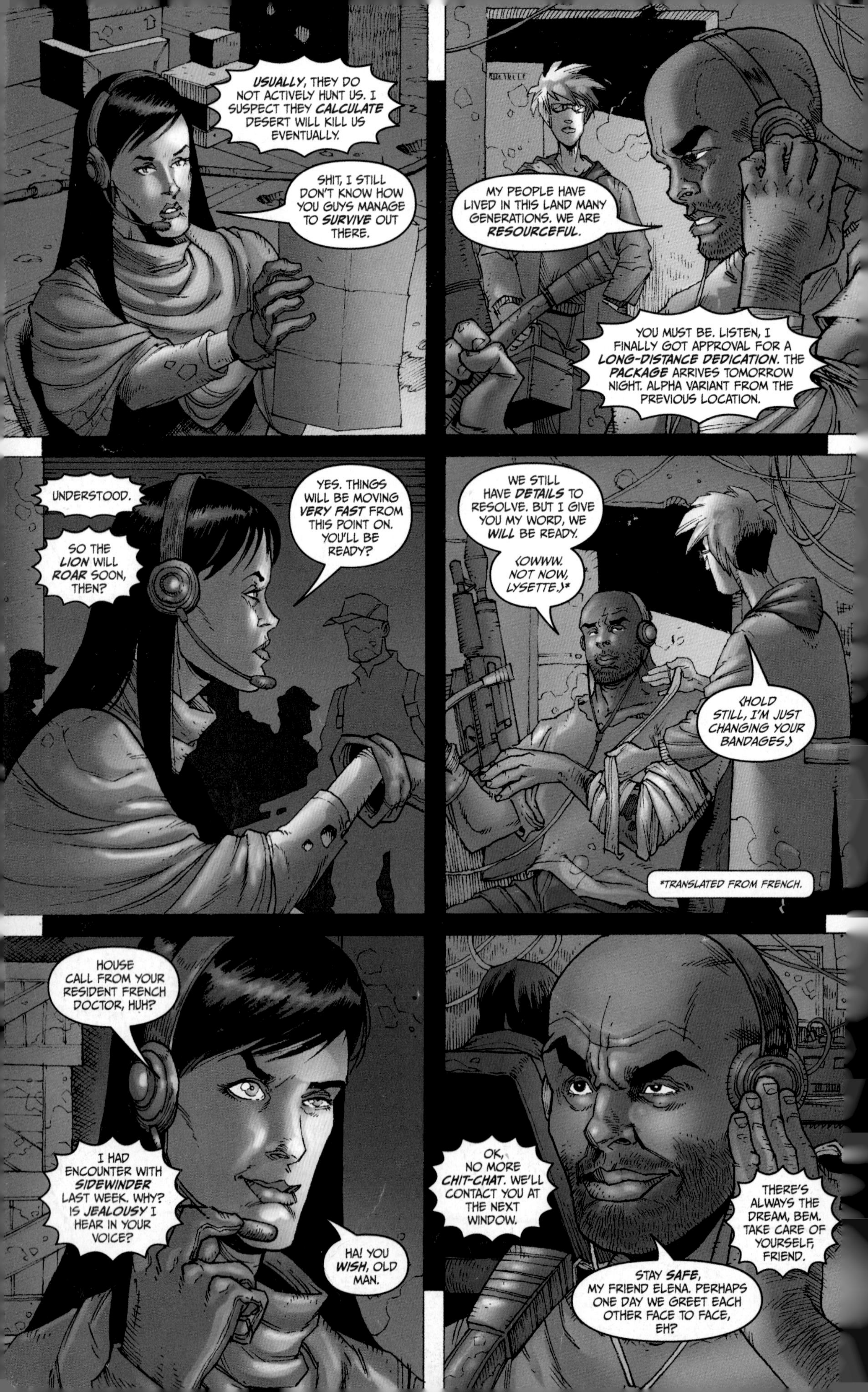
USUALLY, THEY DO NOT ACTIVELY HUNT US. I SUSPECT THEY CALCULATE DESERT WILL KILL US EVENTUALLY.
SHIT, I STILL DON'T KNOW HOW YOU GUYS MANAGE TO SURVIVE OUT THERE.
MY PEOPLE HAVE LIVED IN THIS LAND MANY GENERATIONS. WE ARE RESOURCEFUL.
YOU MUST BE. LISTEN, I FINALLY GOT APPROVAL FOR A LONG-DISTANCE DEDICATION. THE PACKAGE ARRIVES TOMORROW NIGHT. ALPHA VARIANT FROM THE PREVIOUS LOCATION.
UNDERSTOOD.
SO THE LION WILL ROAR SOON, THEN?
YES. THINGS WILL BE MOVING VERY FAST FROM THIS POINT ON. YOU'LL BE READY?
WE STILL HAVE DETAILS TO RESOLVE. BUT I GIVE YOU MY WORD, WE WILL BE READY.
‹OWWW. NOT NOW, LYSETTE.›*
‹HOLD STILL, I'M JUST CHANGING YOUR BANDAGES.›
*TRANSLATED FROM FRENCH.
HOUSE CALL FROM YOUR RESIDENT FRENCH DOCTOR, HUH?
I HAD ENCOUNTER WITH SIDEWINDER LAST WEEK. WHY? IS JEALOUSY I HEAR IN YOUR VOICE?
HA! YOU WISH, OLD MAN.
OK, NO MORE CHIT-CHAT. WE'LL CONTACT YOU AT THE NEXT WINDOW.
STAY SAFE, MY FRIEND ELENA. PERHAPS ONE DAY WE GREET EACH OTHER FACE TO FACE, EH?
THERE'S ALWAYS THE DREAM, BEM. TAKE CARE OF YOURSELF, FRIEND.

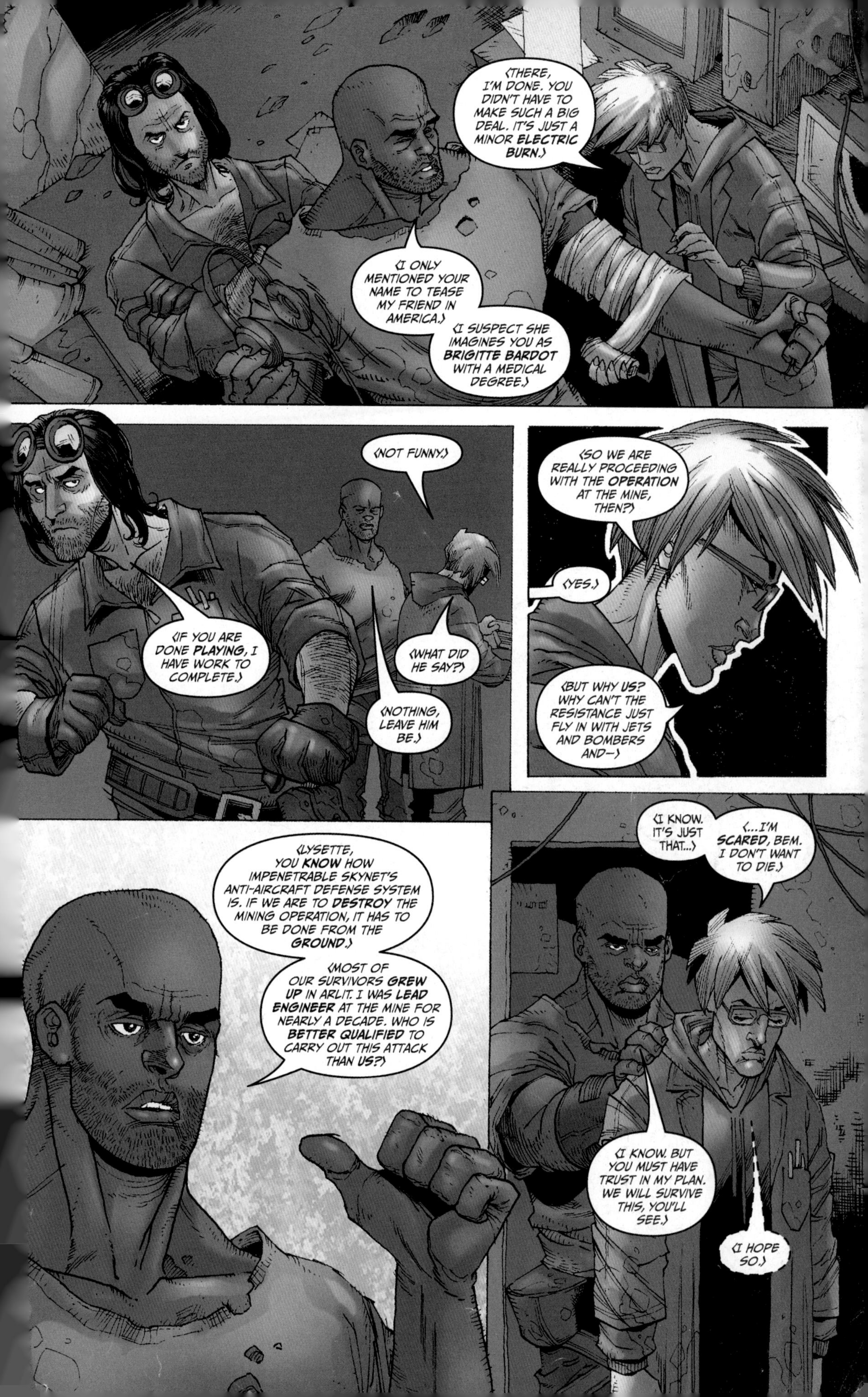
⟨THERE, I'M DONE. YOU DIDN'T HAVE TO MAKE SUCH A BIG DEAL. IT'S JUST A MINOR ELECTRIC BURN.⟩
⟨I ONLY MENTIONED YOUR NAME TO TEASE MY FRIEND IN AMERICA.⟩
⟨I SUSPECT SHE IMAGINES YOU AS BRIGITTE BARDOT WITH A MEDICAL DEGREE.⟩
⟨NOT FUNNY.⟩
⟨IF YOU ARE DONE PLAYING, I HAVE WORK TO COMPLETE.⟩
⟨WHAT DID HE SAY?⟩
⟨NOTHING, LEAVE HIM BE.⟩
⟨SO WE ARE REALLY PROCEEDING WITH THE OPERATION AT THE MINE, THEN?⟩
⟨YES.⟩
⟨BUT WHY US? WHY CAN'T THE RESISTANCE JUST FLY IN WITH JETS AND BOMBERS AND—⟩
⟨LYSETTE, YOU KNOW HOW IMPENETRABLE SKYNET'S ANTI-AIRCRAFT DEFENSE SYSTEM IS. IF WE ARE TO DESTROY THE MINING OPERATION, IT HAS TO BE DONE FROM THE GROUND.⟩
⟨MOST OF OUR SURVIVORS GREW UP IN ARLIT. I WAS LEAD ENGINEER AT THE MINE FOR NEARLY A DECADE. WHO IS BETTER QUALIFIED TO CARRY OUT THIS ATTACK THAN US?⟩
⟨I KNOW. IT'S JUST THAT...⟩
⟨...I'M SCARED, BEM. I DON'T WANT TO DIE.⟩
⟨I KNOW. BUT YOU MUST HAVE TRUST IN MY PLAN. WE WILL SURVIVE THIS, YOU'LL SEE.⟩
⟨I HOPE SO.⟩

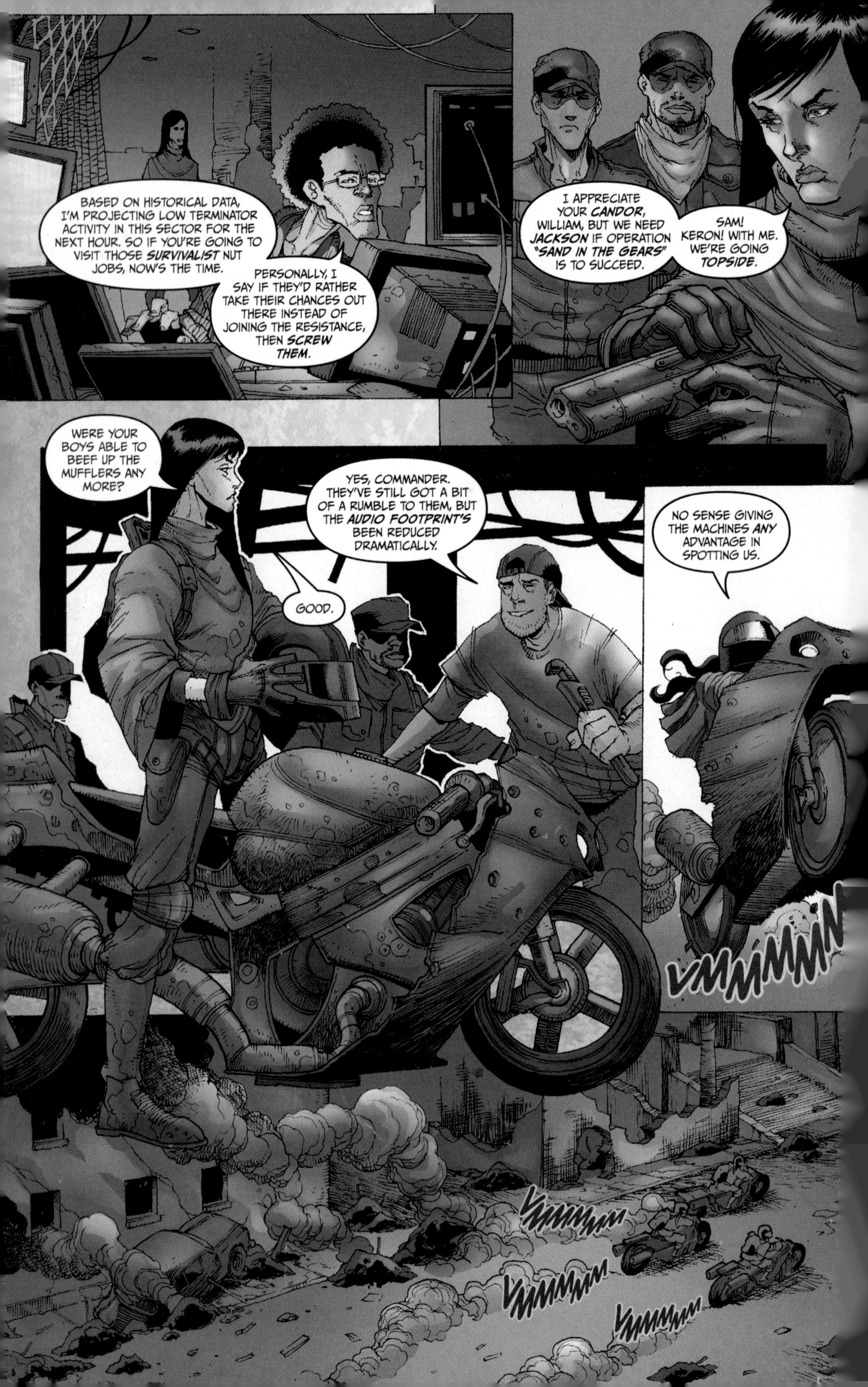

BASED ON HISTORICAL DATA, I'M PROJECTING LOW TERMINATOR ACTIVITY IN THIS SECTOR FOR THE NEXT HOUR. SO IF YOU'RE GOING TO VISIT THOSE SURVIVALIST NUT JOBS, NOW'S THE TIME.
PERSONALLY, I SAY IF THEY'D RATHER TAKE THEIR CHANCES OUT THERE INSTEAD OF JOINING THE RESISTANCE, THEN SCREW THEM.
I APPRECIATE YOUR CANDOR, WILLIAM, BUT WE NEED JACKSON IF OPERATION "SAND IN THE GEARS" IS TO SUCCEED.
SAM! KERON! WITH ME. WE'RE GOING TOPSIDE.
WERE YOUR BOYS ABLE TO BEEF UP THE MUFFLERS ANY MORE?
YES, COMMANDER. THEY'VE STILL GOT A BIT OF A RUMBLE TO THEM, BUT THE AUDIO FOOTPRINT'S BEEN REDUCED DRAMATICALLY.
GOOD.
NO SENSE GIVING THE MACHINES ANY ADVANTAGE IN SPOTTING US.
VMMMMMN
VMMMMMM
VMMMMMM
VMMMMM

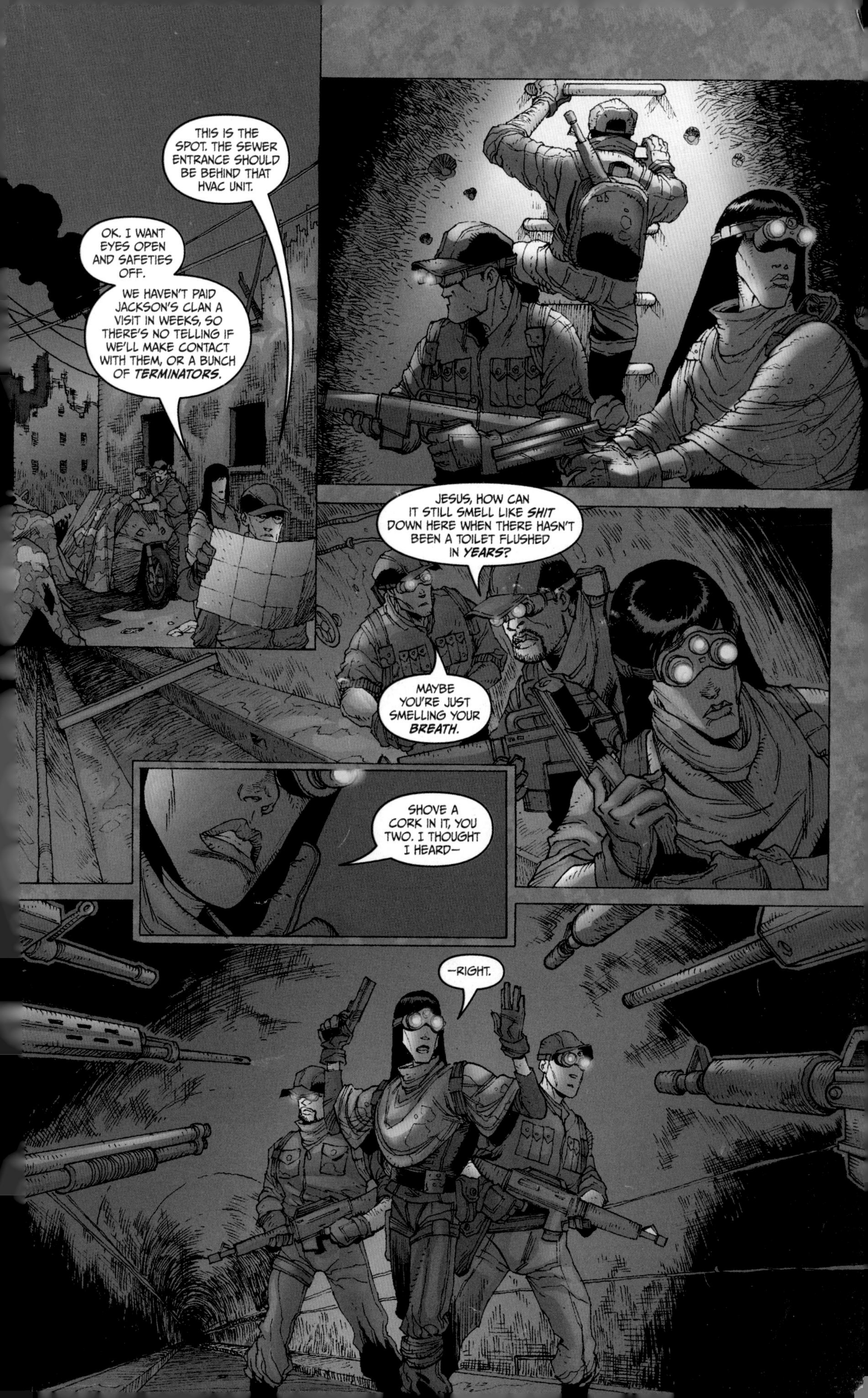
THIS IS THE SPOT. THE SEWER ENTRANCE SHOULD BE BEHIND THAT HVAC UNIT.
OK. I WANT EYES OPEN AND SAFETIES OFF.
WE HAVEN'T PAID JACKSON'S CLAN A VISIT IN WEEKS, SO THERE'S NO TELLING IF WE'LL MAKE CONTACT WITH THEM, OR A BUNCH OF TERMINATORS.
JESUS, HOW CAN IT STILL SMELL LIKE SHIT DOWN HERE WHEN THERE HASN'T BEEN A TOILET FLUSHED IN YEARS?
MAYBE YOU'RE JUST SMELLING YOUR BREATH.
SHOVE A CORK IN IT, YOU TWO. I THOUGHT I HEARD—
—RIGHT.

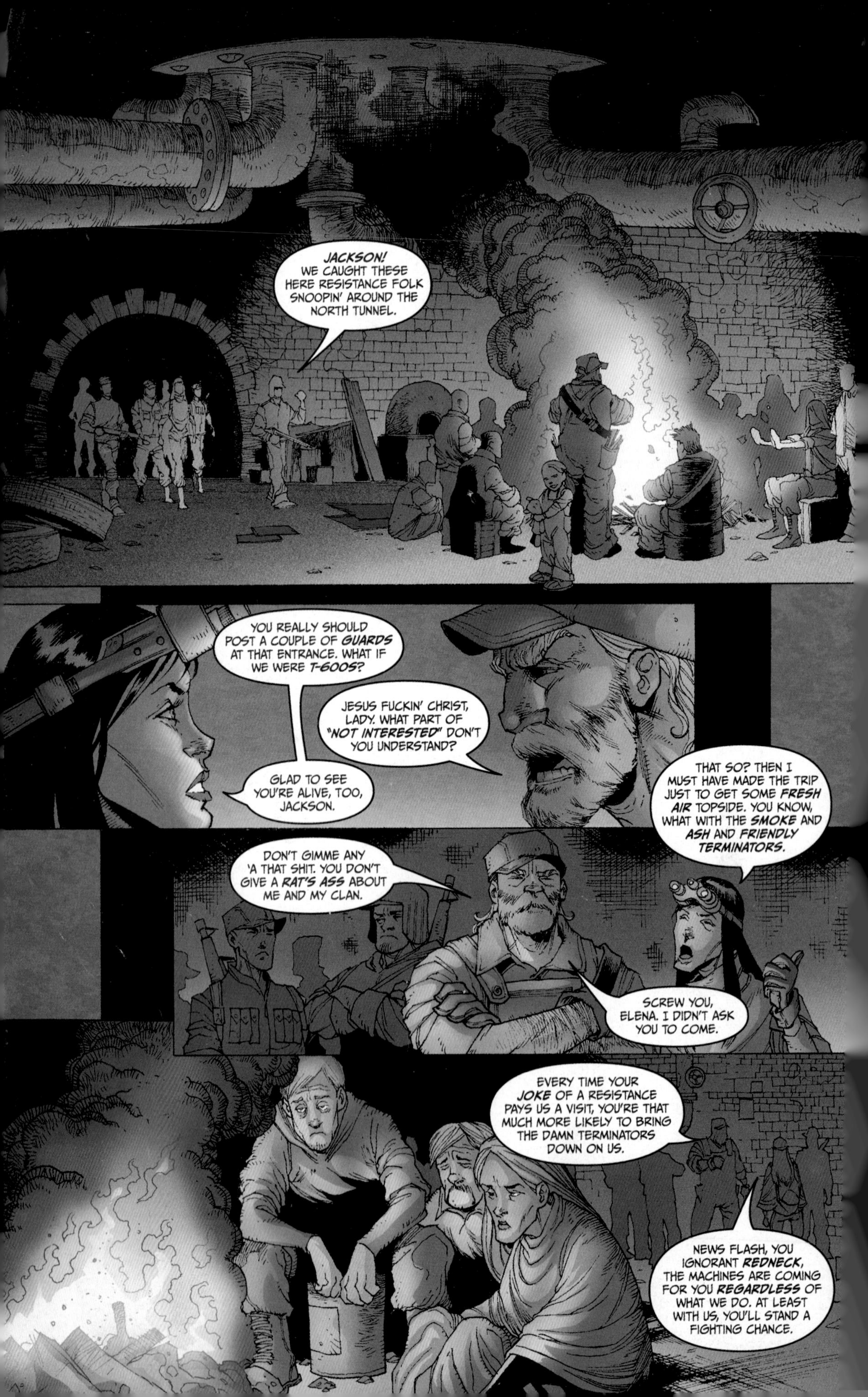

JACKSON! WE CAUGHT THESE HERE RESISTANCE FOLK SNOOPIN' AROUND THE NORTH TUNNEL.
YOU REALLY SHOULD POST A COUPLE OF GUARDS AT THAT ENTRANCE. WHAT IF WE WERE T-600S?
GLAD TO SEE YOU'RE ALIVE, TOO, JACKSON.
JESUS FUCKIN' CHRIST, LADY. WHAT PART OF "NOT INTERESTED" DON'T YOU UNDERSTAND?
THAT SO? THEN I MUST HAVE MADE THE TRIP JUST TO GET SOME FRESH AIR TOPSIDE. YOU KNOW, WHAT WITH THE SMOKE AND ASH AND FRIENDLY TERMINATORS.
DON'T GIMME ANY 'A THAT SHIT. YOU DON'T GIVE A RAT'S ASS ABOUT ME AND MY CLAN.
SCREW YOU, ELENA. I DIDN'T ASK YOU TO COME.
EVERY TIME YOUR JOKE OF A RESISTANCE PAYS US A VISIT, YOU'RE THAT MUCH MORE LIKELY TO BRING THE DAMN TERMINATORS DOWN ON US.
NEWS FLASH, YOU IGNORANT REDNECK, THE MACHINES ARE COMING FOR YOU REGARDLESS OF WHAT WE DO. AT LEAST WITH US, YOU'LL STAND A FIGHTING CHANCE.

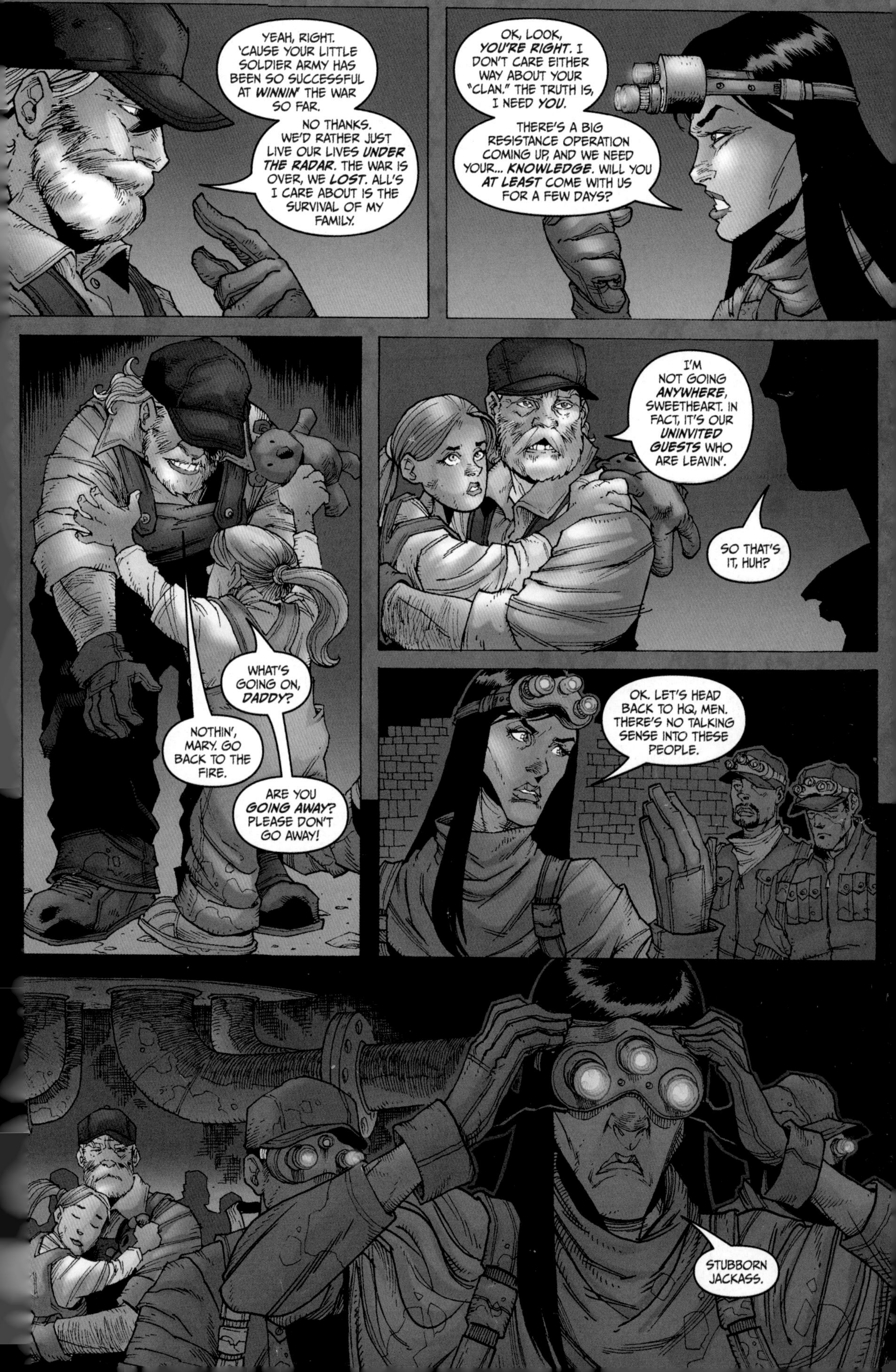
YEAH, RIGHT. 'CAUSE YOUR LITTLE SOLDIER ARMY HAS BEEN SO SUCCESSFUL AT WINNIN' THE WAR SO FAR.
NO THANKS. WE'D RATHER JUST LIVE OUR LIVES UNDER THE RADAR. THE WAR IS OVER, WE LOST. ALL'S I CARE ABOUT IS THE SURVIVAL OF MY FAMILY.
OK, LOOK, YOU'RE RIGHT. I DON'T CARE EITHER WAY ABOUT YOUR "CLAN." THE TRUTH IS, I NEED YOU.
THERE'S A BIG RESISTANCE OPERATION COMING UP, AND WE NEED YOUR... KNOWLEDGE. WILL YOU AT LEAST COME WITH US FOR A FEW DAYS?
WHAT'S GOING ON, DADDY?
NOTHIN', MARY. GO BACK TO THE FIRE.
ARE YOU GOING AWAY? PLEASE DON'T GO AWAY!
I'M NOT GOING ANYWHERE, SWEETHEART. IN FACT, IT'S OUR UNINVITED GUESTS WHO ARE LEAVIN'.
SO THAT'S IT, HUH?
OK. LET'S HEAD BACK TO HQ, MEN. THERE'S NO TALKING SENSE INTO THESE PEOPLE.
STUBBORN JACKASS.

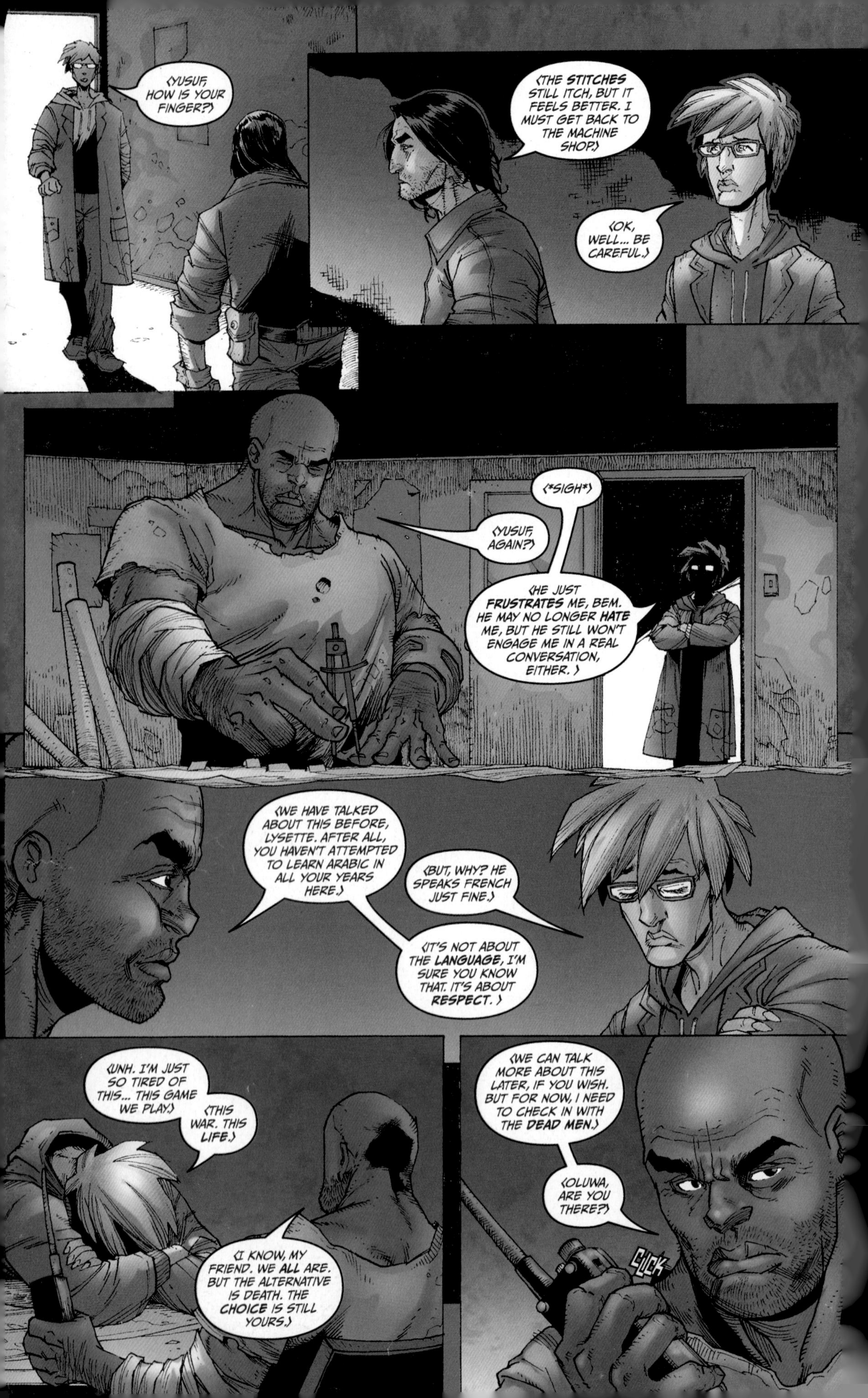

‹YUSUF, HOW IS YOUR FINGER?›
‹THE STITCHES STILL ITCH, BUT IT FEELS BETTER. I MUST GET BACK TO THE MACHINE SHOP.›
‹OK, WELL... BE CAREFUL.›
‹*SIGH*›
‹YUSUF, AGAIN?›
‹HE JUST FRUSTRATES ME, BEM. HE MAY NO LONGER HATE ME, BUT HE STILL WON'T ENGAGE ME IN A REAL CONVERSATION, EITHER.›
‹WE HAVE TALKED ABOUT THIS BEFORE, LYSETTE. AFTER ALL, YOU HAVEN'T ATTEMPTED TO LEARN ARABIC IN ALL YOUR YEARS HERE.›
‹BUT, WHY? HE SPEAKS FRENCH JUST FINE.›
‹IT'S NOT ABOUT THE LANGUAGE, I'M SURE YOU KNOW THAT. IT'S ABOUT RESPECT.›
‹UNH. I'M JUST SO TIRED OF THIS... THIS GAME WE PLAY.›
‹THIS WAR. THIS LIFE.›
‹I KNOW, MY FRIEND. WE ALL ARE. BUT THE ALTERNATIVE IS DEATH. THE CHOICE IS STILL YOURS.›
‹WE CAN TALK MORE ABOUT THIS LATER, IF YOU WISH. BUT FOR NOW, I NEED TO CHECK IN WITH THE DEAD MEN.›
‹OLUWA, ARE YOU THERE?›
CLICK

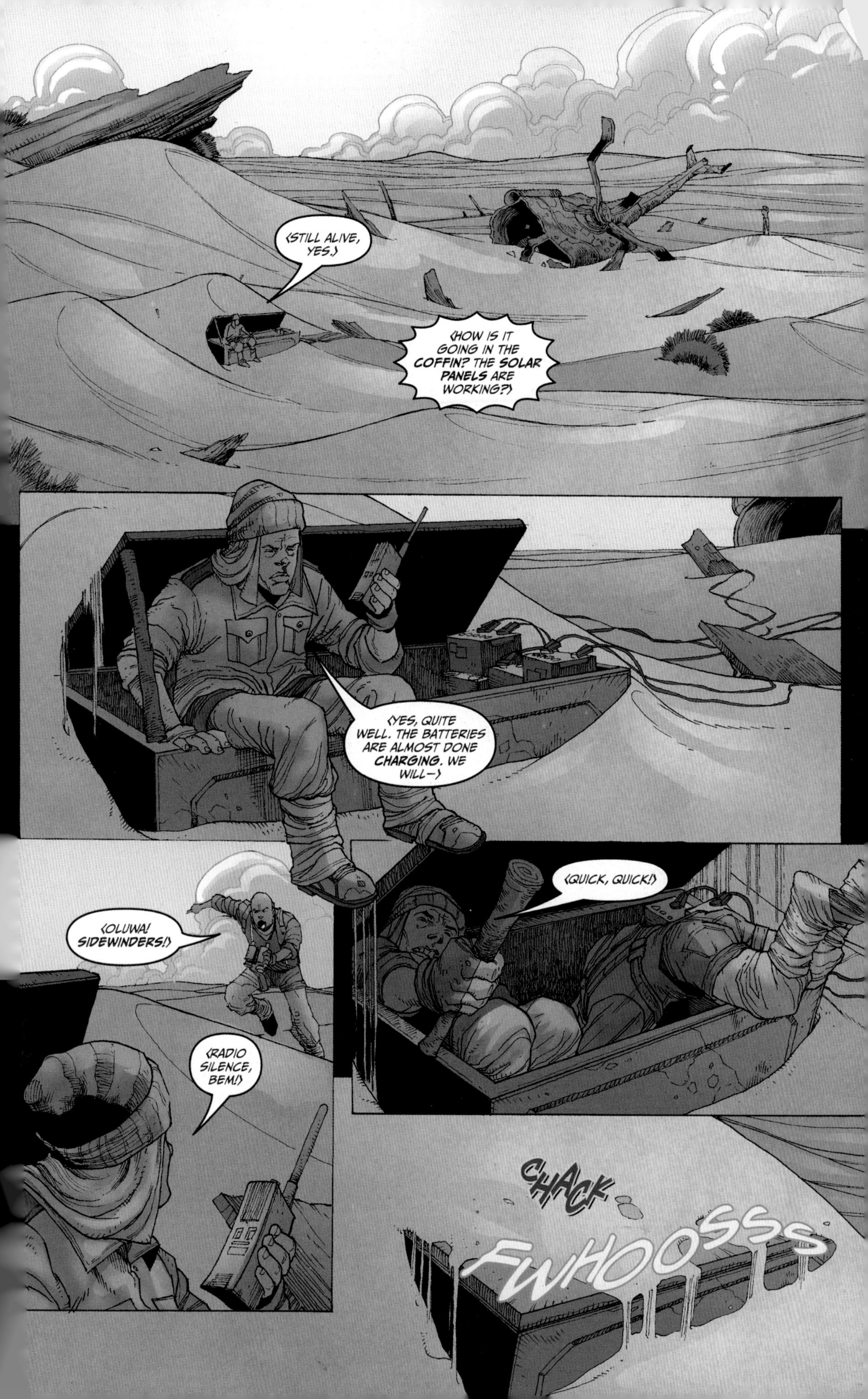
‹STILL ALIVE, YES.›
‹HOW IS IT GOING IN THE COFFIN? THE SOLAR PANELS ARE WORKING?›
‹YES, QUITE WELL. THE BATTERIES ARE ALMOST DONE CHARGING. WE WILL—›
‹OLUWA! SIDEWINDERS!›
‹RADIO SILENCE, BEM!›
‹QUICK, QUICK!›
CHACK
FWHOOSSSS

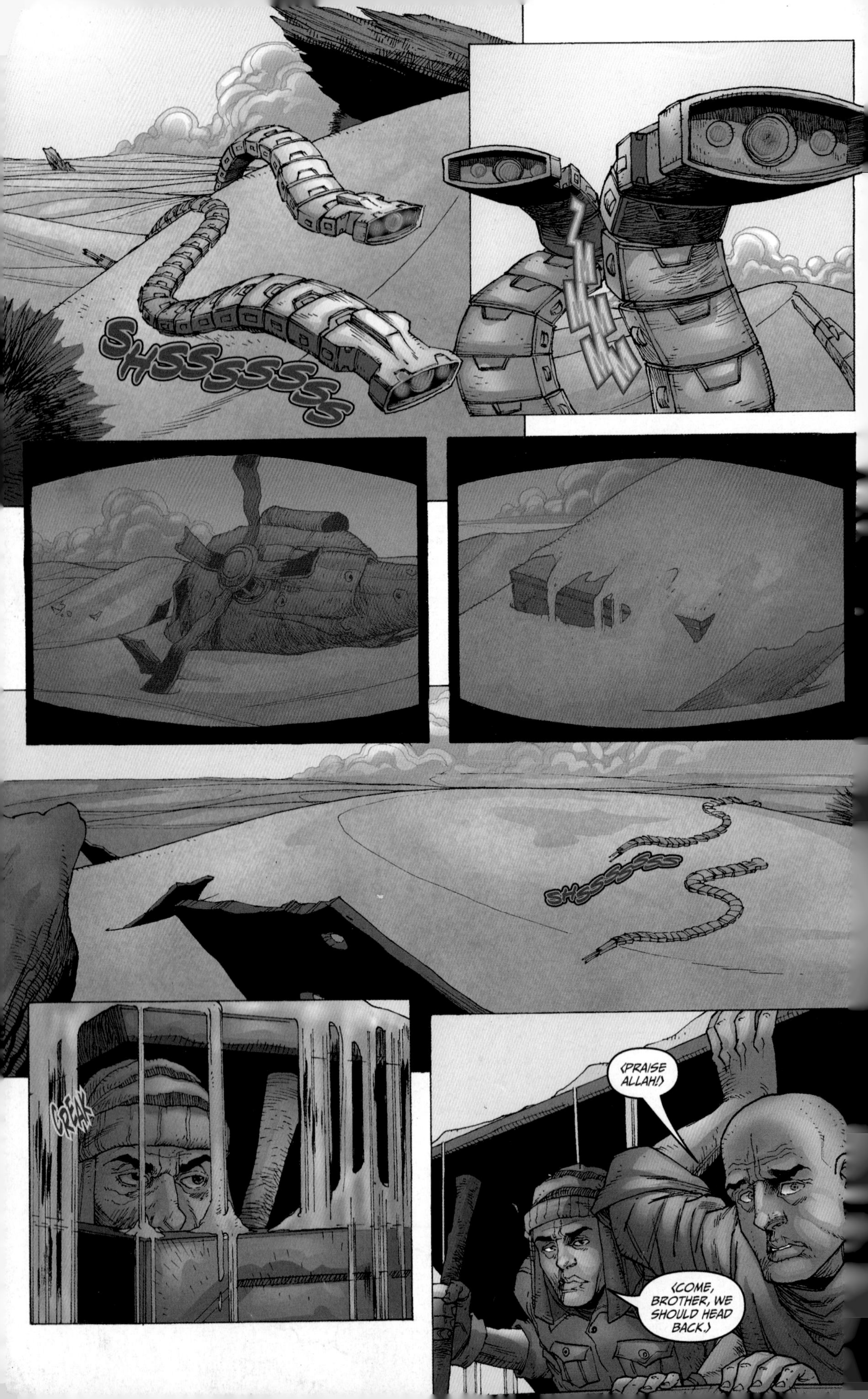
SHSSSSSSS
ZMMMMMM
SHSSSSSS
CREAK
‹PRAISE ALLAH!›
‹COME, BROTHER, WE SHOULD HEAD BACK.›

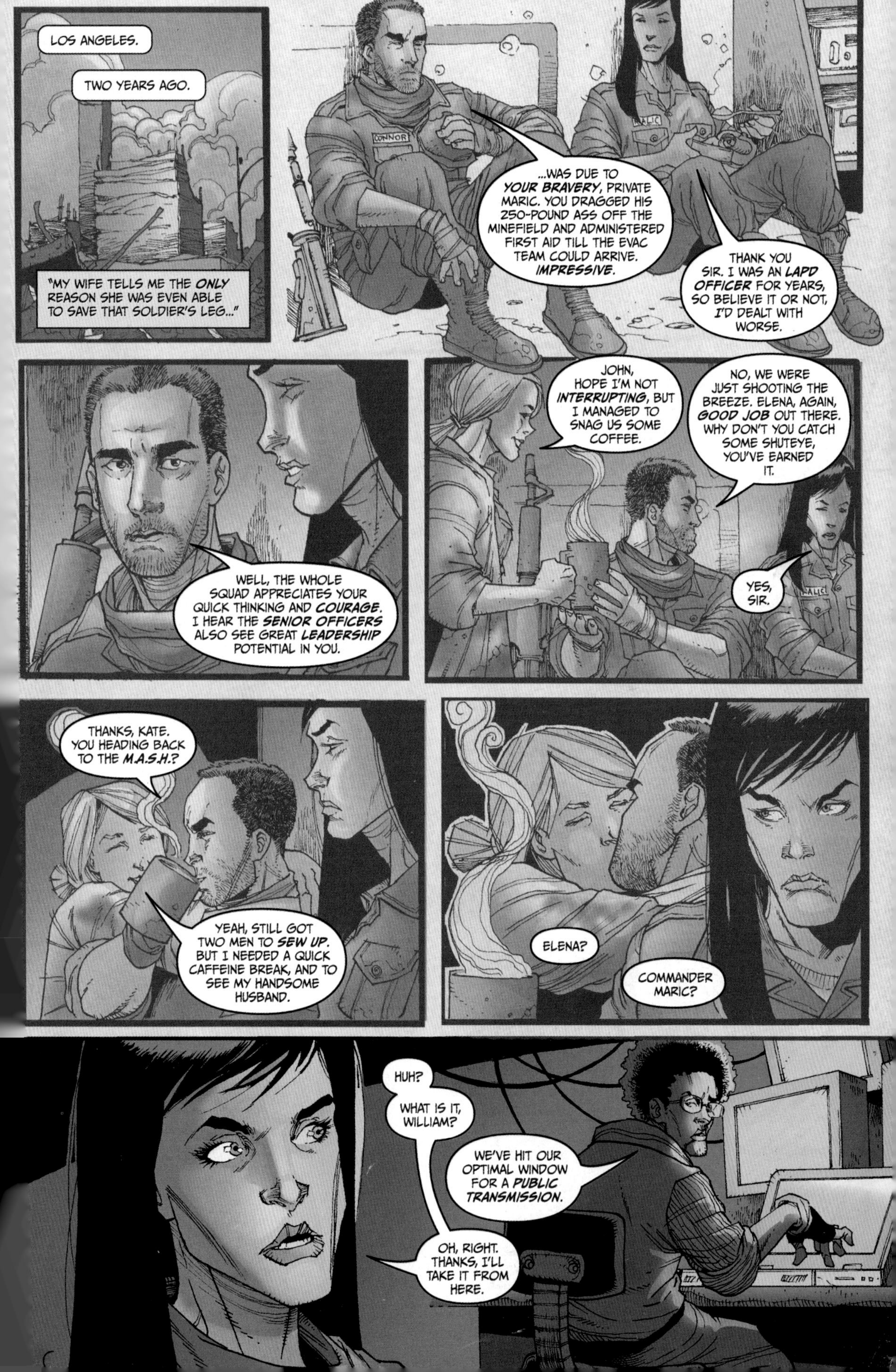

LOS ANGELES.
TWO YEARS AGO.
"MY WIFE TELLS ME THE ONLY REASON SHE WAS EVEN ABLE TO SAVE THAT SOLDIER'S LEG..."
...WAS DUE TO YOUR BRAVERY, PRIVATE MARIC. YOU DRAGGED HIS 250-POUND ASS OFF THE MINEFIELD AND ADMINISTERED FIRST AID TILL THE EVAC TEAM COULD ARRIVE. IMPRESSIVE.
THANK YOU SIR. I WAS AN LAPD OFFICER FOR YEARS, SO BELIEVE IT OR NOT, I'D DEALT WITH WORSE.
WELL, THE WHOLE SQUAD APPRECIATES YOUR QUICK THINKING AND COURAGE. I HEAR THE SENIOR OFFICERS ALSO SEE GREAT LEADERSHIP POTENTIAL IN YOU.
JOHN, HOPE I'M NOT INTERRUPTING, BUT I MANAGED TO SNAG US SOME COFFEE.
NO, WE WERE JUST SHOOTING THE BREEZE. ELENA, AGAIN, GOOD JOB OUT THERE. WHY DON'T YOU CATCH SOME SHUTEYE, YOU'VE EARNED IT.
YES, SIR.
THANKS, KATE. YOU HEADING BACK TO THE M.A.S.H.?
YEAH, STILL GOT TWO MEN TO SEW UP. BUT I NEEDED A QUICK CAFFEINE BREAK, AND TO SEE MY HANDSOME HUSBAND.
ELENA?
COMMANDER MARIC?
HUH?
WHAT IS IT, WILLIAM?
WE'VE HIT OUR OPTIMAL WINDOW FOR A PUBLIC TRANSMISSION.
OH, RIGHT. THANKS, I'LL TAKE IT FROM HERE.

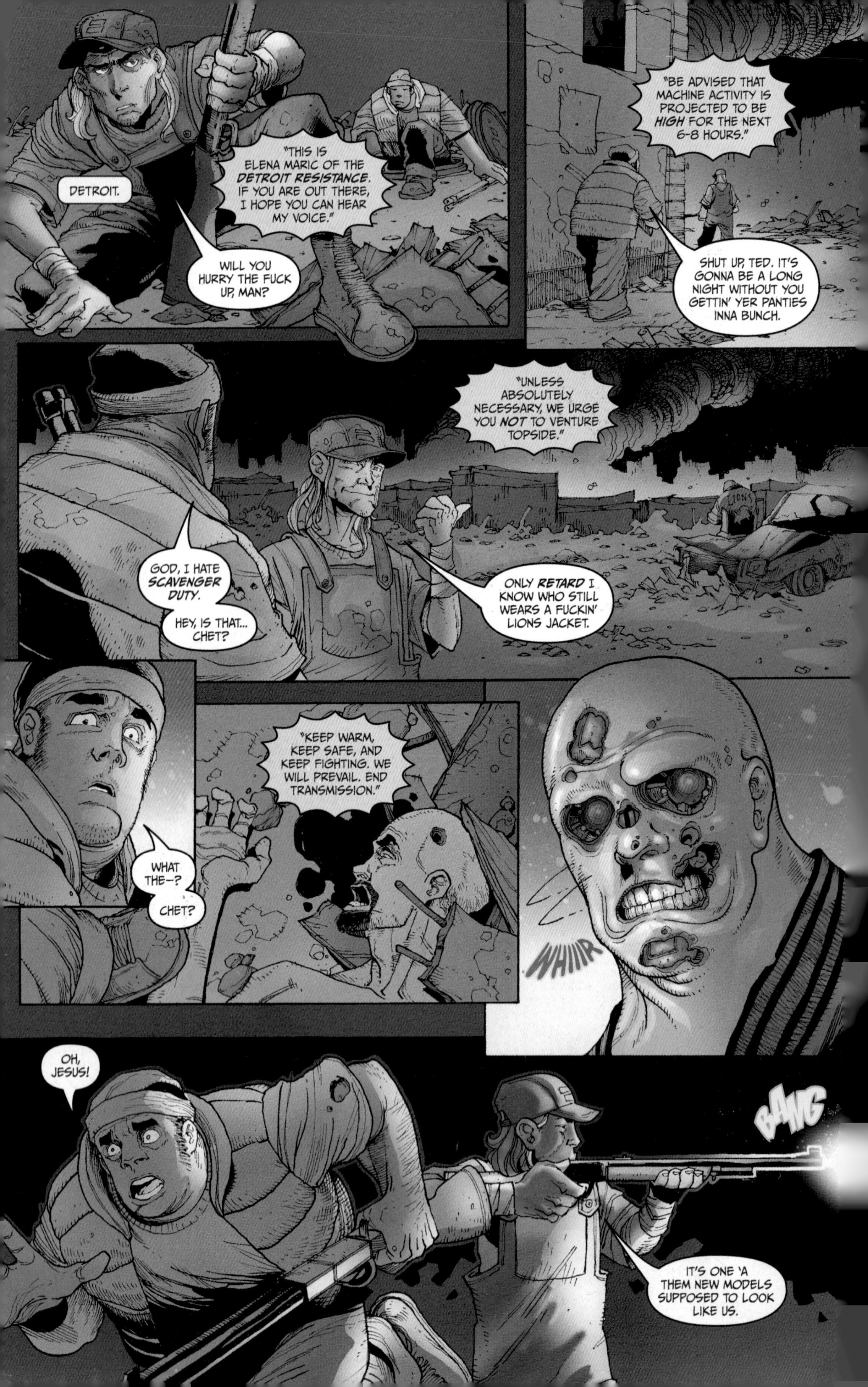
DETROIT.
"THIS IS ELENA MARIC OF THE DETROIT RESISTANCE. IF YOU ARE OUT THERE, I HOPE YOU CAN HEAR MY VOICE."
WILL YOU HURRY THE FUCK UP, MAN?
"BE ADVISED THAT MACHINE ACTIVITY IS PROJECTED TO BE HIGH FOR THE NEXT 6-8 HOURS."
SHUT UP, TED. IT'S GONNA BE A LONG NIGHT WITHOUT YOU GETTIN' YER PANTIES INNA BUNCH.
"UNLESS ABSOLUTELY NECESSARY, WE URGE YOU NOT TO VENTURE TOPSIDE."
GOD, I HATE SCAVENGER DUTY.
HEY, IS THAT... CHET?
ONLY RETARD I KNOW WHO STILL WEARS A FUCKIN' LIONS JACKET.
WHAT THE-?
CHET?
"KEEP WARM, KEEP SAFE, AND KEEP FIGHTING. WE WILL PREVAIL. END TRANSMISSION."
WHIIIR
OH, JESUS!
BANG
IT'S ONE 'A THEM NEW MODELS SUPPOSED TO LOOK LIKE US.

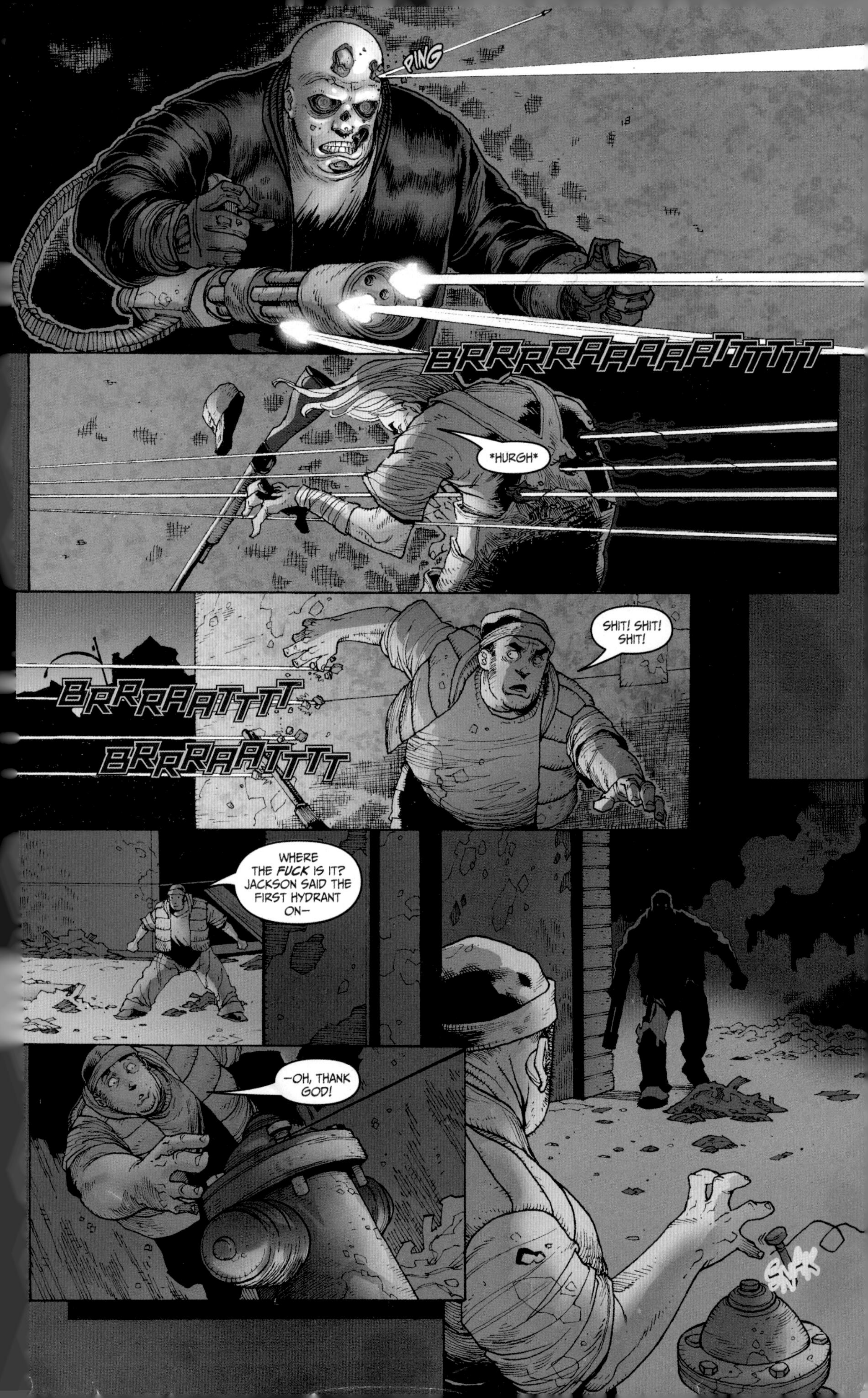
PING
BRRRRAAAAAATTTTT
HURGH
SHIT! SHIT! SHIT!
BRRRAATTTT
BRRRAATTTT
WHERE THE FUCK IS IT? JACKSON SAID THE FIRST HYDRANT ON–
–OH, THANK GOD!
SNAK

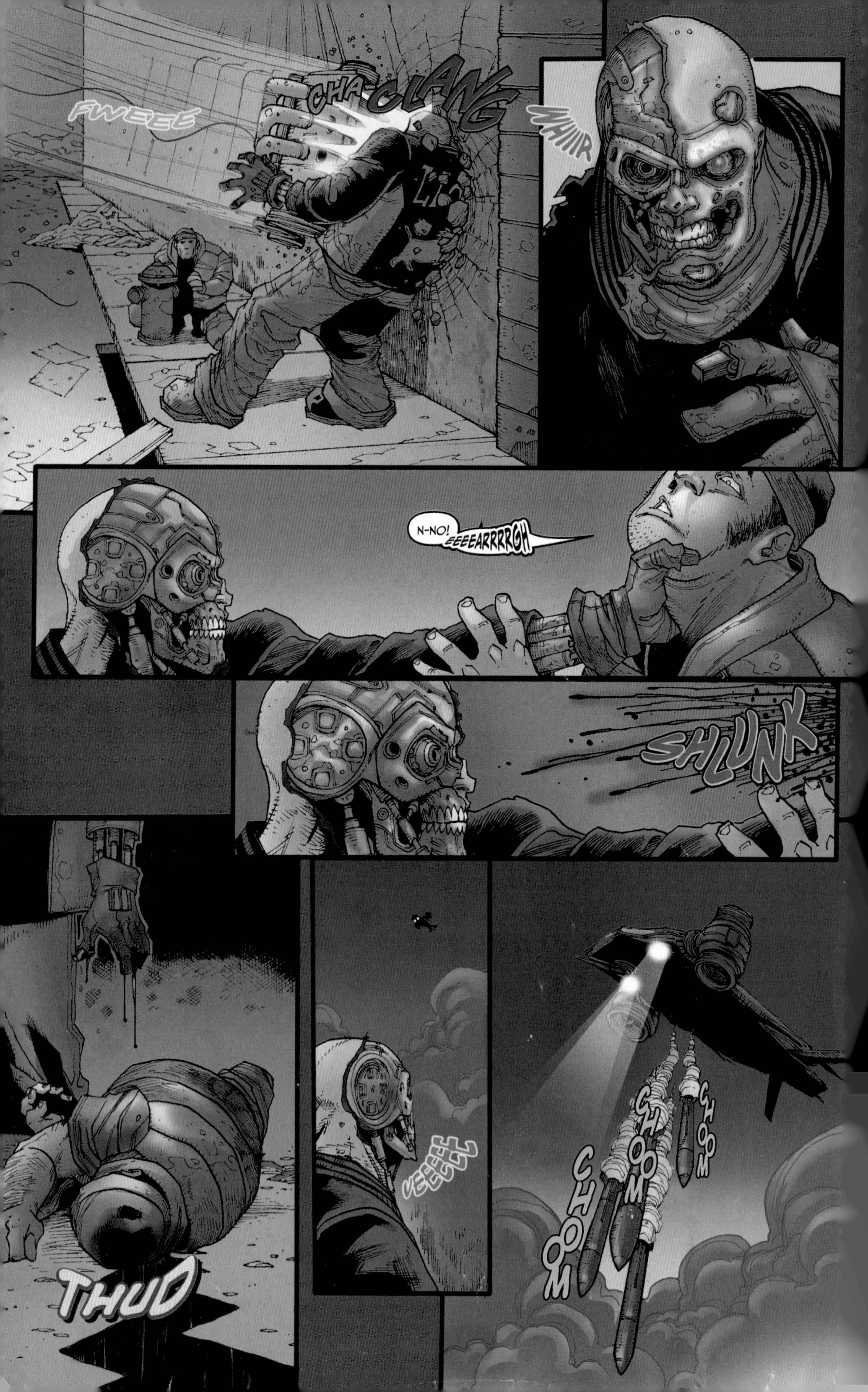
FWEEÉ
CHA-CLANG
WHIIIR
N-NO! EEEEARRRRGH
SHLUNK
THUD
VEEEEEE
CHOOM
CHOOM
CHOOM

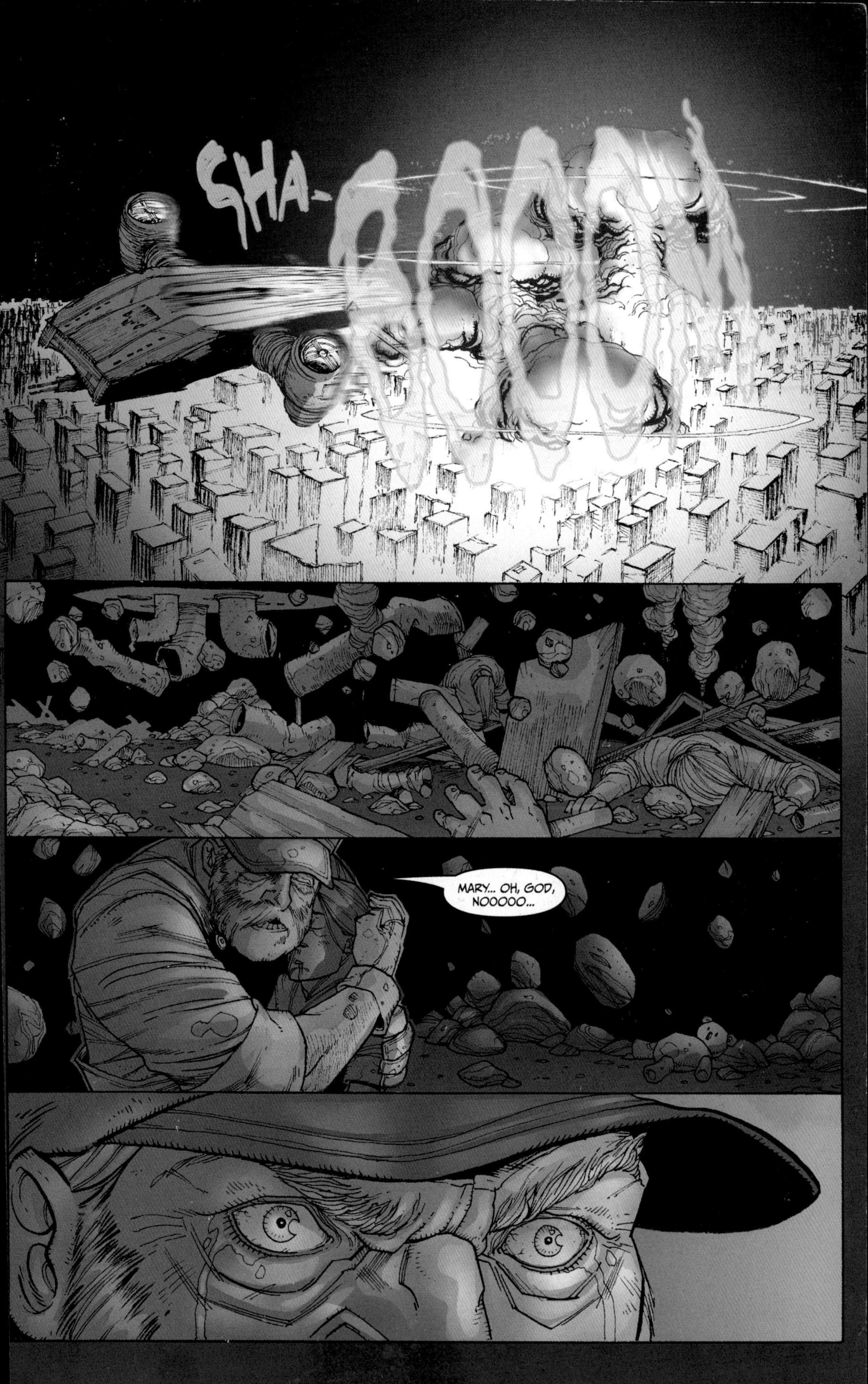
SHA-BOOOM
MARY... OH, GOD, NOOOOO...

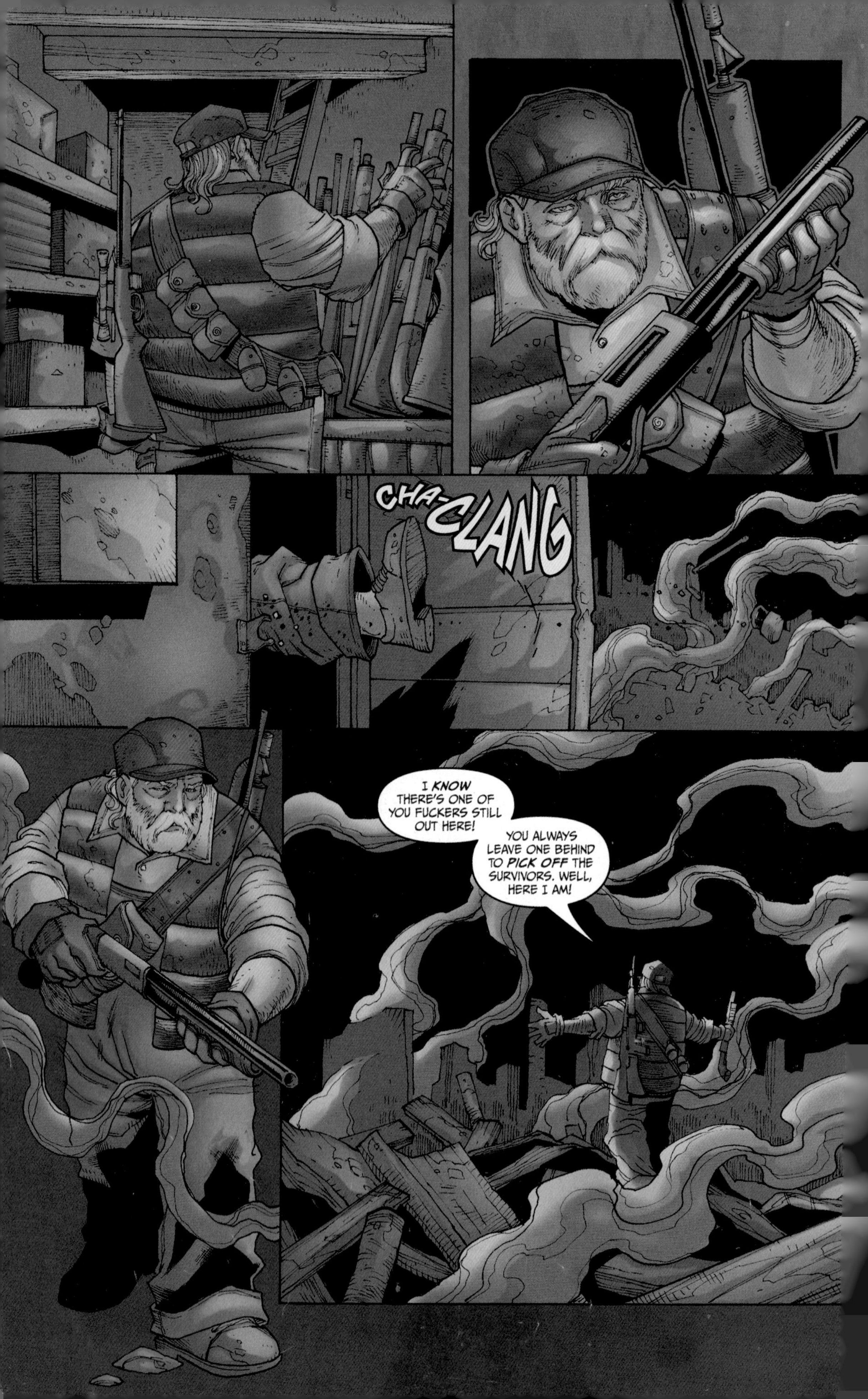
CHA-CLANG
I KNOW THERE'S ONE OF YOU FUCKERS STILL OUT HERE!
YOU ALWAYS LEAVE ONE BEHIND TO PICK OFF THE SURVIVORS. WELL, HERE I AM!

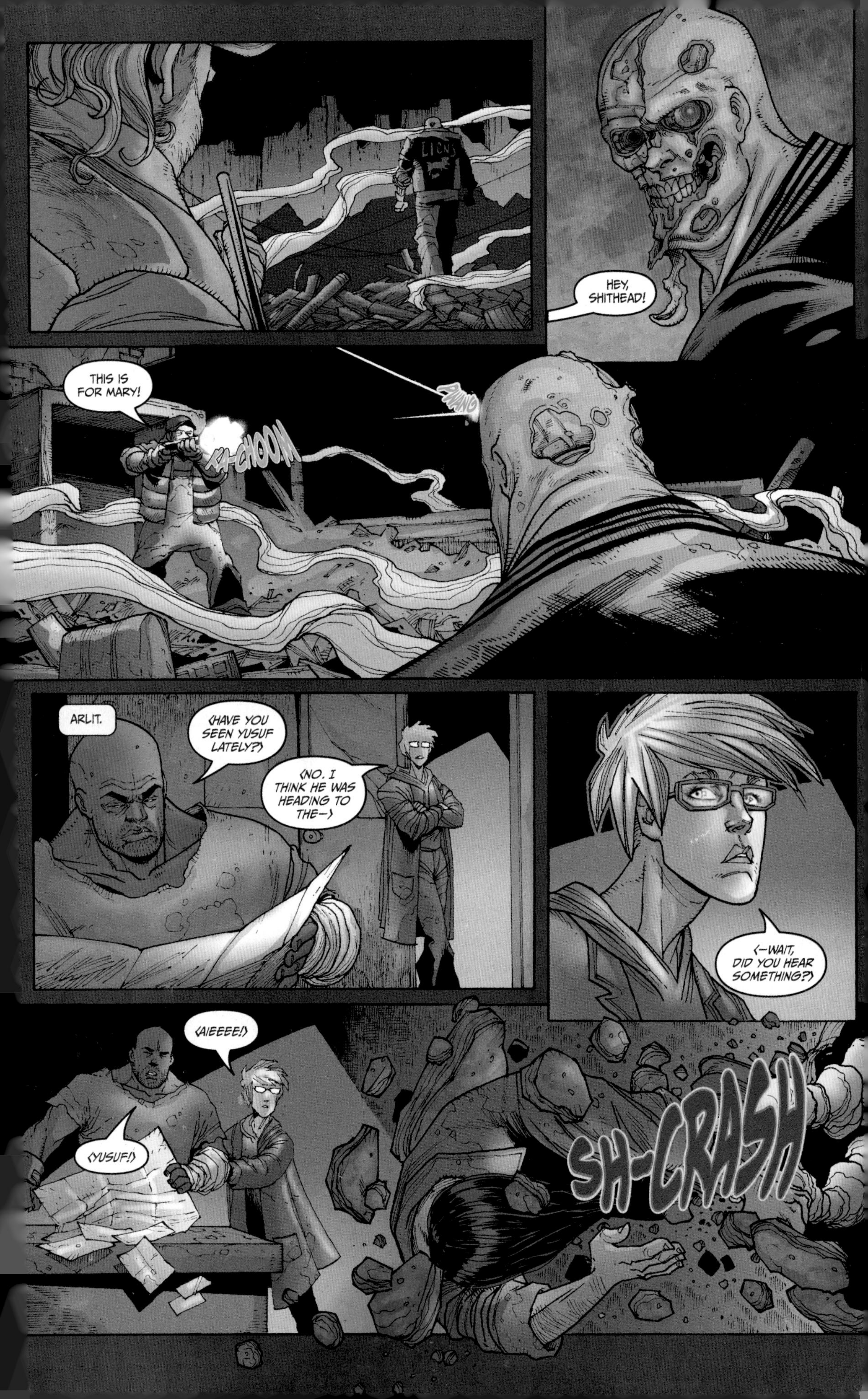
LIONS
HEY, SHITHEAD!
THIS IS FOR MARY!
KA-CHOOM
PWANG
ARLIT.
‹HAVE YOU SEEN YUSUF LATELY?›
‹NO. I THINK HE WAS HEADING TO THE--›
‹--WAIT, DID YOU HEAR SOMETHING?›
‹AIEEEE!›
‹YUSUF!›
SH-CRASH

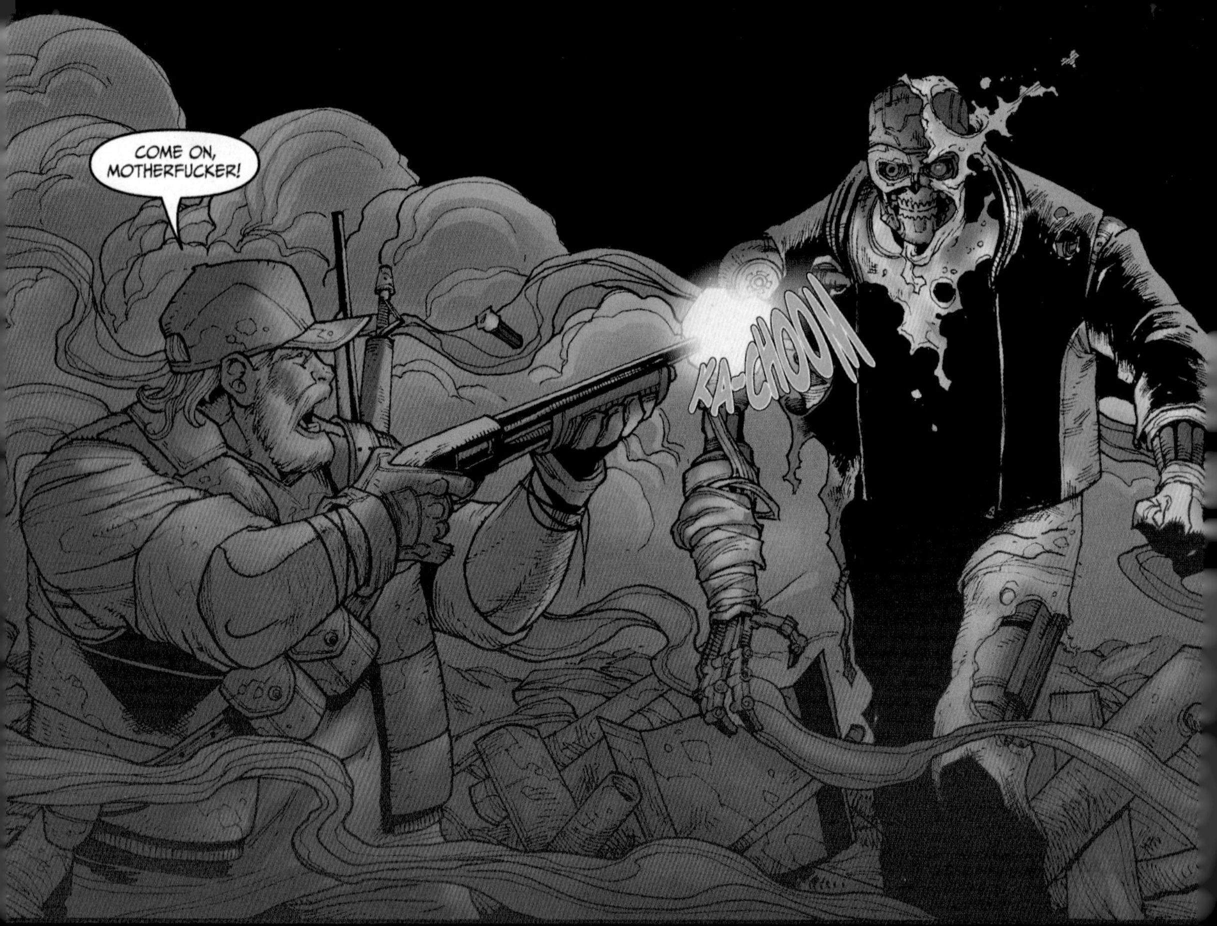
COME ON, MOTHERFUCKER!
KA-CHOOM

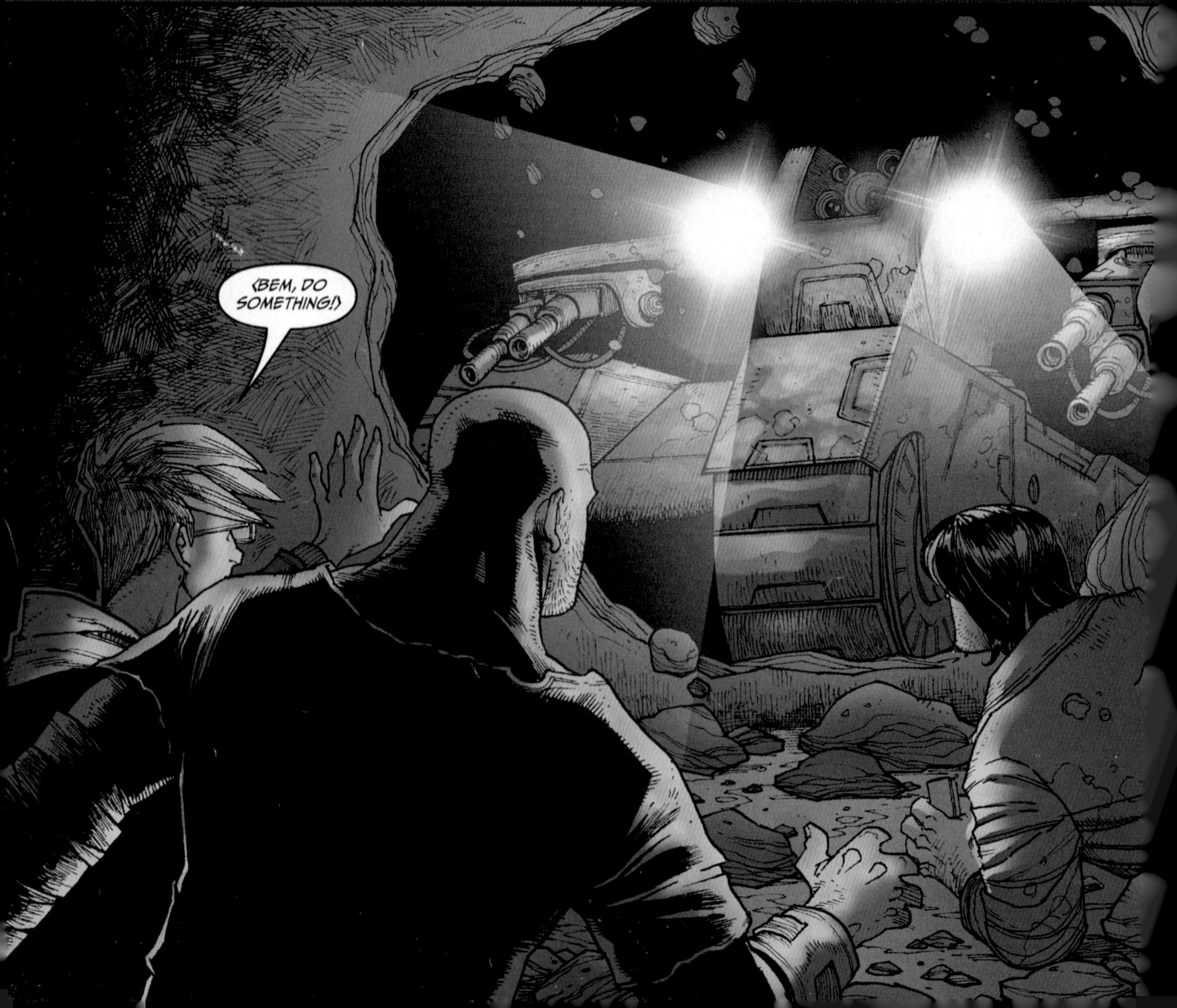
‹BEM, DO SOMETHING!›

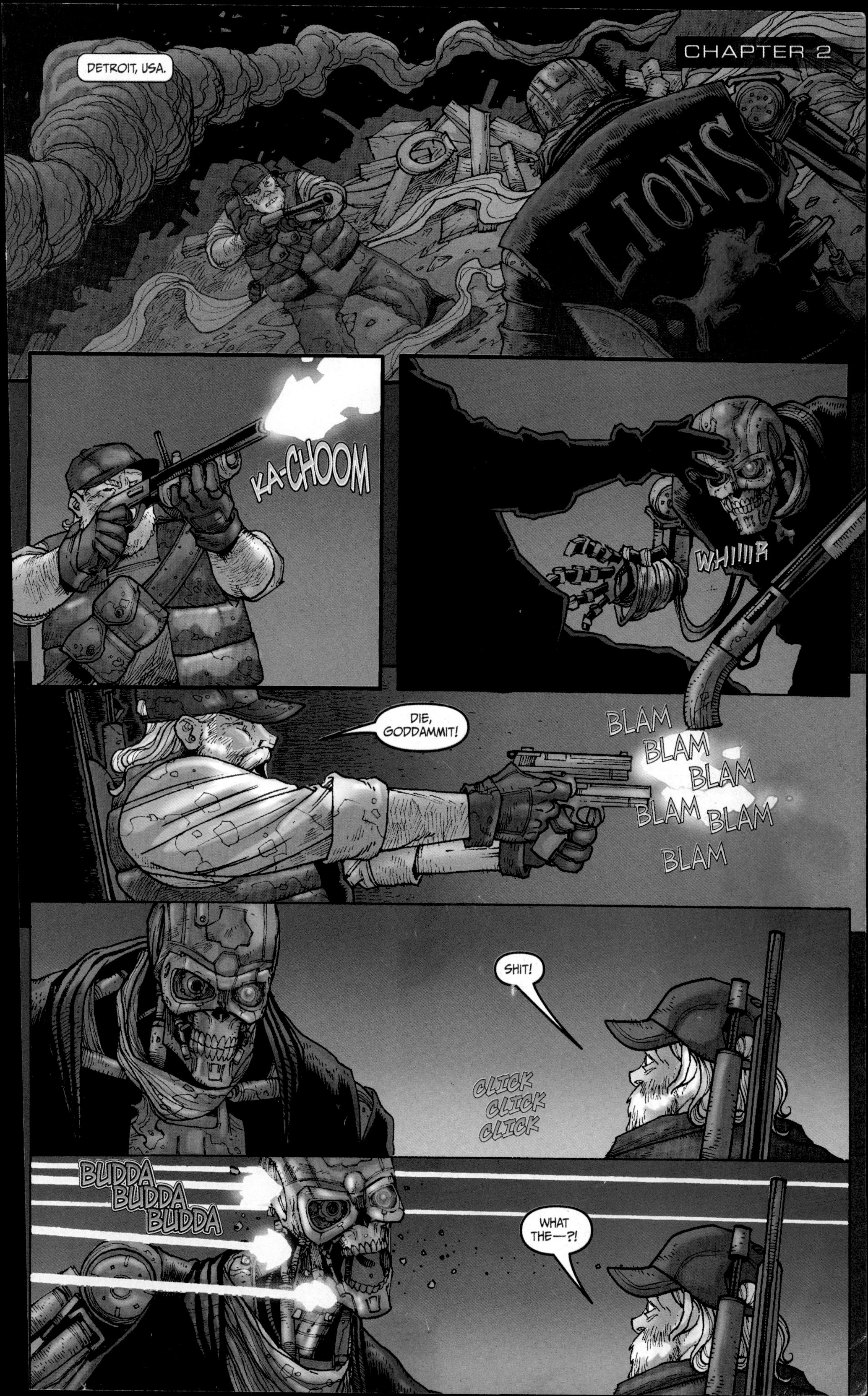
CHAPTER 2
DETROIT, USA.
LIONS
KA-CHOOM
WHIIIIR
DIE, GODDAMMIT!
BLAM BLAM BLAM BLAM BLAM BLAM
SHIT!
CLICK CLICK CLICK
BUDDA BUDDA BUDDA
WHAT THE—?!

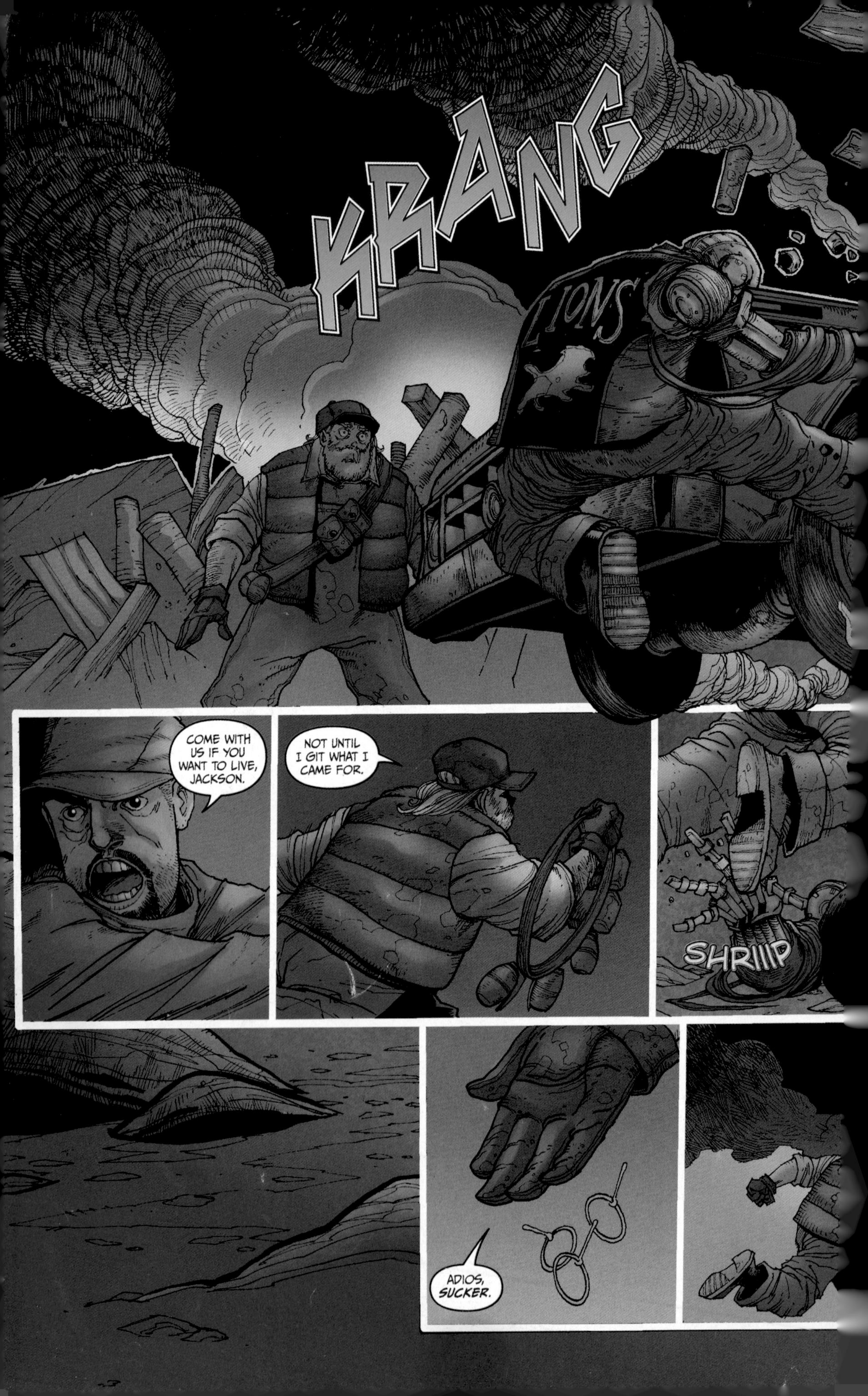
KRANG
LIONS
COME WITH US IF YOU WANT TO LIVE, JACKSON.
NOT UNTIL I GIT WHAT I CAME FOR.
SHRIIP
ADIOS, SUCKER.

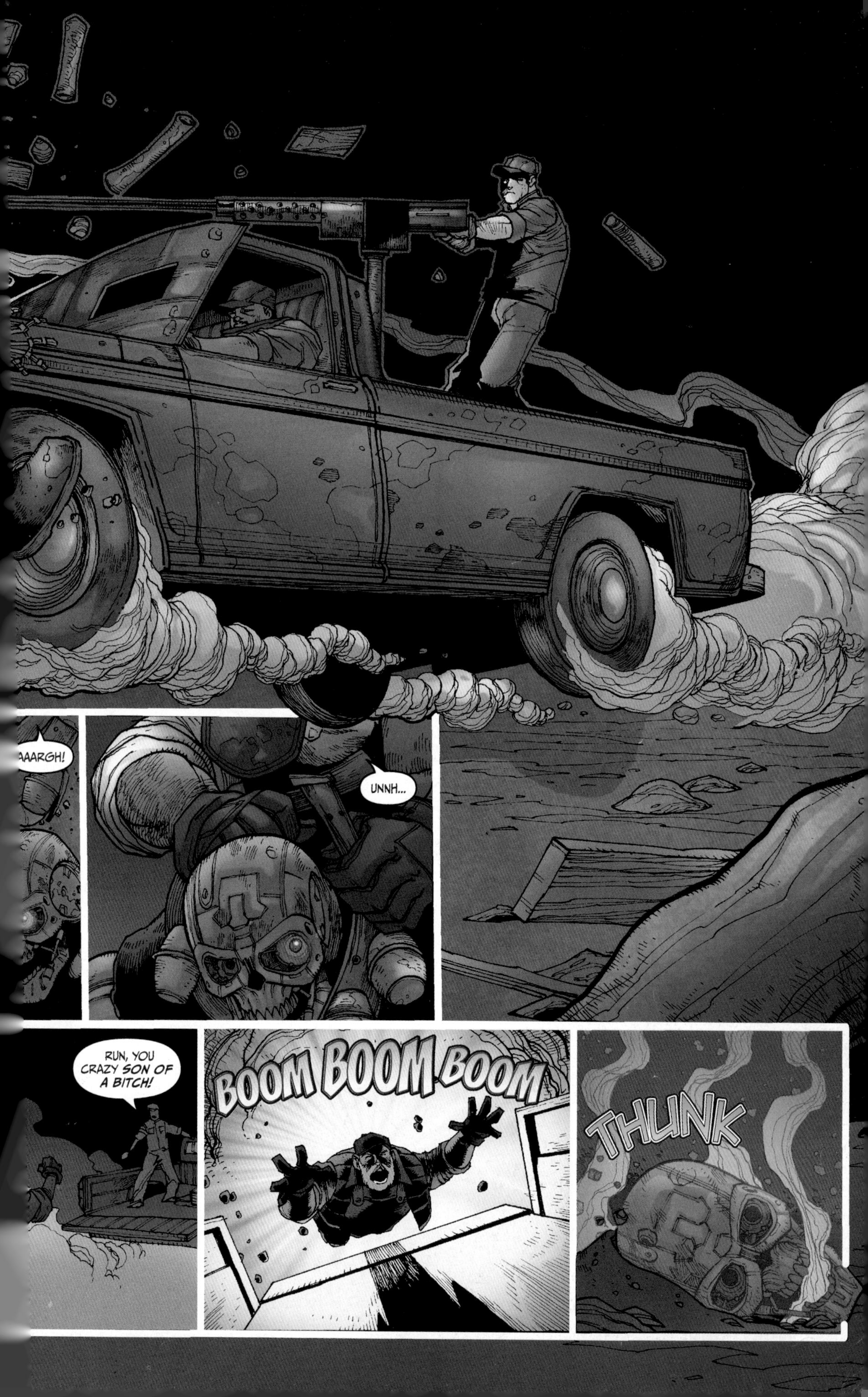
AAARGH!
UNNH...
RUN, YOU CRAZY SON OF A BITCH!
BOOM BOOM BOOM
THUNK

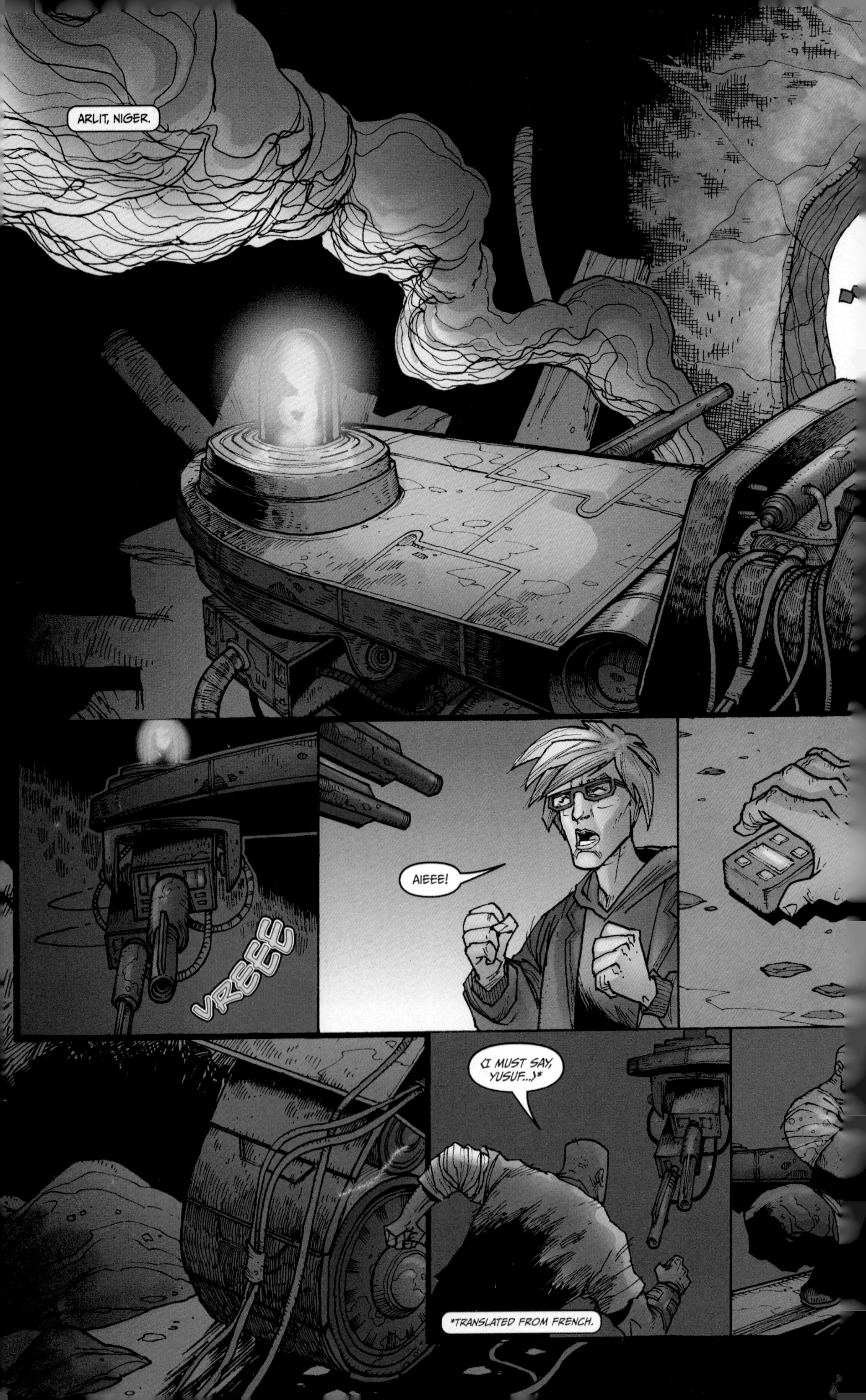
ARLIT, NIGER.
VREEE
AIEEE!
‹I MUST SAY, YUSUF...›*
*TRANSLATED FROM FRENCH.

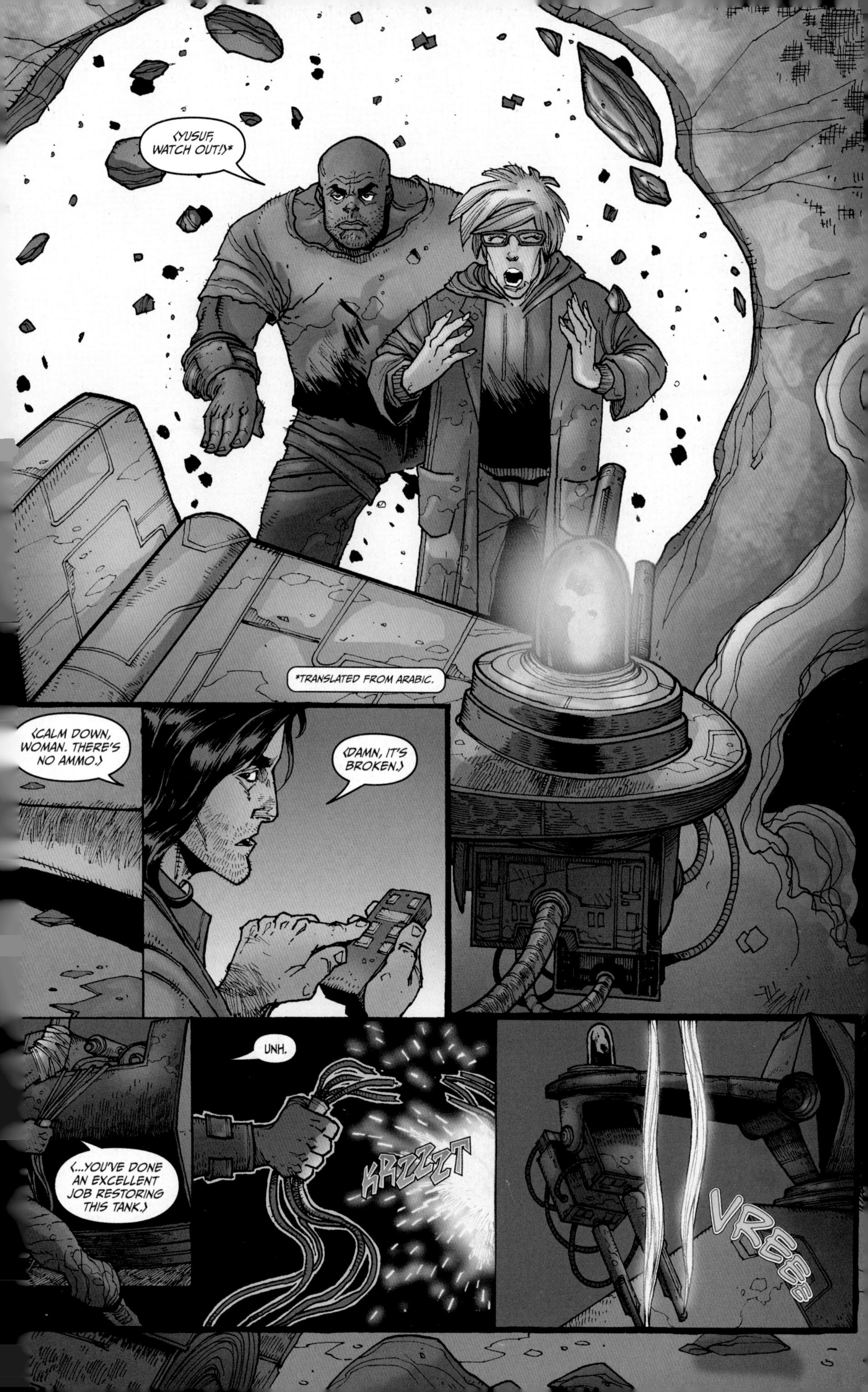
<YUSUF, WATCH OUT!>*
*TRANSLATED FROM ARABIC.
<CALM DOWN, WOMAN. THERE'S NO AMMO.>
<DAMN, IT'S BROKEN.>
UNH.
<...YOU'VE DONE AN EXCELLENT JOB RESTORING THIS TANK.>
KRZZZT
VREEEE

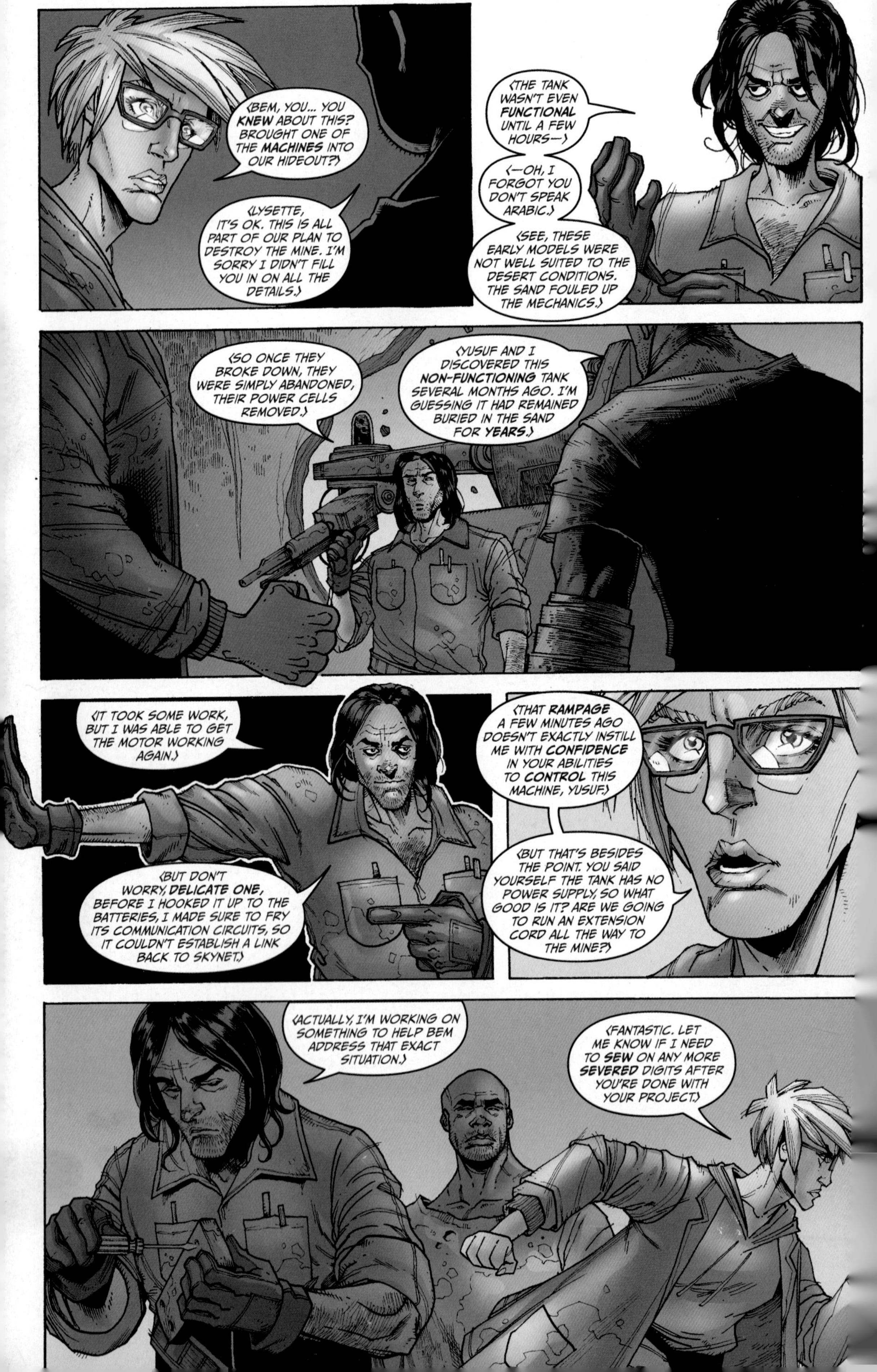
‹BEM, YOU... YOU KNEW ABOUT THIS? BROUGHT ONE OF THE MACHINES INTO OUR HIDEOUT?›
‹LYSETTE, IT'S OK. THIS IS ALL PART OF OUR PLAN TO DESTROY THE MINE. I'M SORRY I DIDN'T FILL YOU IN ON ALL THE DETAILS.›
‹THE TANK WASN'T EVEN FUNCTIONAL UNTIL A FEW HOURS—›
‹—OH, I FORGOT YOU DON'T SPEAK ARABIC.›
‹SEE, THESE EARLY MODELS WERE NOT WELL SUITED TO THE DESERT CONDITIONS. THE SAND FOULED UP THE MECHANICS.›
‹SO ONCE THEY BROKE DOWN, THEY WERE SIMPLY ABANDONED, THEIR POWER CELLS REMOVED.›
‹YUSUF AND I DISCOVERED THIS NON-FUNCTIONING TANK SEVERAL MONTHS AGO. I'M GUESSING IT HAD REMAINED BURIED IN THE SAND FOR YEARS.›
‹IT TOOK SOME WORK, BUT I WAS ABLE TO GET THE MOTOR WORKING AGAIN.›
‹BUT DON'T WORRY, DELICATE ONE, BEFORE I HOOKED IT UP TO THE BATTERIES, I MADE SURE TO FRY ITS COMMUNICATION CIRCUITS, SO IT COULDN'T ESTABLISH A LINK BACK TO SKYNET.›
‹THAT RAMPAGE A FEW MINUTES AGO DOESN'T EXACTLY INSTILL ME WITH CONFIDENCE IN YOUR ABILITIES TO CONTROL THIS MACHINE, YUSUF.›
‹BUT THAT'S BESIDES THE POINT. YOU SAID YOURSELF THE TANK HAS NO POWER SUPPLY, SO WHAT GOOD IS IT? ARE WE GOING TO RUN AN EXTENSION CORD ALL THE WAY TO THE MINE?›
‹ACTUALLY, I'M WORKING ON SOMETHING TO HELP BEM ADDRESS THAT EXACT SITUATION.›
‹FANTASTIC. LET ME KNOW IF I NEED TO SEW ON ANY MORE SEVERED DIGITS AFTER YOU'RE DONE WITH YOUR PROJECT.›

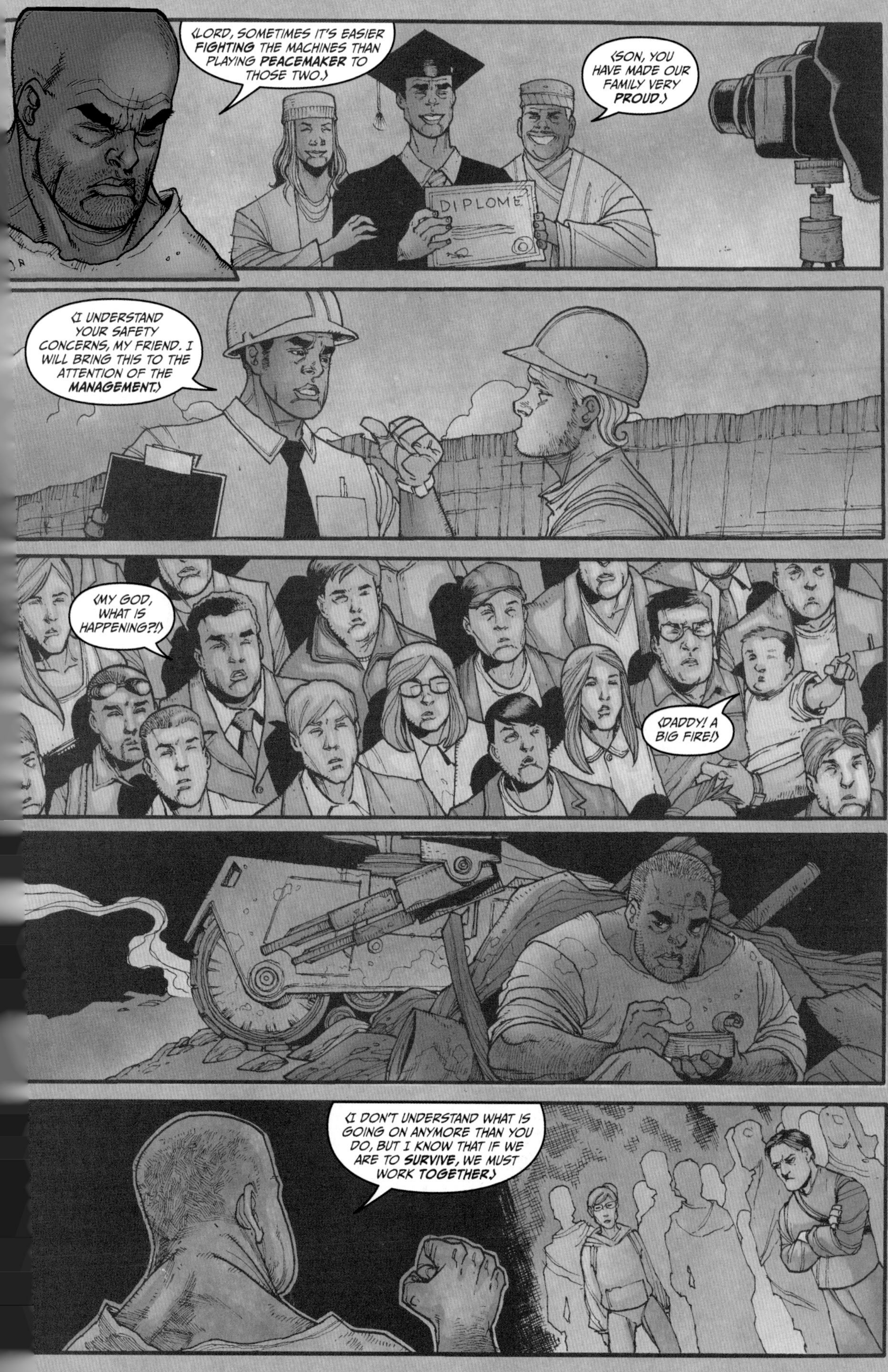

‹LORD, SOMETIMES IT'S EASIER FIGHTING THE MACHINES THAN PLAYING PEACEMAKER TO THOSE TWO.›
‹SON, YOU HAVE MADE OUR FAMILY VERY PROUD.›
DIPLOME
‹I UNDERSTAND YOUR SAFETY CONCERNS, MY FRIEND. I WILL BRING THIS TO THE ATTENTION OF THE MANAGEMENT.›
‹MY GOD, WHAT IS HAPPENING?!›
‹DADDY! A BIG FIRE!›
‹I DON'T UNDERSTAND WHAT IS GOING ON ANYMORE THAN YOU DO, BUT I KNOW THAT IF WE ARE TO SURVIVE, WE MUST WORK TOGETHER.›

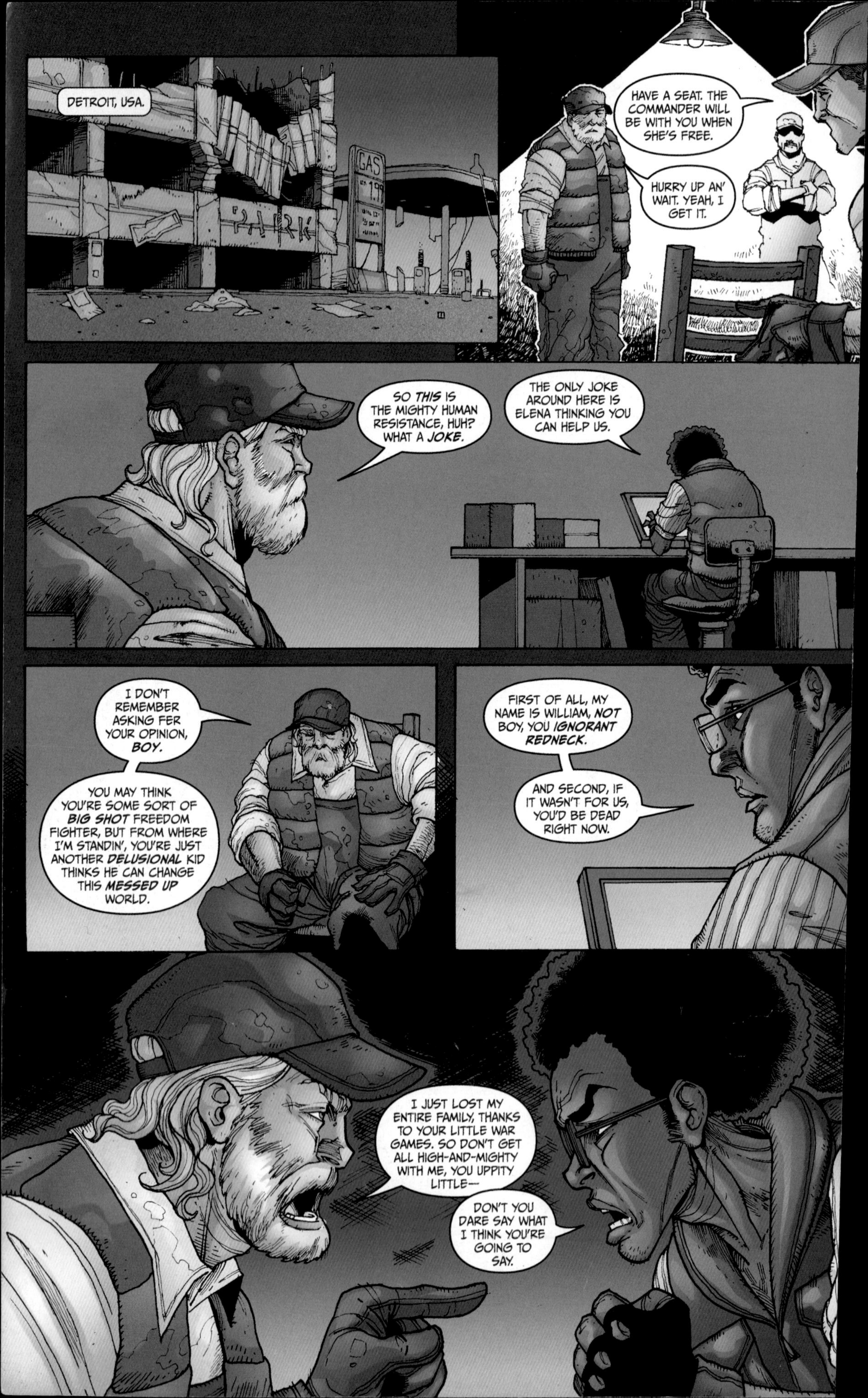
DETROIT, USA.
GAS
PARK
HAVE A SEAT. THE COMMANDER WILL BE WITH YOU WHEN SHE'S FREE.
HURRY UP AN' WAIT. YEAH, I GET IT.
SO THIS IS THE MIGHTY HUMAN RESISTANCE, HUH? WHAT A JOKE.
THE ONLY JOKE AROUND HERE IS ELENA THINKING YOU CAN HELP US.
I DON'T REMEMBER ASKING FER YOUR OPINION, BOY.
YOU MAY THINK YOU'RE SOME SORT OF BIG SHOT FREEDOM FIGHTER, BUT FROM WHERE I'M STANDIN', YOU'RE JUST ANOTHER DELUSIONAL KID THINKS HE CAN CHANGE THIS MESSED UP WORLD.
FIRST OF ALL, MY NAME IS WILLIAM, NOT BOY, YOU IGNORANT REDNECK.
AND SECOND, IF IT WASN'T FOR US, YOU'D BE DEAD RIGHT NOW.
I JUST LOST MY ENTIRE FAMILY, THANKS TO YOUR LITTLE WAR GAMES. SO DON'T GET ALL HIGH-AND-MIGHTY WITH ME, YOU UPPITY LITTLE—
DON'T YOU DARE SAY WHAT I THINK YOU'RE GOING TO SAY.

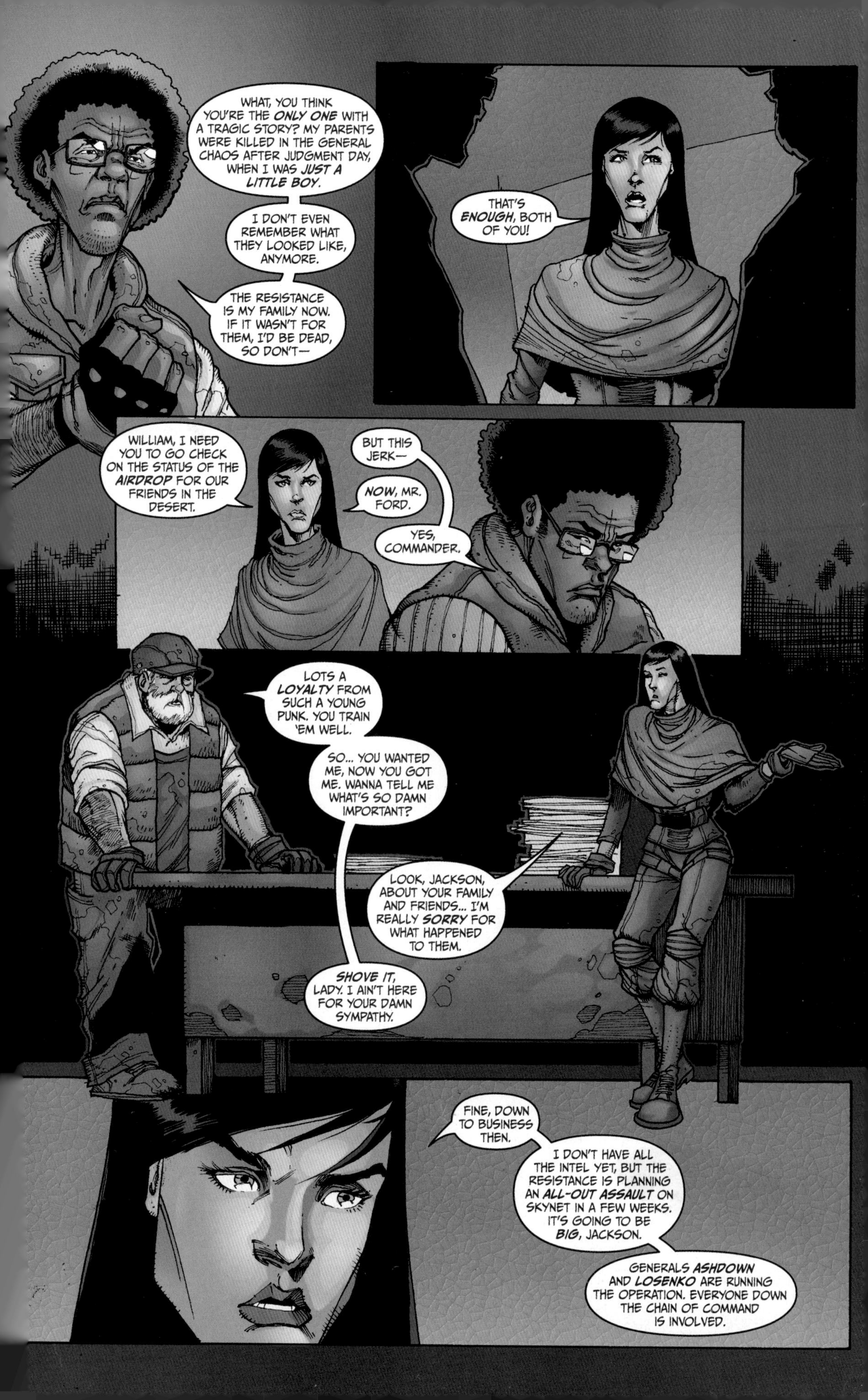
WHAT, YOU THINK YOU'RE THE ONLY ONE WITH A TRAGIC STORY? MY PARENTS WERE KILLED IN THE GENERAL CHAOS AFTER JUDGMENT DAY, WHEN I WAS JUST A LITTLE BOY.
I DON'T EVEN REMEMBER WHAT THEY LOOKED LIKE, ANYMORE.
THE RESISTANCE IS MY FAMILY NOW. IF IT WASN'T FOR THEM, I'D BE DEAD, SO DON'T—
THAT'S ENOUGH, BOTH OF YOU!
WILLIAM, I NEED YOU TO GO CHECK ON THE STATUS OF THE AIRDROP FOR OUR FRIENDS IN THE DESERT.
BUT THIS JERK—
NOW, MR. FORD.
YES, COMMANDER.
LOTS A LOYALTY FROM SUCH A YOUNG PUNK. YOU TRAIN 'EM WELL.
SO... YOU WANTED ME, NOW YOU GOT ME. WANNA TELL ME WHAT'S SO DAMN IMPORTANT?
LOOK, JACKSON, ABOUT YOUR FAMILY AND FRIENDS... I'M REALLY SORRY FOR WHAT HAPPENED TO THEM.
SHOVE IT, LADY. I AIN'T HERE FOR YOUR DAMN SYMPATHY.
FINE, DOWN TO BUSINESS THEN.
I DON'T HAVE ALL THE INTEL YET, BUT THE RESISTANCE IS PLANNING AN ALL-OUT ASSAULT ON SKYNET IN A FEW WEEKS. IT'S GOING TO BE BIG, JACKSON.
GENERALS ASHDOWN AND LOSENKO ARE RUNNING THE OPERATION. EVERYONE DOWN THE CHAIN OF COMMAND IS INVOLVED.

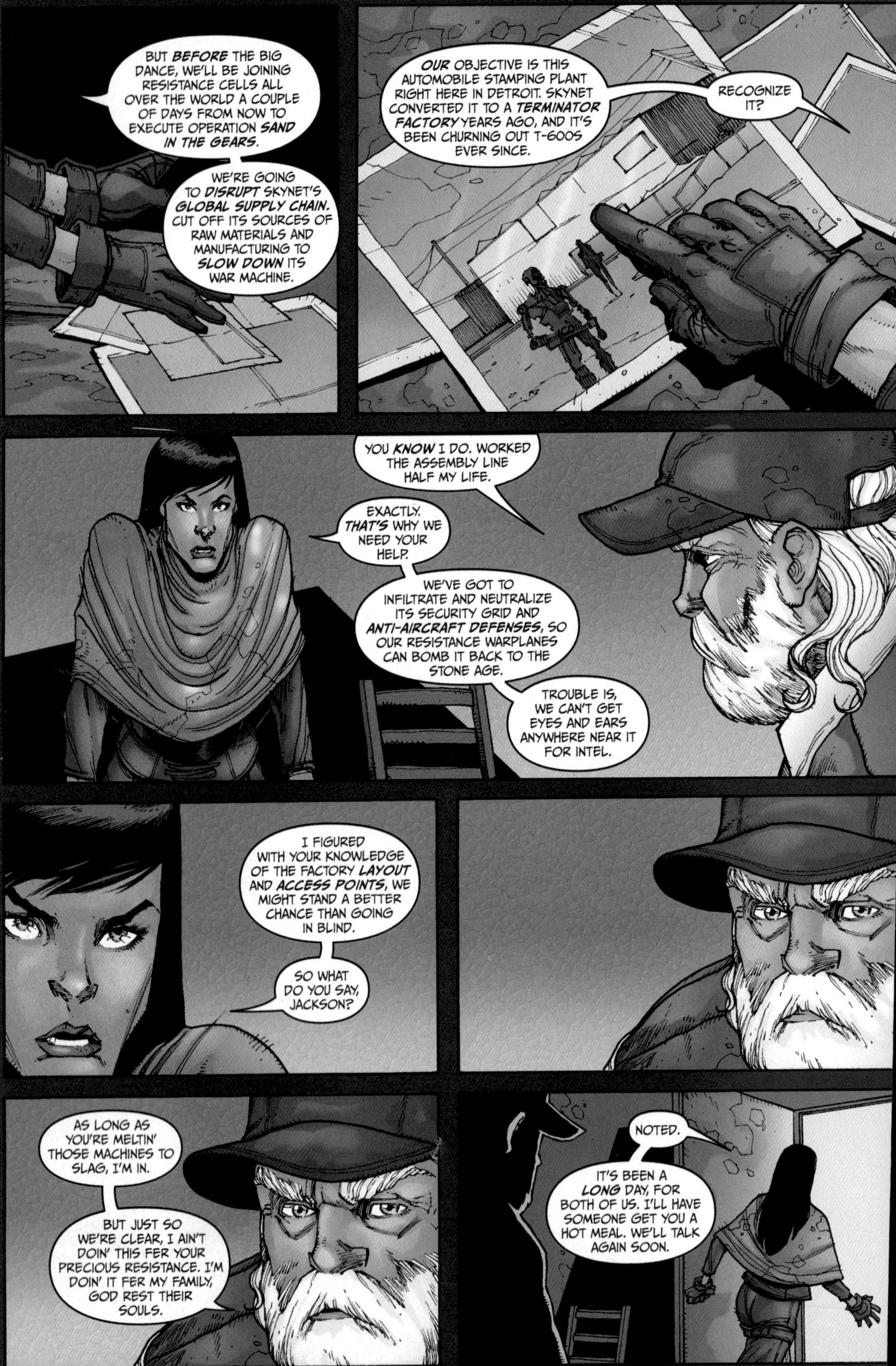
BUT BEFORE THE BIG DANCE, WE'LL BE JOINING RESISTANCE CELLS ALL OVER THE WORLD A COUPLE OF DAYS FROM NOW TO EXECUTE OPERATION SAND IN THE GEARS.
WE'RE GOING TO DISRUPT SKYNET'S GLOBAL SUPPLY CHAIN. CUT OFF ITS SOURCES OF RAW MATERIALS AND MANUFACTURING TO SLOW DOWN ITS WAR MACHINE.
OUR OBJECTIVE IS THIS AUTOMOBILE STAMPING PLANT RIGHT HERE IN DETROIT. SKYNET CONVERTED IT TO A TERMINATOR FACTORY YEARS AGO, AND IT'S BEEN CHURNING OUT T-600S EVER SINCE.
RECOGNIZE IT?
YOU KNOW I DO. WORKED THE ASSEMBLY LINE HALF MY LIFE.
EXACTLY. THAT'S WHY WE NEED YOUR HELP.
WE'VE GOT TO INFILTRATE AND NEUTRALIZE ITS SECURITY GRID AND ANTI-AIRCRAFT DEFENSES, SO OUR RESISTANCE WARPLANES CAN BOMB IT BACK TO THE STONE AGE.
TROUBLE IS, WE CAN'T GET EYES AND EARS ANYWHERE NEAR IT FOR INTEL.
I FIGURED WITH YOUR KNOWLEDGE OF THE FACTORY LAYOUT AND ACCESS POINTS, WE MIGHT STAND A BETTER CHANCE THAN GOING IN BLIND.
SO WHAT DO YOU SAY, JACKSON?
AS LONG AS YOU'RE MELTIN' THOSE MACHINES TO SLAG, I'M IN.
BUT JUST SO WE'RE CLEAR, I AIN'T DOIN' THIS FER YOUR PRECIOUS RESISTANCE. I'M DOIN' IT FER MY FAMILY, GOD REST THEIR SOULS.
NOTED.
IT'S BEEN A LONG DAY, FOR BOTH OF US. I'LL HAVE SOMEONE GET YOU A HOT MEAL. WE'LL TALK AGAIN SOON.

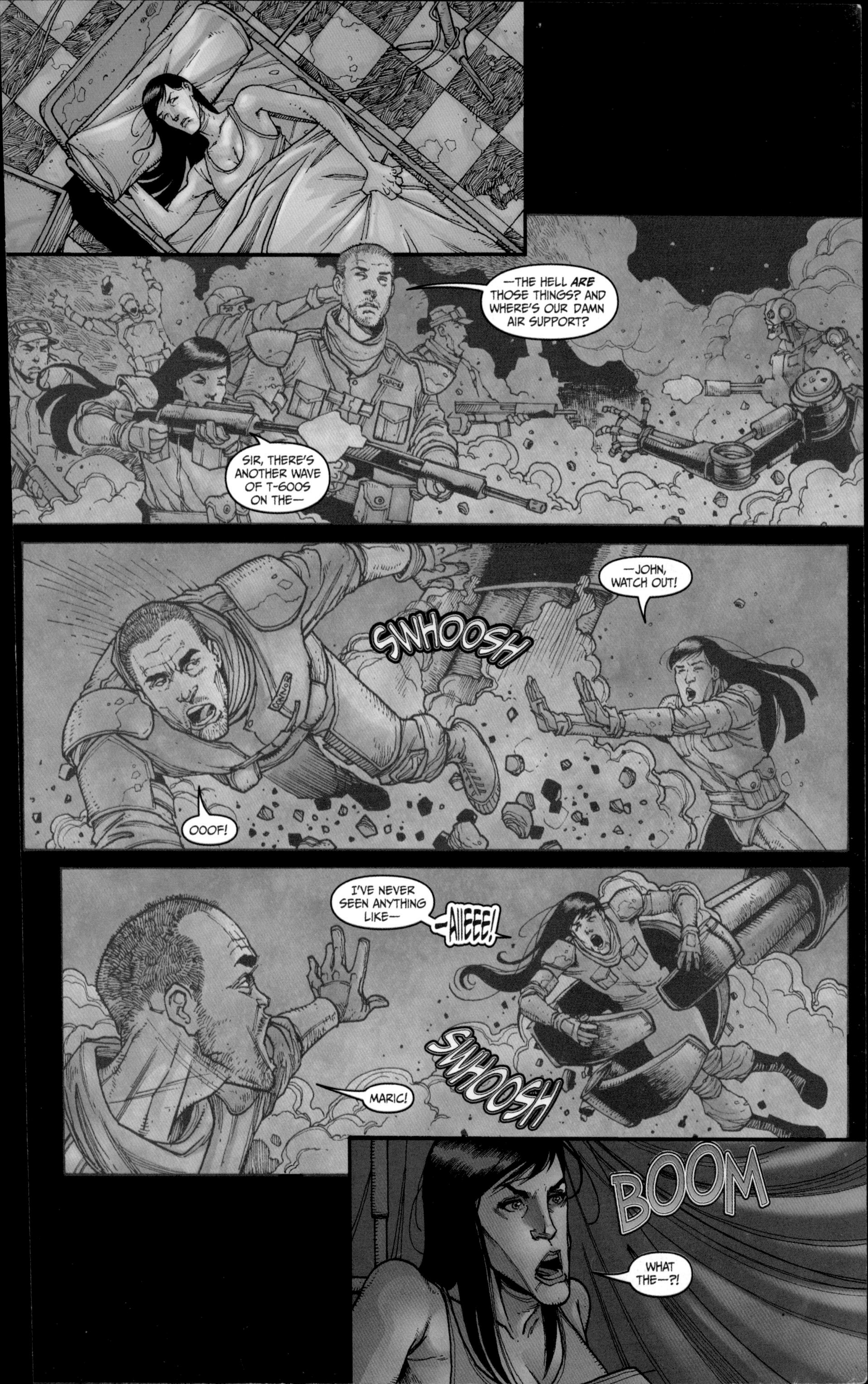
—THE HELL ARE THOSE THINGS? AND WHERE'S OUR DAMN AIR SUPPORT?
SIR, THERE'S ANOTHER WAVE OF T-600S ON THE—
—JOHN, WATCH OUT!
SWHOOSH
OOOF!
I'VE NEVER SEEN ANYTHING LIKE—
—AIIEEE!
SWHOOSH
MARIC!
BOOM
WHAT THE—?!

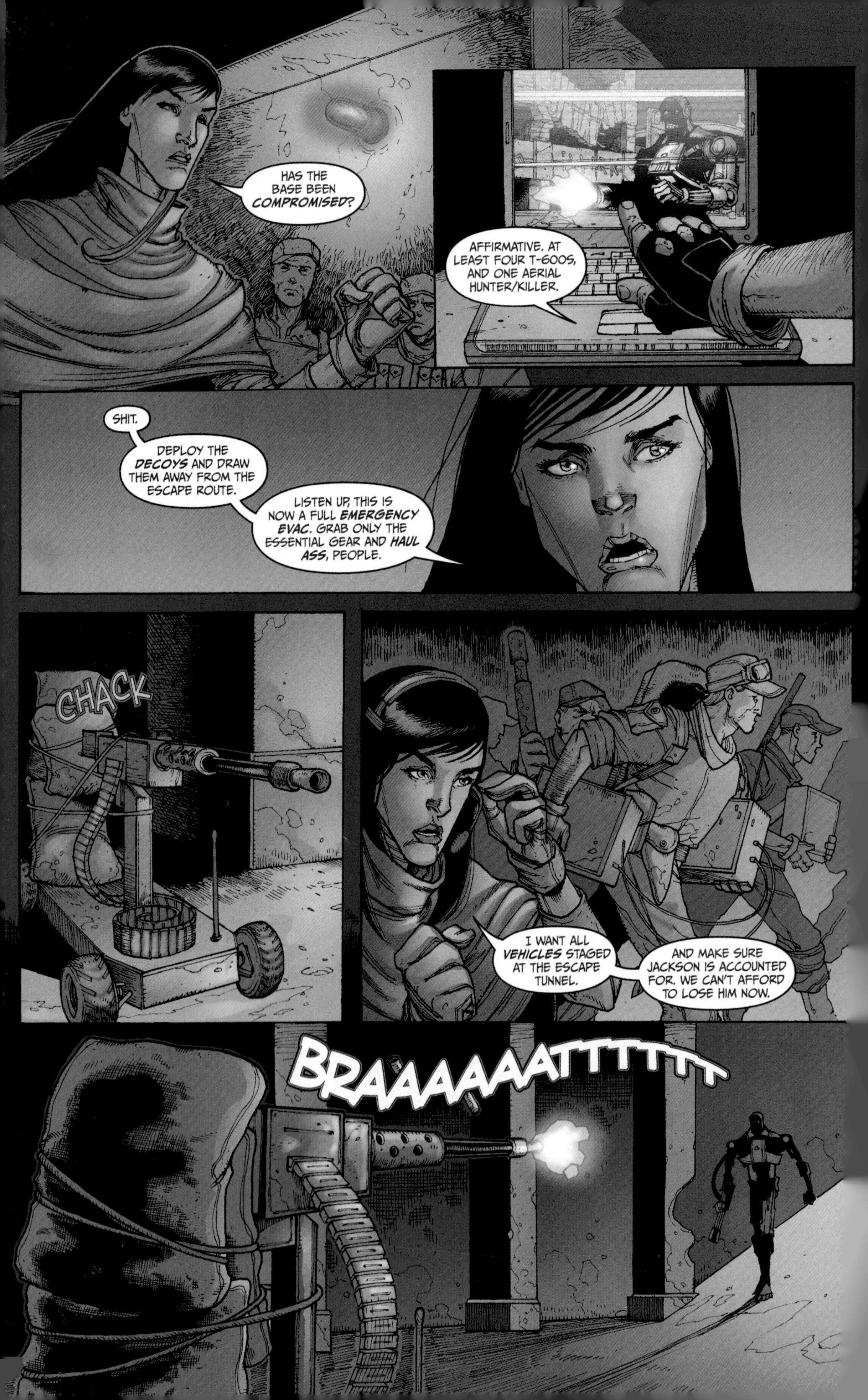
HAS THE BASE BEEN COMPROMISED?
AFFIRMATIVE. AT LEAST FOUR T-600S, AND ONE AERIAL HUNTER/KILLER.
SHIT.
DEPLOY THE DECOYS AND DRAW THEM AWAY FROM THE ESCAPE ROUTE.
LISTEN UP, THIS IS NOW A FULL EMERGENCY EVAC. GRAB ONLY THE ESSENTIAL GEAR AND HAUL ASS, PEOPLE.
CHACK
I WANT ALL VEHICLES STAGED AT THE ESCAPE TUNNEL.
AND MAKE SURE JACKSON IS ACCOUNTED FOR. WE CAN'T AFFORD TO LOSE HIM NOW.
BRAAAAAATTTTTT

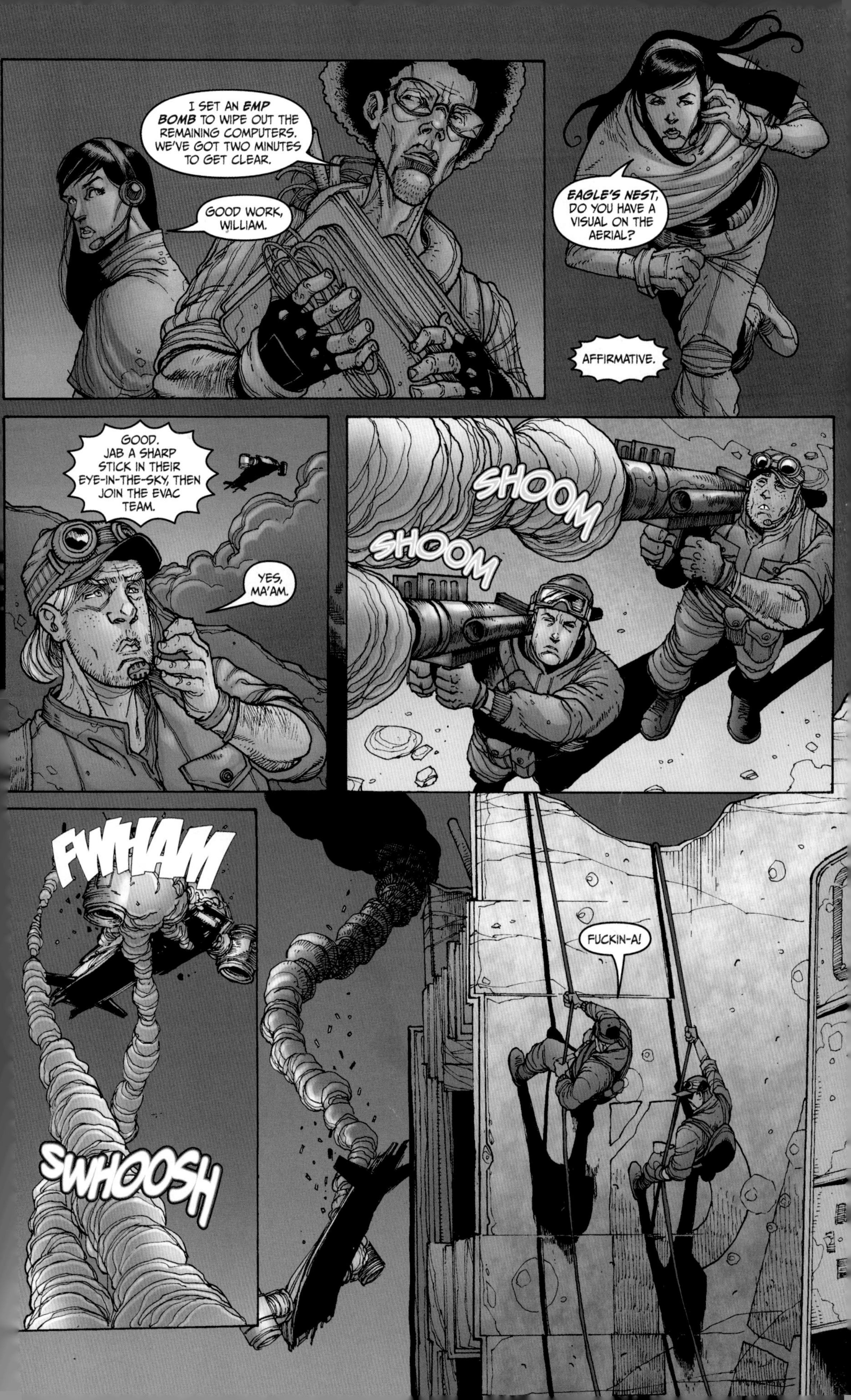
I SET AN EMP BOMB TO WIPE OUT THE REMAINING COMPUTERS. WE'VE GOT TWO MINUTES TO GET CLEAR.
GOOD WORK, WILLIAM.
EAGLE'S NEST, DO YOU HAVE A VISUAL ON THE AERIAL?
AFFIRMATIVE.
GOOD. JAB A SHARP STICK IN THEIR EYE-IN-THE-SKY, THEN JOIN THE EVAC TEAM.
YES, MA'AM.
SHOOM
SHOOM
FWHAM
SWHOOSH
FUCKIN-A!

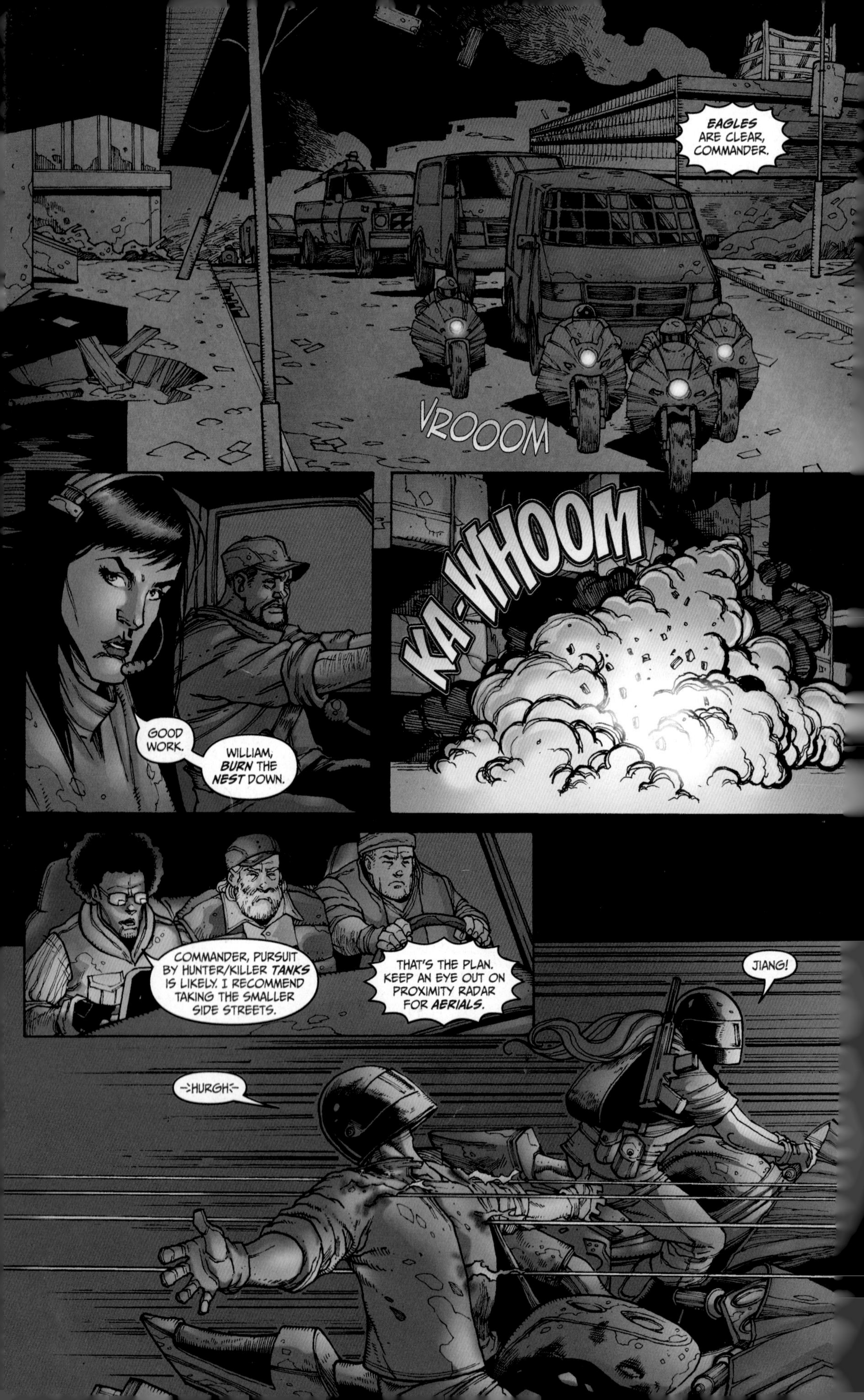
EAGLES ARE CLEAR, COMMANDER.
VROOOM
GOOD WORK.
WILLIAM, BURN THE NEST DOWN.
KA-WHOOM
COMMANDER, PURSUIT BY HUNTER/KILLER TANKS IS LIKELY. I RECOMMEND TAKING THE SMALLER SIDE STREETS.
THAT'S THE PLAN. KEEP AN EYE OUT ON PROXIMITY RADAR FOR AERIALS.
JIANG!
HURGH

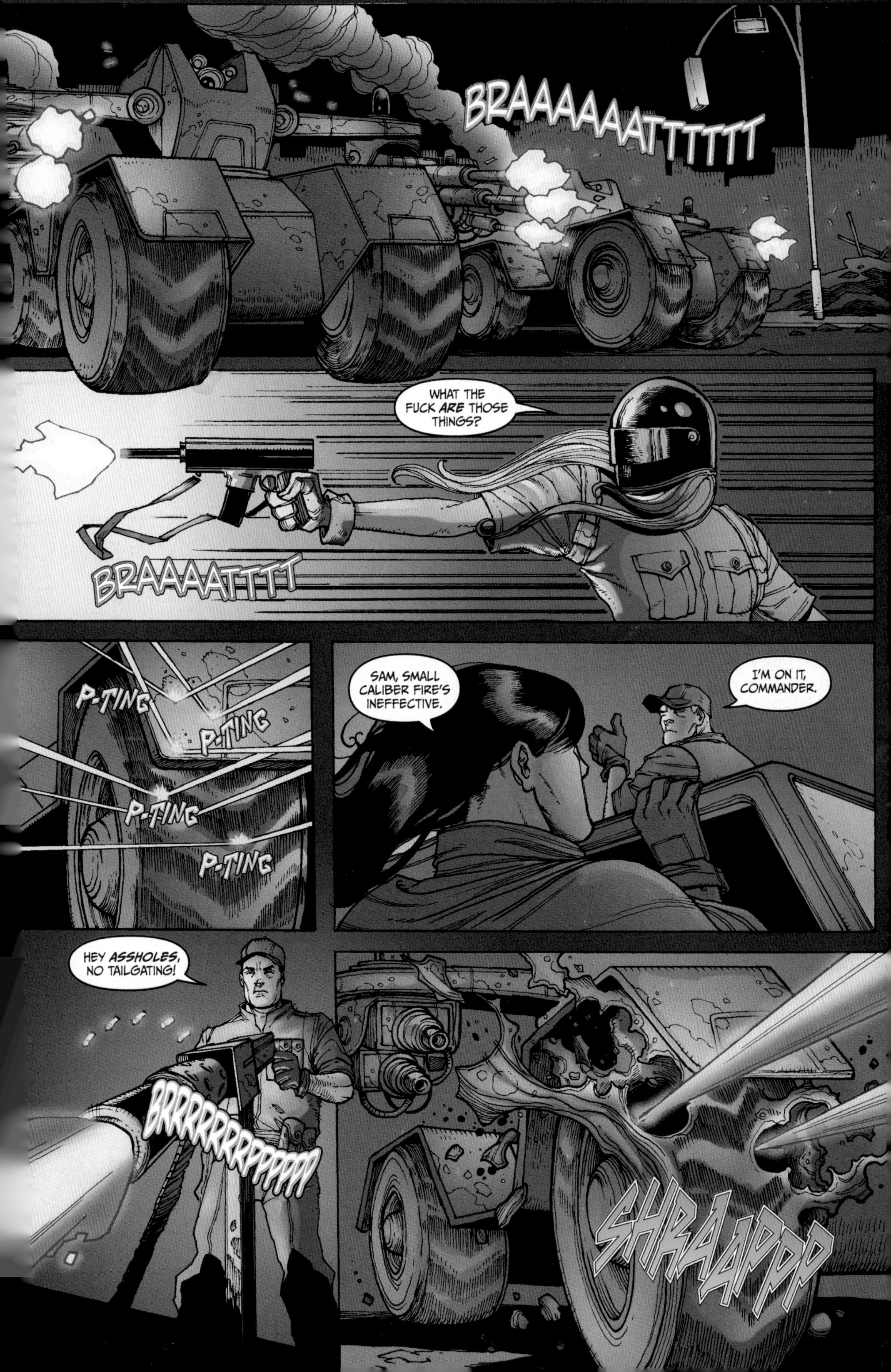

BRAAAAAAATTTTTT
WHAT THE FUCK *ARE* THOSE THINGS?
BRAAAATTTTT
P-TING
P-TING
P-T-ING
P-TING
SAM, SMALL CALIBER FIRE'S INEFFECTIVE.
I'M ON IT, COMMANDER.
HEY *ASSHOLES*, NO TAILGATING!
BRRRRRRRPPPPPP
SHRAAPPPP

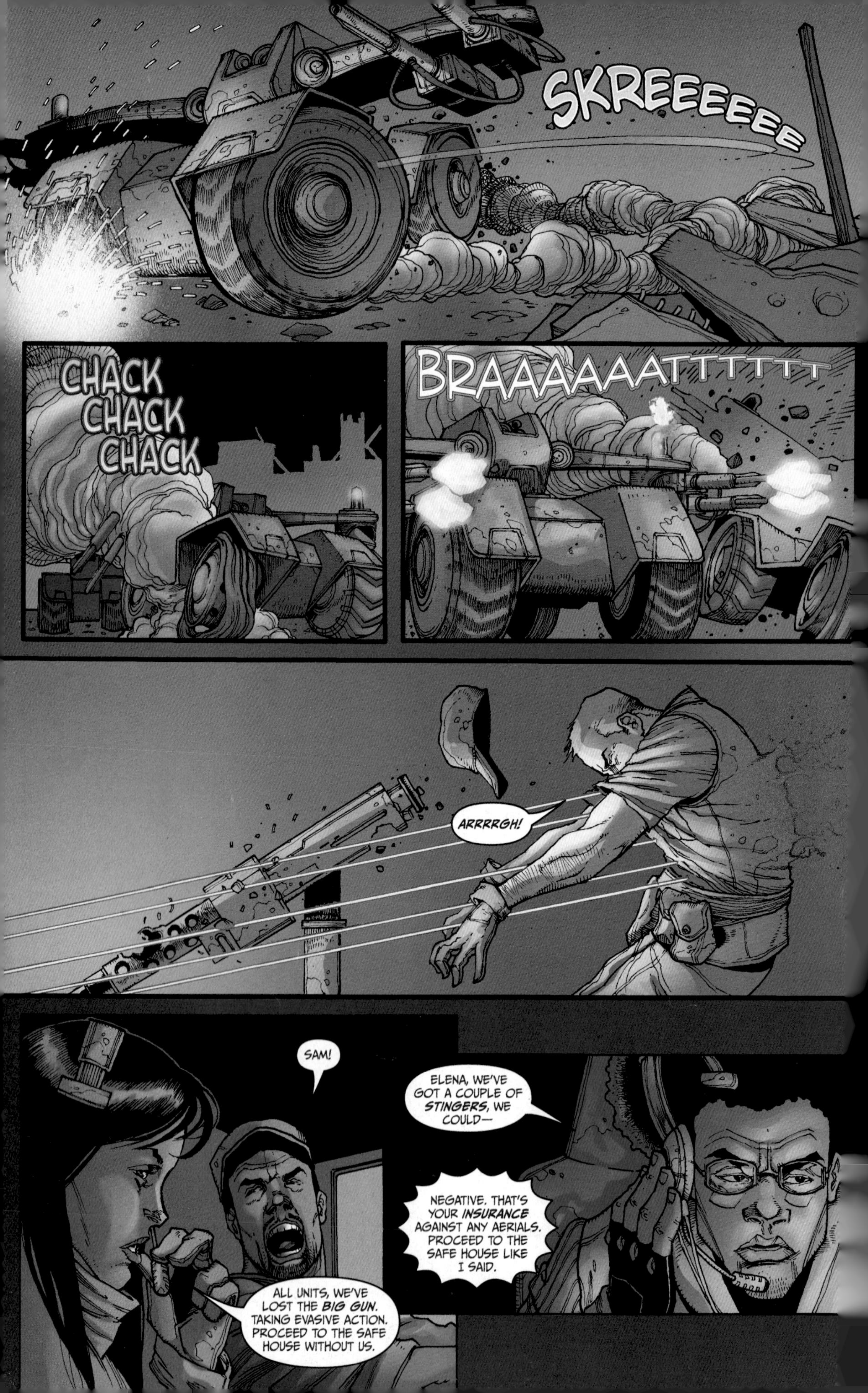
SKREEEEEEE
CHACK CHACK CHACK
BRAAAAAATTTTTT
ARRRRGH!
SAM!
ALL UNITS, WE'VE LOST THE *BIG GUN*. TAKING EVASIVE ACTION. PROCEED TO THE SAFE HOUSE WITHOUT US.
ELENA, WE'VE GOT A COUPLE OF *STINGERS*, WE COULD—
NEGATIVE. THAT'S YOUR *INSURANCE* AGAINST ANY AERIALS. PROCEED TO THE SAFE HOUSE LIKE I SAID.

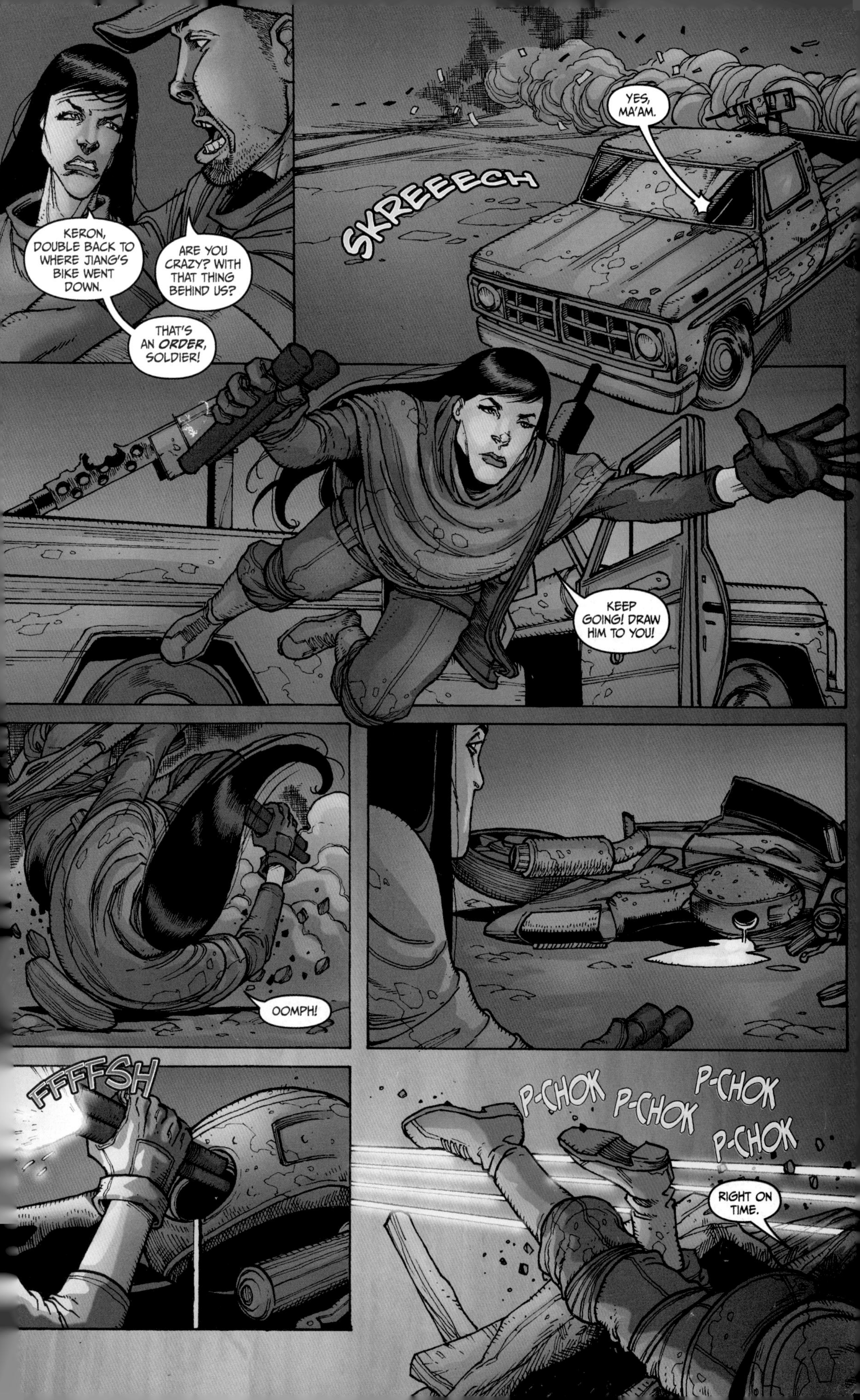
KERON, DOUBLE BACK TO WHERE JIANG'S BIKE WENT DOWN.
ARE YOU CRAZY? WITH THAT THING BEHIND US?
THAT'S AN *ORDER*, SOLDIER!
SKREEECH
YES, MA'AM.
KEEP GOING! DRAW HIM TO YOU!
OOMPH!
FFFFSH
P-CHOK
P-CHOK
P-CHOK
P-CHOK
RIGHT ON TIME.

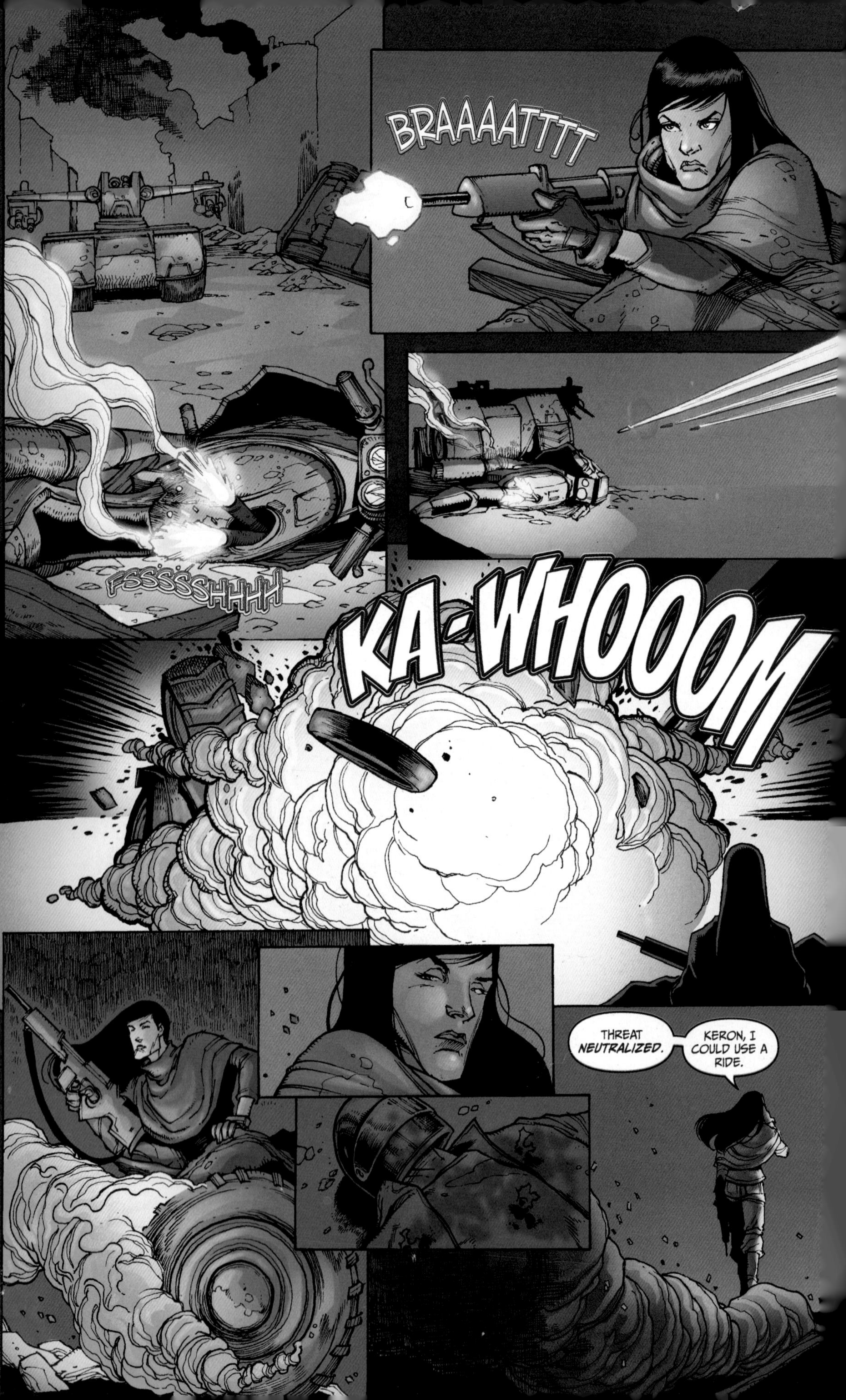
BRAAAATTTT
FSSSSSHHHH
KA-WHOOOM
THREAT NEUTRALIZED.
KERON, I COULD USE A RIDE.

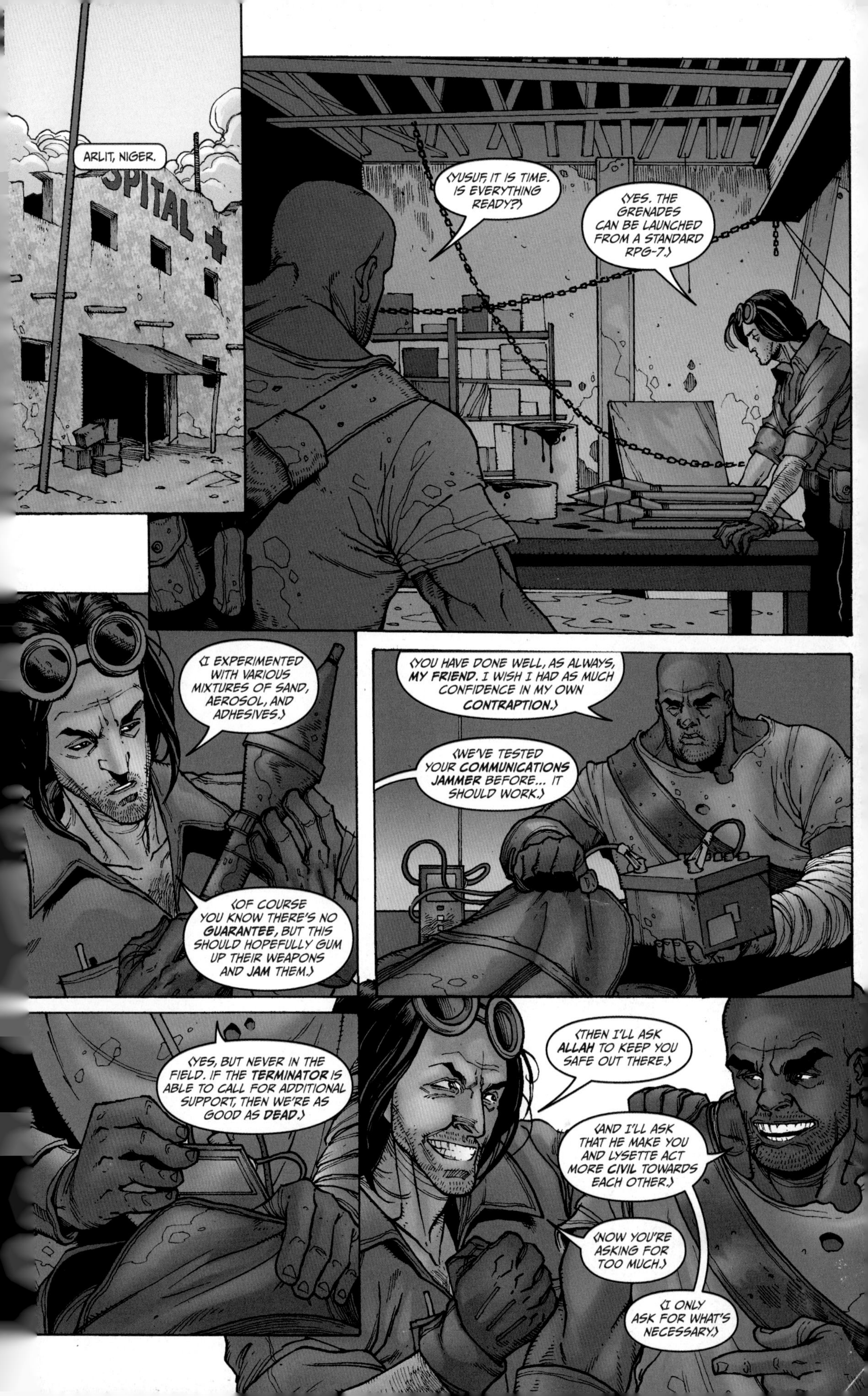

ARLIT, NIGER.
SPITAL
‹YUSUF, IT IS TIME. IS EVERYTHING READY?›
‹YES. THE GRENADES CAN BE LAUNCHED FROM A STANDARD RPG-7.›
‹I EXPERIMENTED WITH VARIOUS MIXTURES OF SAND, AEROSOL, AND ADHESIVES.›
‹OF COURSE YOU KNOW THERE'S NO GUARANTEE, BUT THIS SHOULD HOPEFULLY GUM UP THEIR WEAPONS AND JAM THEM.›
‹YOU HAVE DONE WELL, AS ALWAYS, MY FRIEND. I WISH I HAD AS MUCH CONFIDENCE IN MY OWN CONTRAPTION.›
‹WE'VE TESTED YOUR COMMUNICATIONS JAMMER BEFORE... IT SHOULD WORK.›
‹YES, BUT NEVER IN THE FIELD. IF THE TERMINATOR IS ABLE TO CALL FOR ADDITIONAL SUPPORT, THEN WE'RE AS GOOD AS DEAD.›
‹THEN I'LL ASK ALLAH TO KEEP YOU SAFE OUT THERE.›
‹AND I'LL ASK THAT HE MAKE YOU AND LYSETTE ACT MORE CIVIL TOWARDS EACH OTHER.›
‹NOW YOU'RE ASKING FOR TOO MUCH.›
‹I ONLY ASK FOR WHAT'S NECESSARY.›

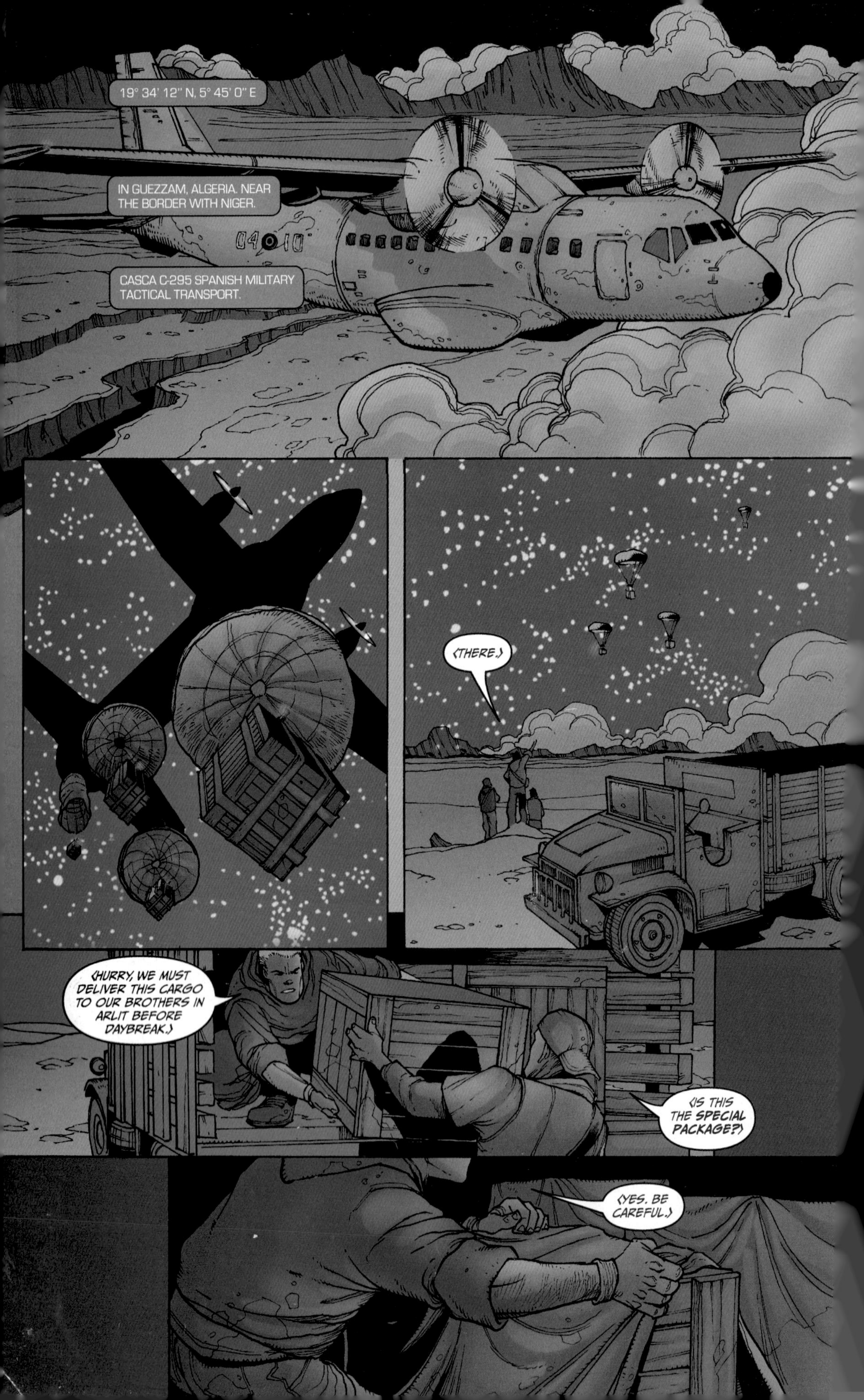
19° 34' 12" N, 5° 45' 0" E
IN GUEZZAM, ALGERIA. NEAR THE BORDER WITH NIGER.
CASCA C-295 SPANISH MILITARY TACTICAL TRANSPORT.
04 10
‹THERE.›
‹HURRY, WE MUST DELIVER THIS CARGO TO OUR BROTHERS IN ARLIT BEFORE DAYBREAK.›
‹IS THIS THE SPECIAL PACKAGE?›
‹YES. BE CAREFUL.›

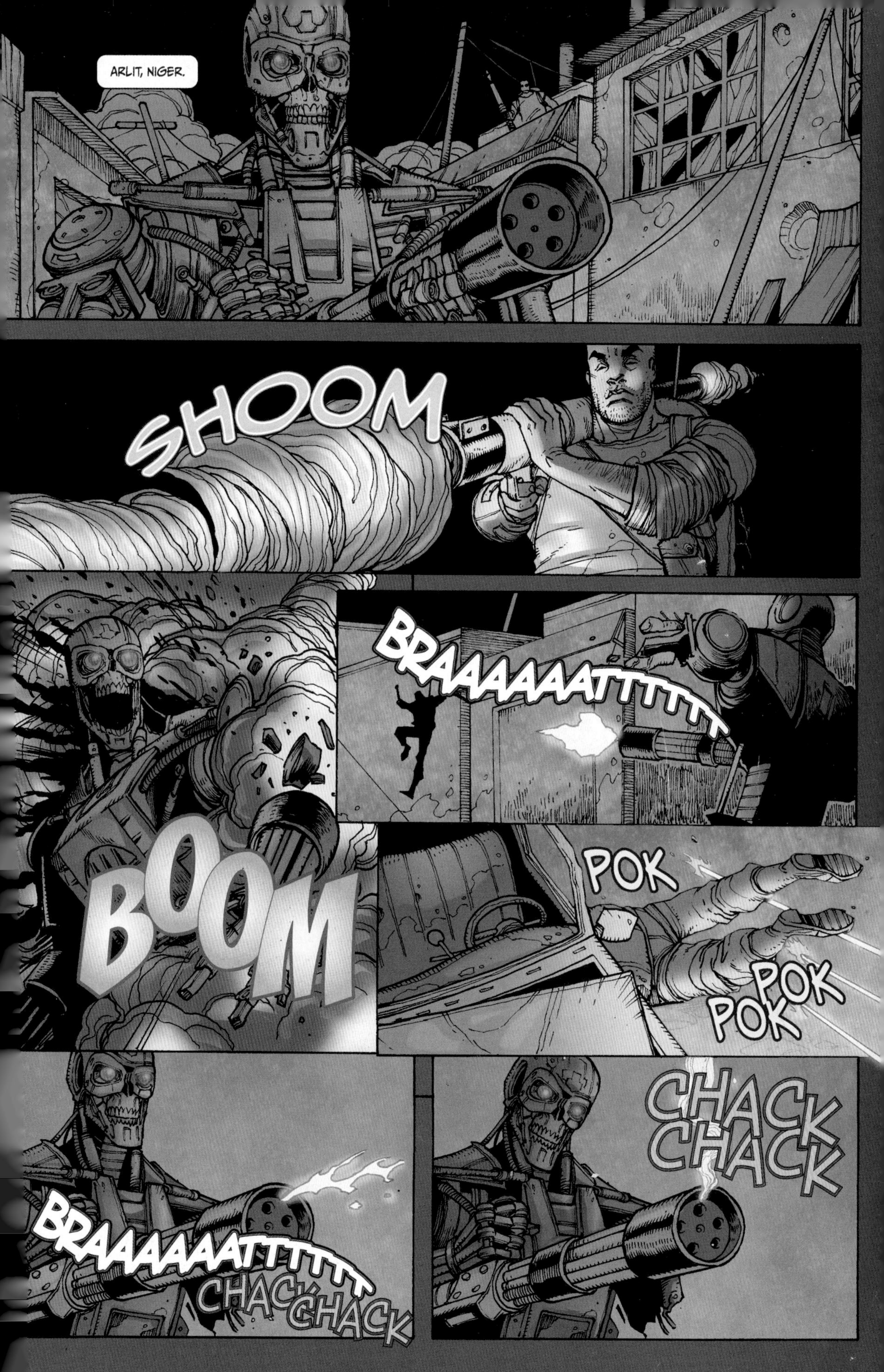
ARLIT, NIGER.
SHOOM
BRAAAAAATTTTTTT
BOOM
POK
POK POK POK
BRAAAAAATTTTTTT
CHACK CHACK
CHACK
CHACK

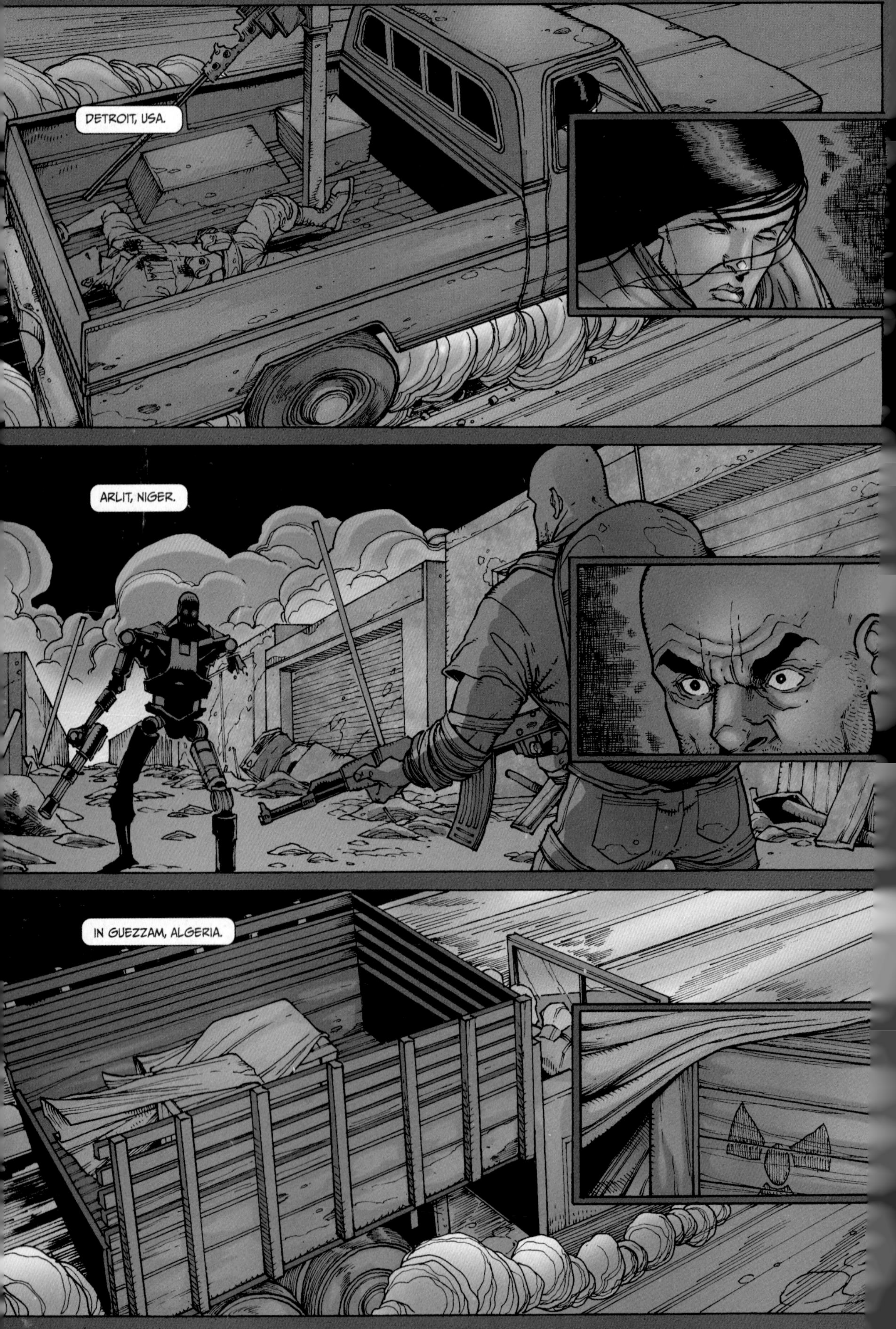
DETROIT, USA.
ARLIT, NIGER.
IN GUEZZAM, ALGERIA.

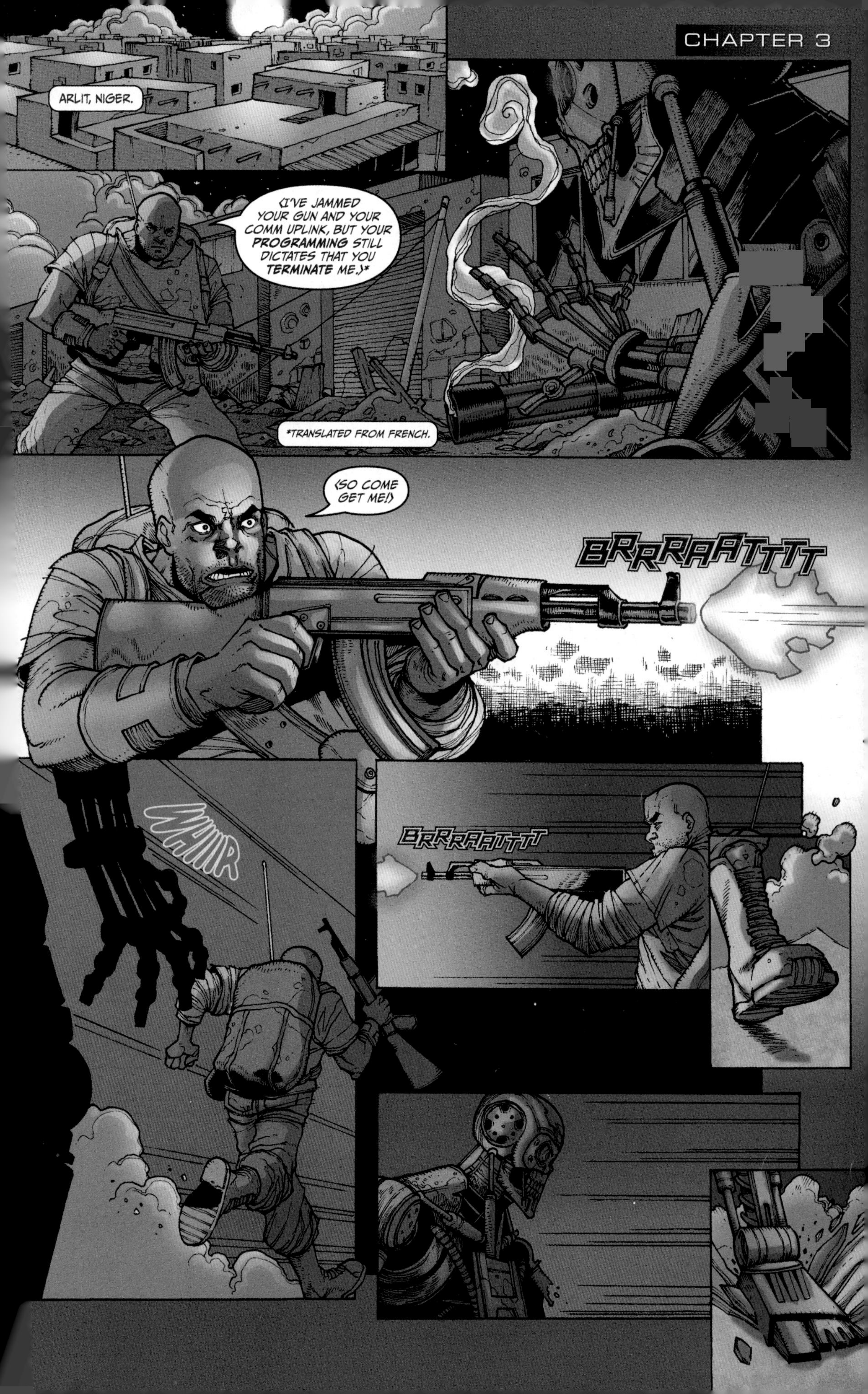
ARLIT, NIGER.
‹I'VE JAMMED YOUR GUN AND YOUR COMM UPLINK, BUT YOUR PROGRAMMING STILL DICTATES THAT YOU TERMINATE ME.›*
*TRANSLATED FROM FRENCH.
‹SO COME GET ME!›
BRRRAATTTT
WHIRR
BRRRAATTTT

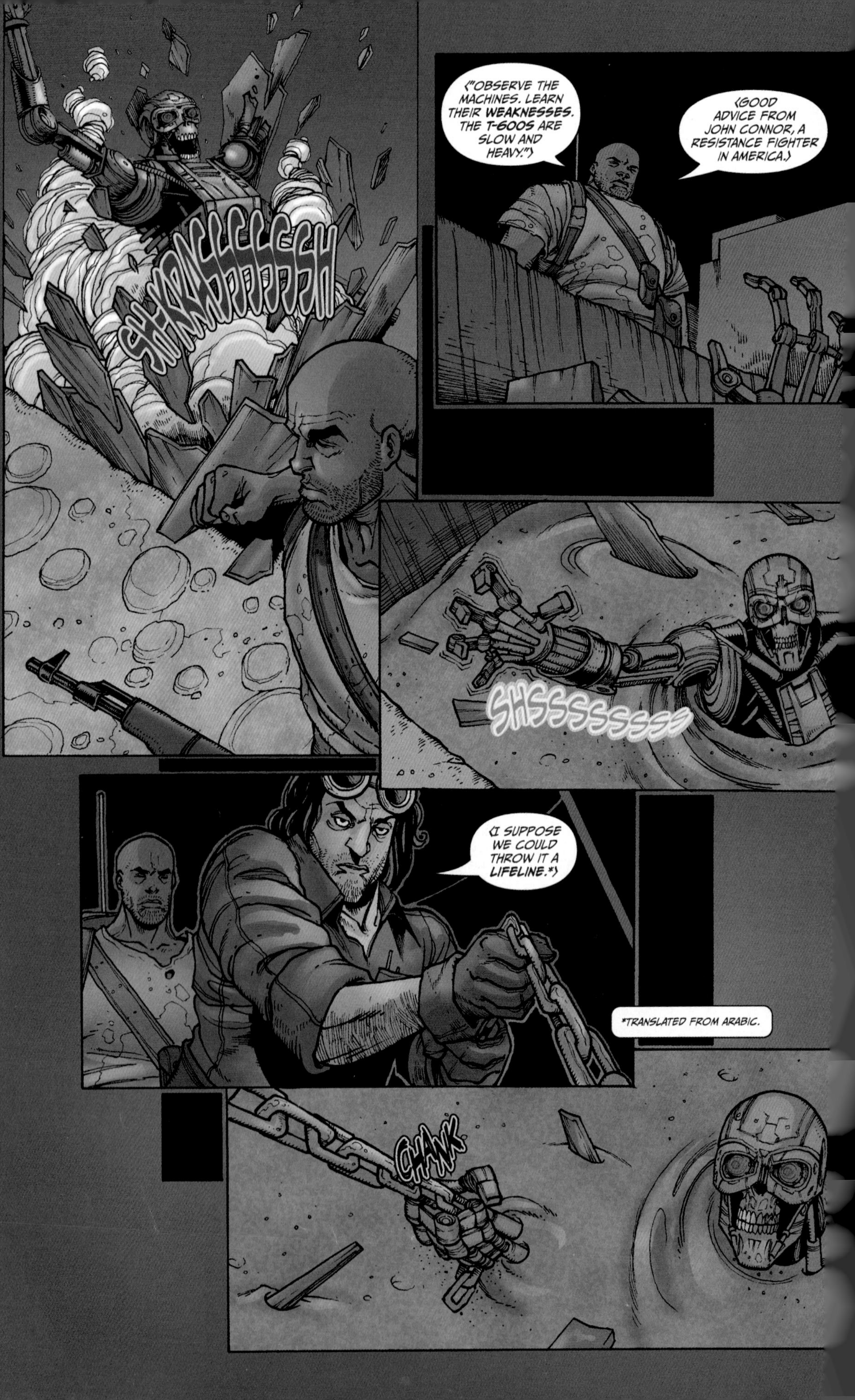
SHKRASSSSSSSH
‹"OBSERVE THE MACHINES. LEARN THEIR WEAKNESSES. THE T-600S ARE SLOW AND HEAVY."›
‹GOOD ADVICE FROM JOHN CONNOR, A RESISTANCE FIGHTER IN AMERICA.›
SHSSSSSSSSS
‹I SUPPOSE WE COULD THROW IT A LIFELINE.*›
*TRANSLATED FROM ARABIC.
CHANK

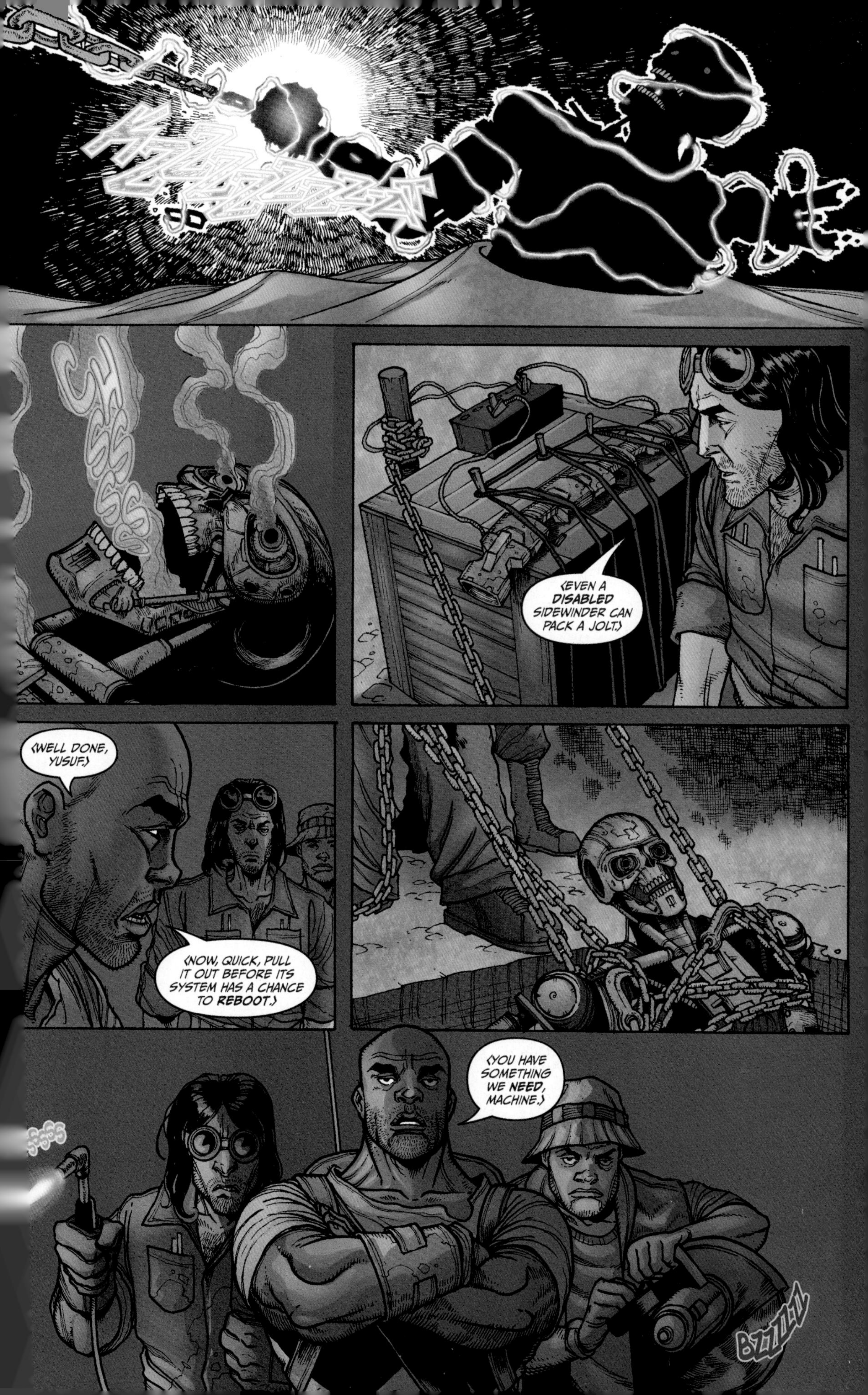

KRZZZZZT
⟨EVEN A DISABLED SIDEWINDER CAN PACK A JOLT.⟩
⟨WELL DONE, YUSUF.⟩
⟨NOW, QUICK, PULL IT OUT BEFORE ITS SYSTEM HAS A CHANCE TO REBOOT.⟩
⟨YOU HAVE SOMETHING WE NEED, MACHINE.⟩
SSSS
BZZZZZ

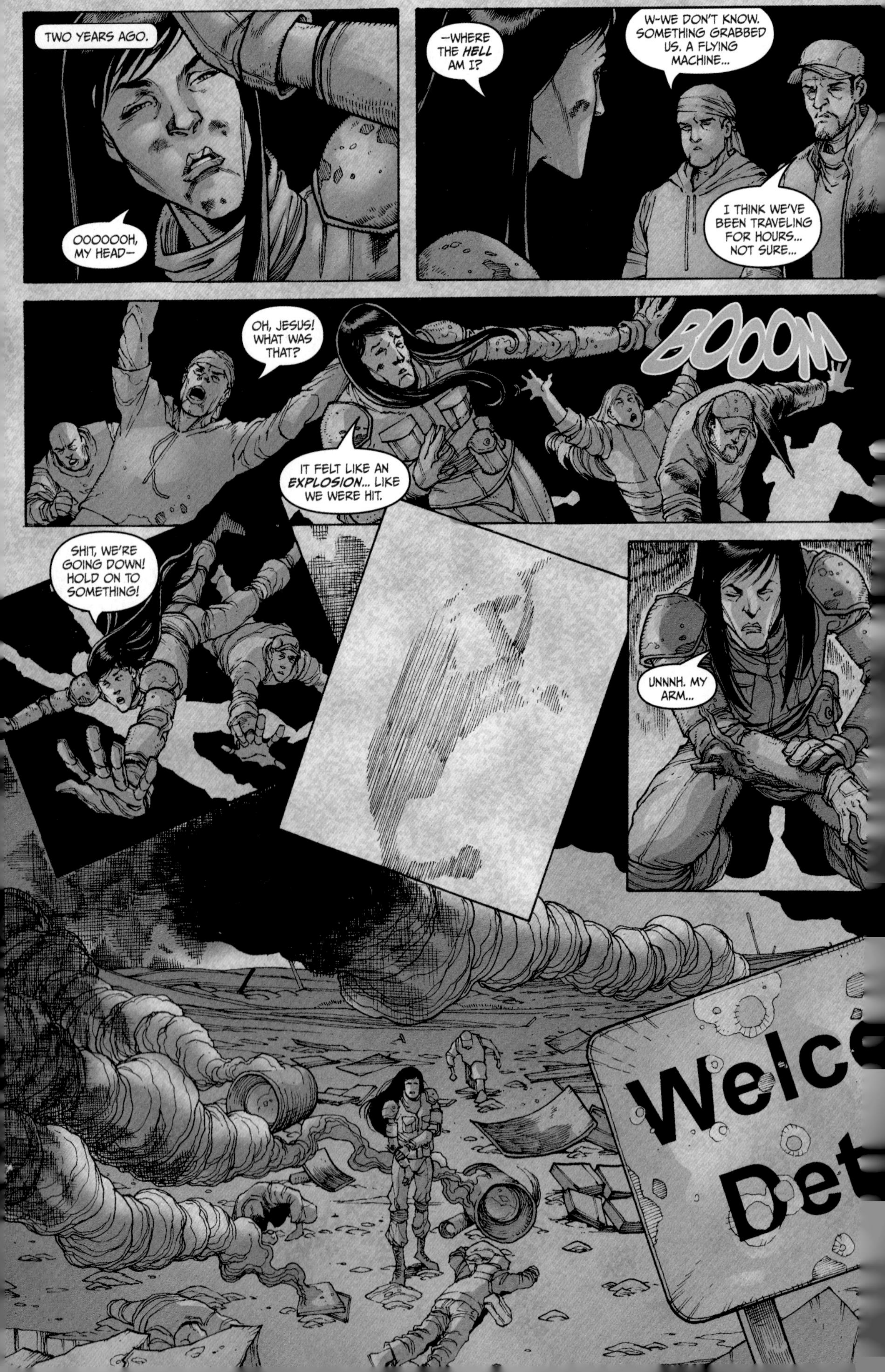
TWO YEARS AGO.
OOOOOOH, MY HEAD—
—WHERE THE *HELL* AM I?
W-WE DON'T KNOW. SOMETHING GRABBED US. A FLYING MACHINE...
I THINK WE'VE BEEN TRAVELING FOR HOURS... NOT SURE...
OH, JESUS! WHAT WAS THAT?
BOOOM
IT FELT LIKE AN *EXPLOSION*... LIKE WE WERE HIT.
SHIT, WE'RE GOING DOWN! HOLD ON TO SOMETHING!
UNNNH. MY ARM...
Welc
Det

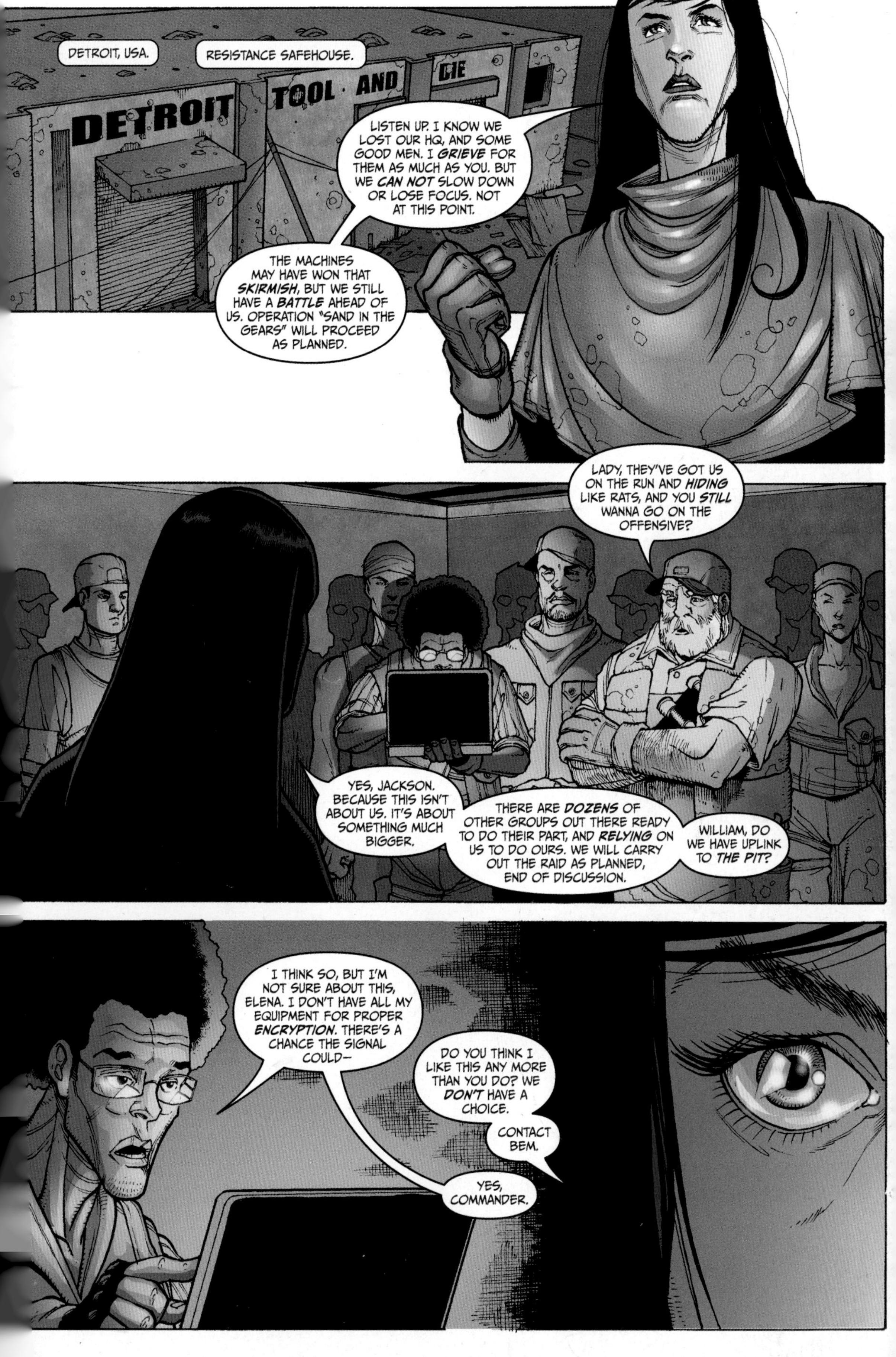
DETROIT, USA.
RESISTANCE SAFEHOUSE.
DETROIT TOOL AND DIE
LISTEN UP. I KNOW WE LOST OUR HQ, AND SOME GOOD MEN. I GRIEVE FOR THEM AS MUCH AS YOU. BUT WE CAN NOT SLOW DOWN OR LOSE FOCUS. NOT AT THIS POINT.
THE MACHINES MAY HAVE WON THAT SKIRMISH, BUT WE STILL HAVE A BATTLE AHEAD OF US. OPERATION "SAND IN THE GEARS" WILL PROCEED AS PLANNED.
LADY, THEY'VE GOT US ON THE RUN AND HIDING LIKE RATS, AND YOU STILL WANNA GO ON THE OFFENSIVE?
YES, JACKSON. BECAUSE THIS ISN'T ABOUT US. IT'S ABOUT SOMETHING MUCH BIGGER.
THERE ARE DOZENS OF OTHER GROUPS OUT THERE READY TO DO THEIR PART, AND RELYING ON US TO DO OURS. WE WILL CARRY OUT THE RAID AS PLANNED, END OF DISCUSSION.
WILLIAM, DO WE HAVE UPLINK TO THE PIT?
I THINK SO, BUT I'M NOT SURE ABOUT THIS, ELENA. I DON'T HAVE ALL MY EQUIPMENT FOR PROPER ENCRYPTION. THERE'S A CHANCE THE SIGNAL COULD–
DO YOU THINK I LIKE THIS ANY MORE THAN YOU DO? WE DON'T HAVE A CHOICE.
CONTACT BEM.
YES, COMMANDER.

CHAPTER 3

KZZZT THERE? REPEAT: ARE YOU THERE?

ELENA, MY FRIEND. YOUR TRANSMISSION IS LATE. I WAS FEARING THE WORST.

WE HAD A SMALL *SETBACK*.

IS EVERYTHING READY ON YOUR END?

YES, WE GOT LAST PIECE OF PUZZLE. WE WILL BE READY ON TIME.

GOOD. *KZZZT* KNEW YOU *KZZZT*.

YOU'LL OBVIOUSLY HAVE TO *RELOCATE* AFTER THE LION ROARS.

I WANTED TO MAKE SUR DIRECTIONS TO NEW *SUMMER HO* WERE DELIVER ALONG WITH T PACKAGE.

YES. I APPRECIATE ALL YOUR HELP. IT IS NOW *OUR* TIME.

I WILL NOT SAY GOODBYE, FOR I KNOW WE *WILL* SPEAK AGAIN WHEN THIS IS ALL OVER.

UNTIL *KZZZT* MAY GOD WATCH OVER *KZZZT*

YOU'RE BREAKING UP. BUT *GOOD LUCK* TO YOU, TOO, MY FRIEND.

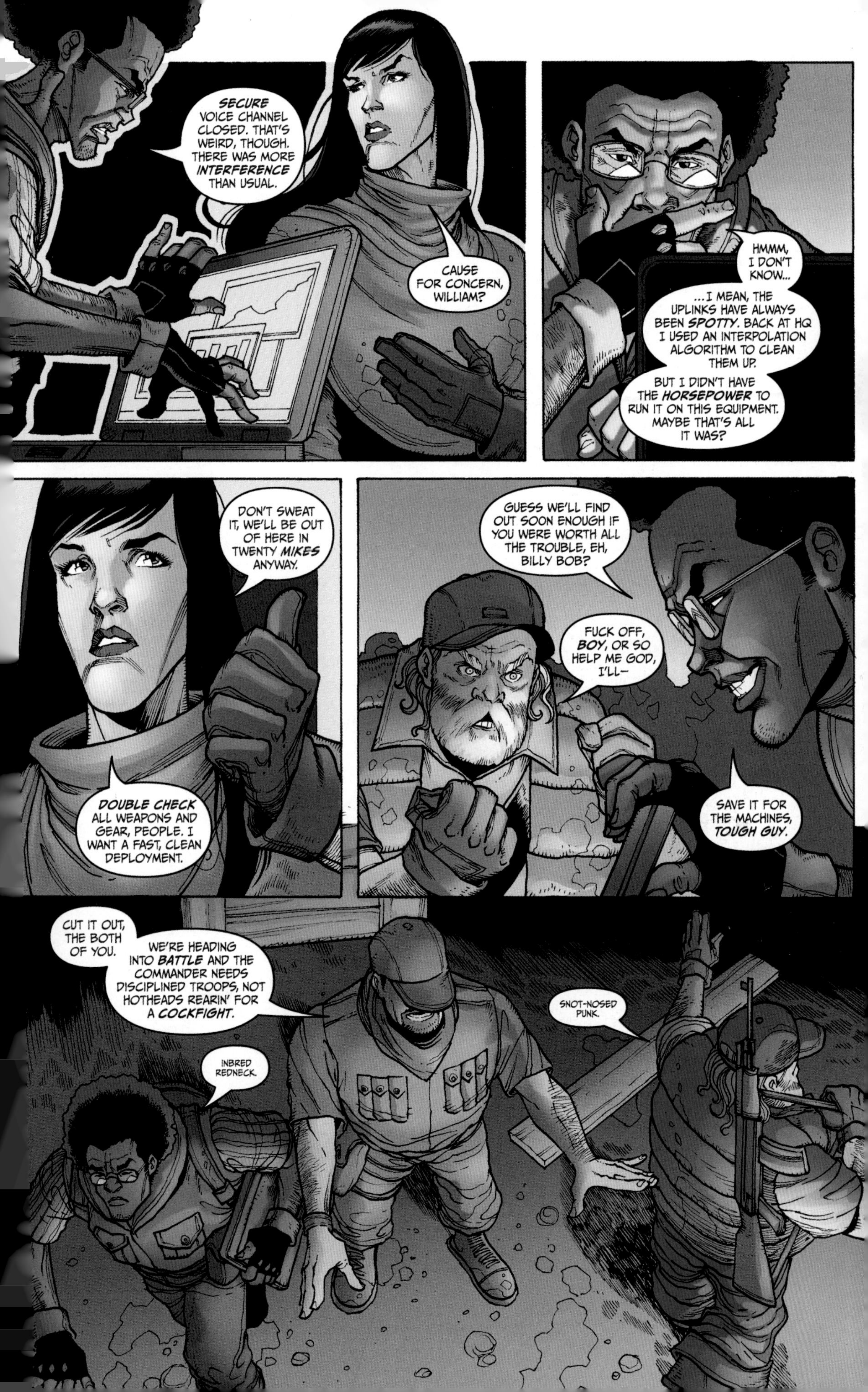
SECURE VOICE CHANNEL CLOSED. THAT'S WEIRD, THOUGH. THERE WAS MORE INTERFERENCE THAN USUAL.
CAUSE FOR CONCERN, WILLIAM?
HMMM, I DON'T KNOW...
...I MEAN, THE UPLINKS HAVE ALWAYS BEEN SPOTTY. BACK AT HQ I USED AN INTERPOLATION ALGORITHM TO CLEAN THEM UP.
BUT I DIDN'T HAVE THE HORSEPOWER TO RUN IT ON THIS EQUIPMENT. MAYBE THAT'S ALL IT WAS?
DON'T SWEAT IT, WE'LL BE OUT OF HERE IN TWENTY MIKES ANYWAY.
DOUBLE CHECK ALL WEAPONS AND GEAR, PEOPLE. I WANT A FAST, CLEAN DEPLOYMENT.
GUESS WE'LL FIND OUT SOON ENOUGH IF YOU WERE WORTH ALL THE TROUBLE, EH, BILLY BOB?
FUCK OFF, BOY, OR SO HELP ME GOD, I'LL—
SAVE IT FOR THE MACHINES, TOUGH GUY.
CUT IT OUT, THE BOTH OF YOU.
WE'RE HEADING INTO BATTLE AND THE COMMANDER NEEDS DISCIPLINED TROOPS, NOT HOTHEADS REARIN' FOR A COCKFIGHT.
SNOT-NOSED PUNK.
INBRED REDNECK.

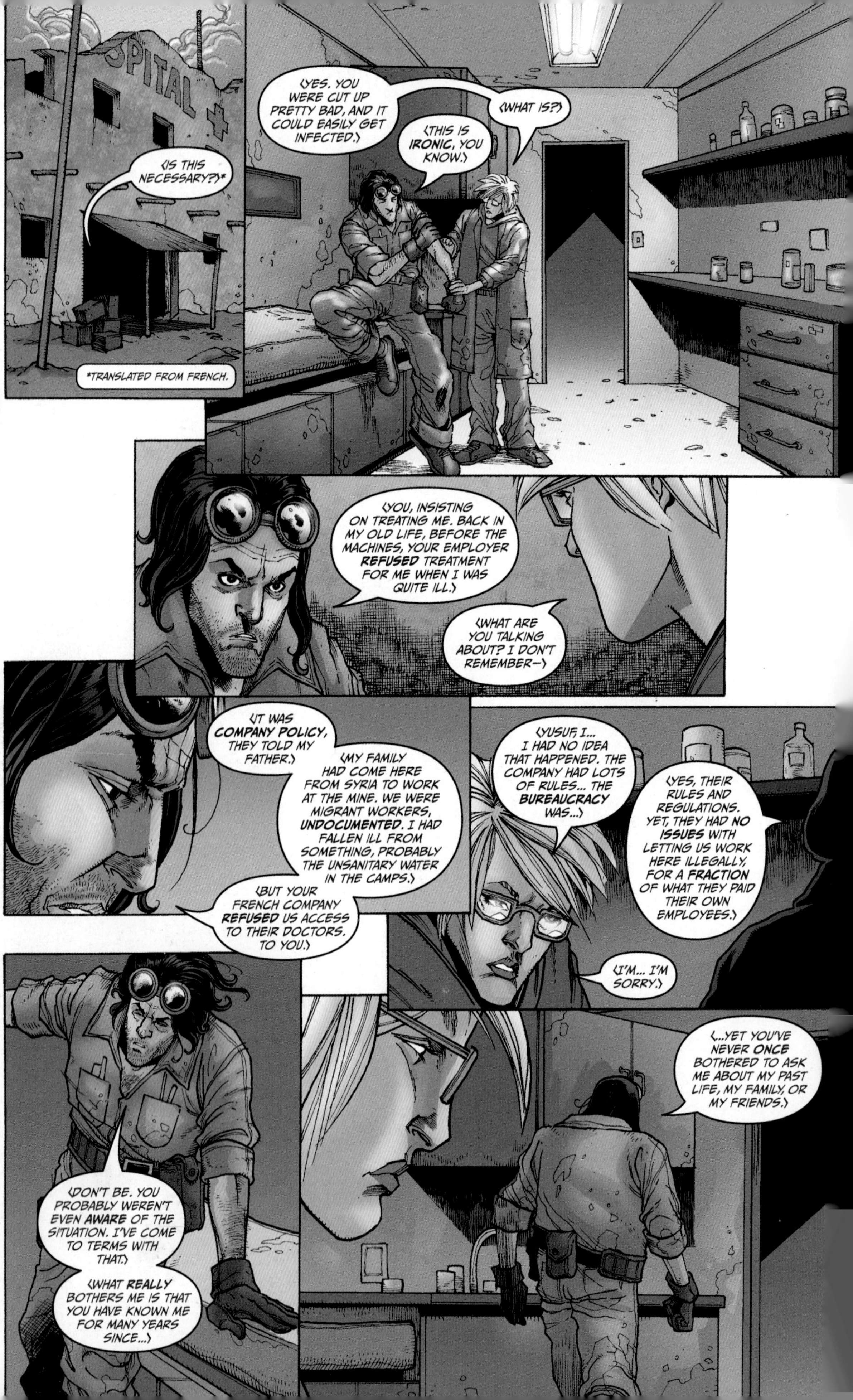
SPITAL
‹IS THIS NECESSARY?›*
*TRANSLATED FROM FRENCH.
‹YES. YOU WERE CUT UP PRETTY BAD, AND IT COULD EASILY GET INFECTED.›
‹THIS IS IRONIC, YOU KNOW.›
‹WHAT IS?›
‹YOU, INSISTING ON TREATING ME. BACK IN MY OLD LIFE, BEFORE THE MACHINES, YOUR EMPLOYER REFUSED TREATMENT FOR ME WHEN I WAS QUITE ILL.›
‹WHAT ARE YOU TALKING ABOUT? I DON'T REMEMBER—›
‹IT WAS COMPANY POLICY, THEY TOLD MY FATHER.›
‹MY FAMILY HAD COME HERE FROM SYRIA TO WORK AT THE MINE. WE WERE MIGRANT WORKERS, UNDOCUMENTED. I HAD FALLEN ILL FROM SOMETHING, PROBABLY THE UNSANITARY WATER IN THE CAMPS.›
‹BUT YOUR FRENCH COMPANY REFUSED US ACCESS TO THEIR DOCTORS. TO YOU.›
‹YUSUF, I... I HAD NO IDEA THAT HAPPENED. THE COMPANY HAD LOTS OF RULES... THE BUREAUCRACY WAS...›
‹YES, THEIR RULES AND REGULATIONS. YET, THEY HAD NO ISSUES WITH LETTING US WORK HERE ILLEGALLY, FOR A FRACTION OF WHAT THEY PAID THEIR OWN EMPLOYEES.›
‹I'M... I'M SORRY.›
‹DON'T BE. YOU PROBABLY WEREN'T EVEN AWARE OF THE SITUATION. I'VE COME TO TERMS WITH THAT.›
‹WHAT REALLY BOTHERS ME IS THAT YOU HAVE KNOWN ME FOR MANY YEARS SINCE...›
‹...YET YOU'VE NEVER ONCE BOTHERED TO ASK ME ABOUT MY PAST LIFE, MY FAMILY, OR MY FRIENDS.›

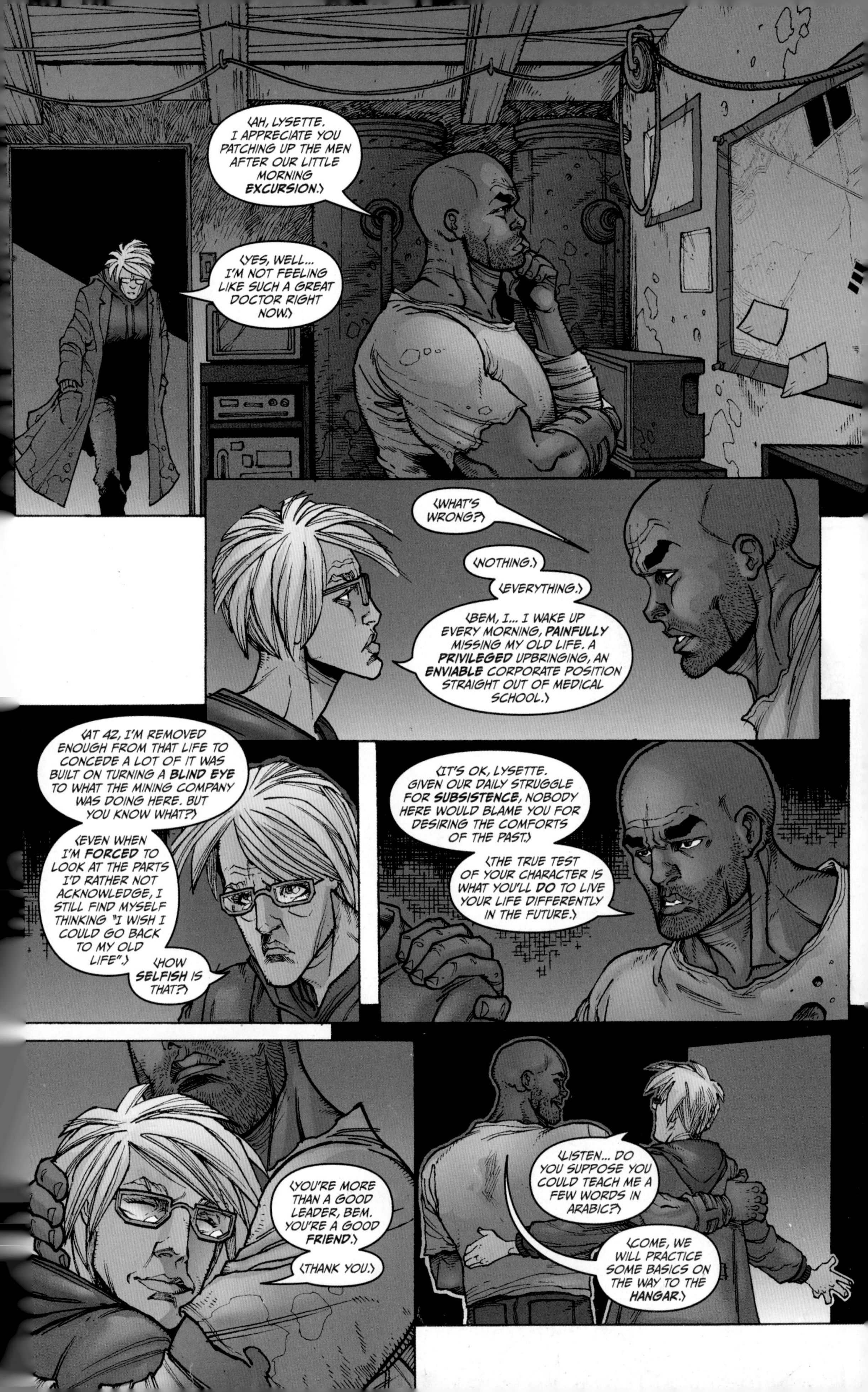
‹AH, LYSETTE. I APPRECIATE YOU PATCHING UP THE MEN AFTER OUR LITTLE MORNING **EXCURSION**.›
‹YES, WELL... I'M NOT FEELING LIKE SUCH A GREAT DOCTOR RIGHT NOW.›
‹WHAT'S WRONG?›
‹NOTHING.›
‹EVERYTHING.›
‹BEM, I... I WAKE UP EVERY MORNING, **PAINFULLY** MISSING MY OLD LIFE. A **PRIVILEGED** UPBRINGING, AN **ENVIABLE** CORPORATE POSITION STRAIGHT OUT OF MEDICAL SCHOOL.›
‹AT 42, I'M REMOVED ENOUGH FROM THAT LIFE TO CONCEDE A LOT OF IT WAS BUILT ON TURNING A **BLIND EYE** TO WHAT THE MINING COMPANY WAS DOING HERE. BUT YOU KNOW WHAT?›
‹EVEN WHEN I'M **FORCED** TO LOOK AT THE PARTS I'D RATHER NOT ACKNOWLEDGE, I STILL FIND MYSELF THINKING "I WISH I COULD GO BACK TO MY OLD LIFE".›
‹HOW **SELFISH** IS THAT?›
‹IT'S OK, LYSETTE. GIVEN OUR DAILY STRUGGLE FOR **SUBSISTENCE**, NOBODY HERE WOULD BLAME YOU FOR DESIRING THE COMFORTS OF THE PAST.›
‹THE TRUE TEST OF YOUR CHARACTER IS WHAT YOU'LL **DO** TO LIVE YOUR LIFE DIFFERENTLY IN THE FUTURE.›
‹YOU'RE MORE THAN A GOOD LEADER, BEM. YOU'RE A GOOD **FRIEND**.›
‹THANK YOU.›
‹LISTEN... DO YOU SUPPOSE YOU COULD TEACH ME A FEW WORDS IN ARABIC?›
‹COME, WE WILL PRACTICE SOME BASICS ON THE WAY TO THE **HANGAR**.›

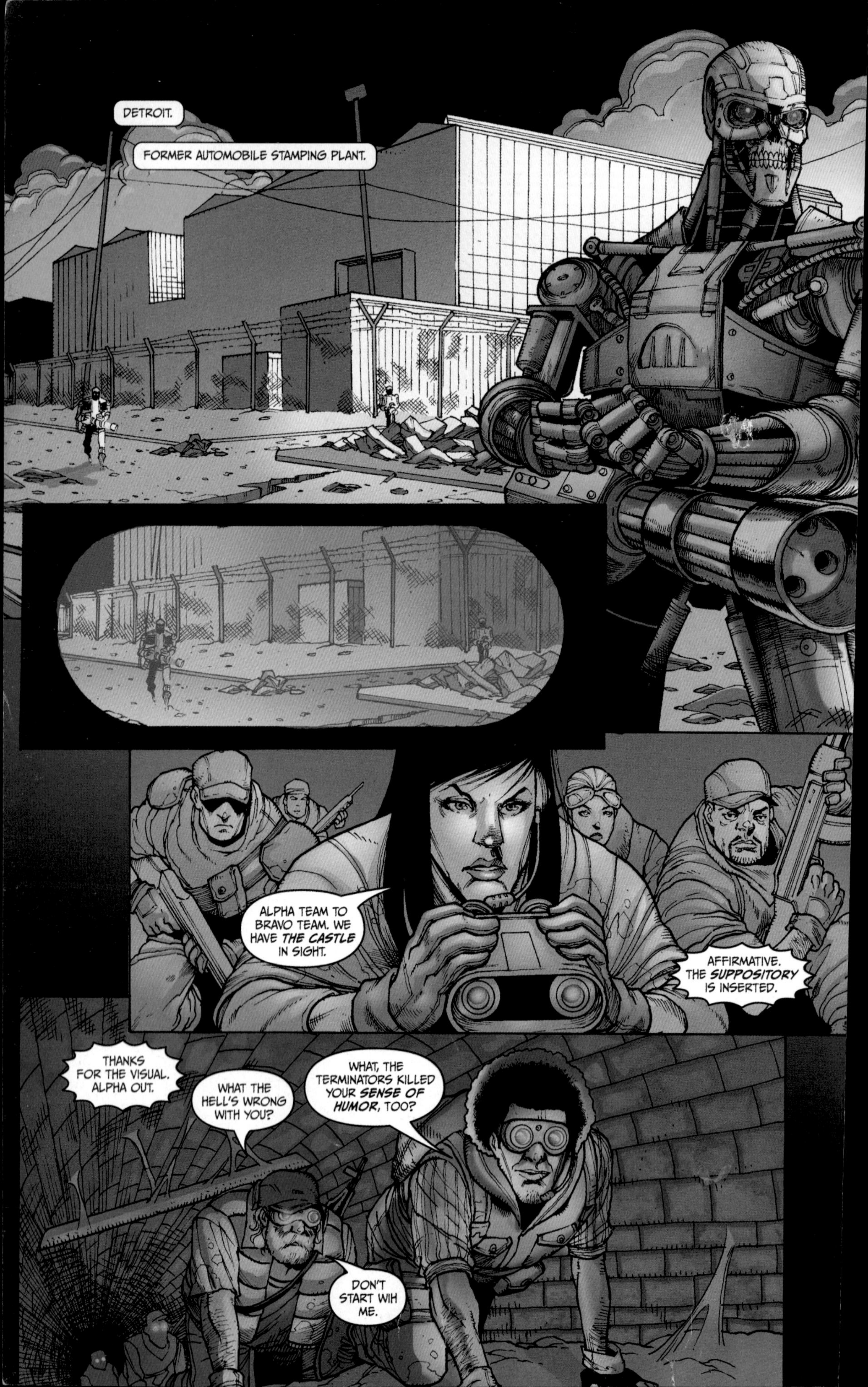
DETROIT.
FORMER AUTOMOBILE STAMPING PLANT.
ALPHA TEAM TO BRAVO TEAM. WE HAVE *THE CASTLE* IN SIGHT.
AFFIRMATIVE. THE *SUPPOSITORY* IS INSERTED.
THANKS FOR THE VISUAL. ALPHA OUT.
WHAT THE HELL'S WRONG WITH YOU?
WHAT, THE TERMINATORS KILLED YOUR *SENSE OF HUMOR*, TOO?
DON'T START WIH ME.

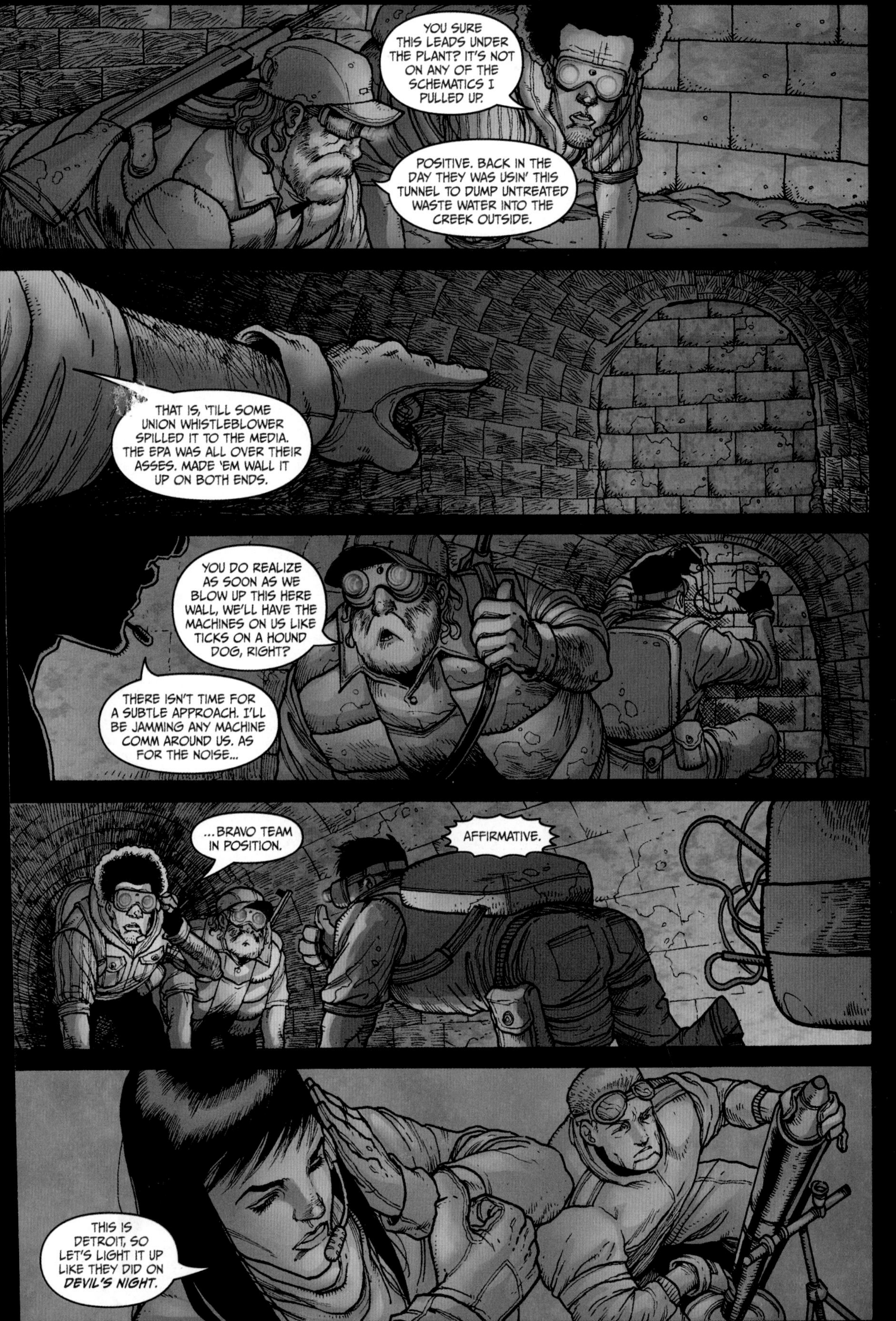
YOU SURE THIS LEADS UNDER THE PLANT? IT'S NOT ON ANY OF THE SCHEMATICS I PULLED UP.
POSITIVE. BACK IN THE DAY THEY WAS USIN' THIS TUNNEL TO DUMP UNTREATED WASTE WATER INTO THE CREEK OUTSIDE.
THAT IS, 'TILL SOME UNION WHISTLEBLOWER SPILLED IT TO THE MEDIA. THE EPA WAS ALL OVER THEIR ASSES. MADE 'EM WALL IT UP ON BOTH ENDS.
YOU DO REALIZE AS SOON AS WE BLOW UP THIS HERE WALL, WE'LL HAVE THE MACHINES ON US LIKE TICKS ON A HOUND DOG, RIGHT?
THERE ISN'T TIME FOR A SUBTLE APPROACH. I'LL BE JAMMING ANY MACHINE COMM AROUND US. AS FOR THE NOISE...
...BRAVO TEAM IN POSITION.
AFFIRMATIVE.
THIS IS DETROIT, SO LET'S LIGHT IT UP LIKE THEY DID ON *DEVIL'S NIGHT*.

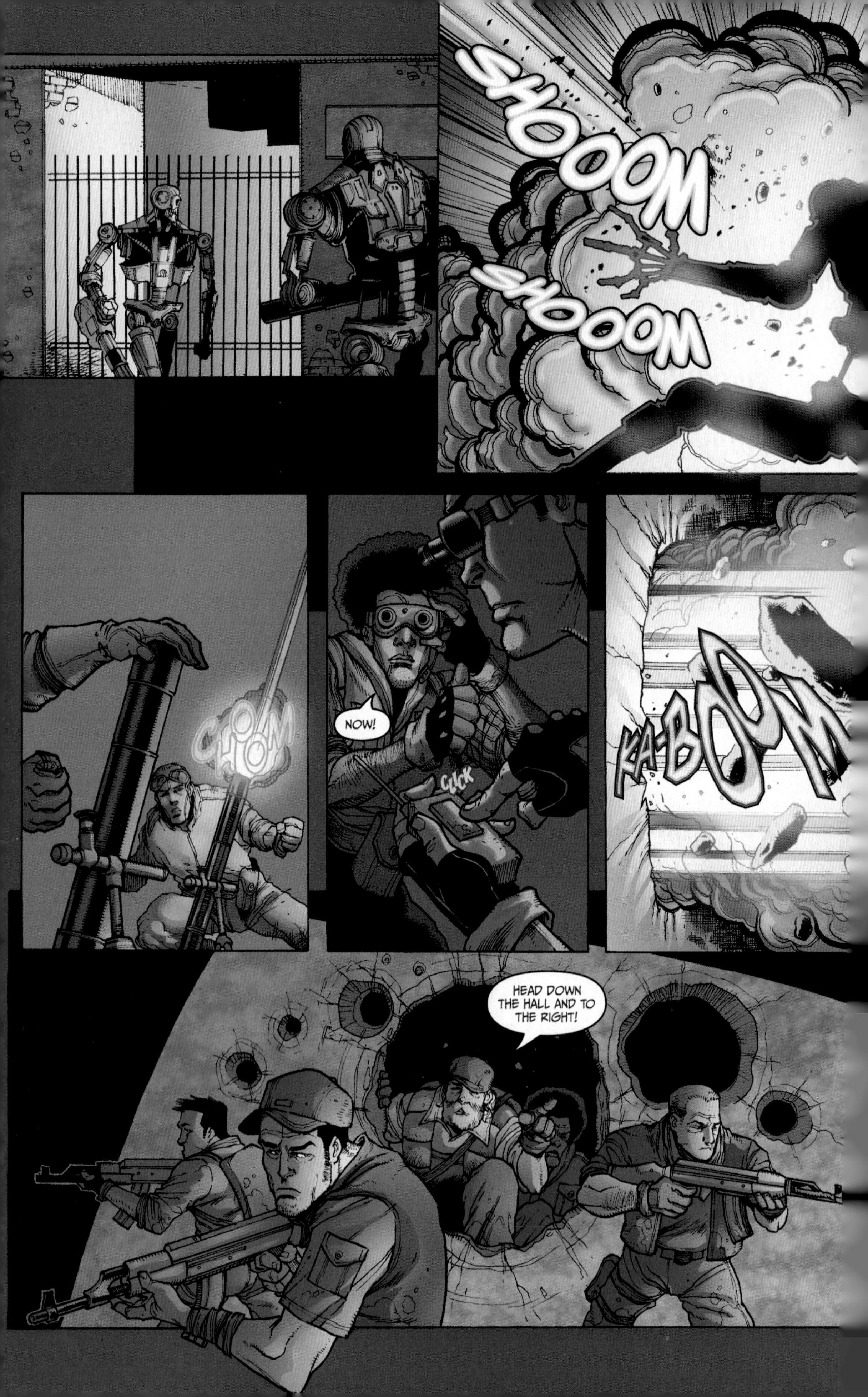
SHOOOM
SHOOOM
CHOOM
NOW!
CLICK
KA-BOOM
HEAD DOWN THE HALL AND TO THE RIGHT!

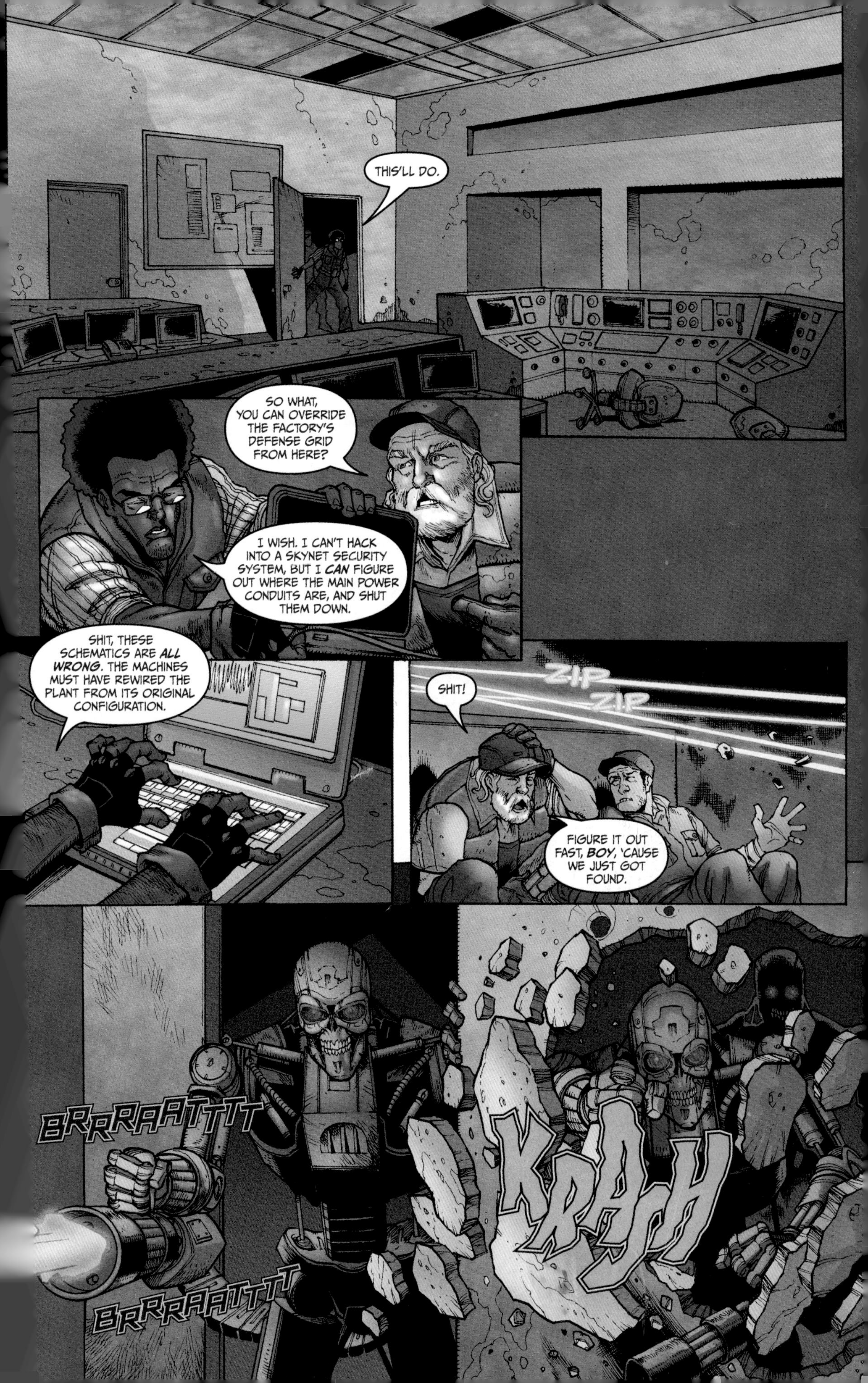
THIS'LL DO.
SO WHAT, YOU CAN OVERRIDE THE FACTORY'S DEFENSE GRID FROM HERE?
I WISH. I CAN'T HACK INTO A SKYNET SECURITY SYSTEM, BUT I *CAN* FIGURE OUT WHERE THE MAIN POWER CONDUITS ARE, AND SHUT THEM DOWN.
SHIT, THESE SCHEMATICS ARE ***ALL WRONG***. THE MACHINES MUST HAVE REWIRED THE PLANT FROM ITS ORIGINAL CONFIGURATION.
ZIP
ZIP
SHIT!
FIGURE IT OUT FAST, ***BOY***, 'CAUSE WE JUST GOT FOUND.
BRRRAATTTT
KRASH
BRRRAATTTT

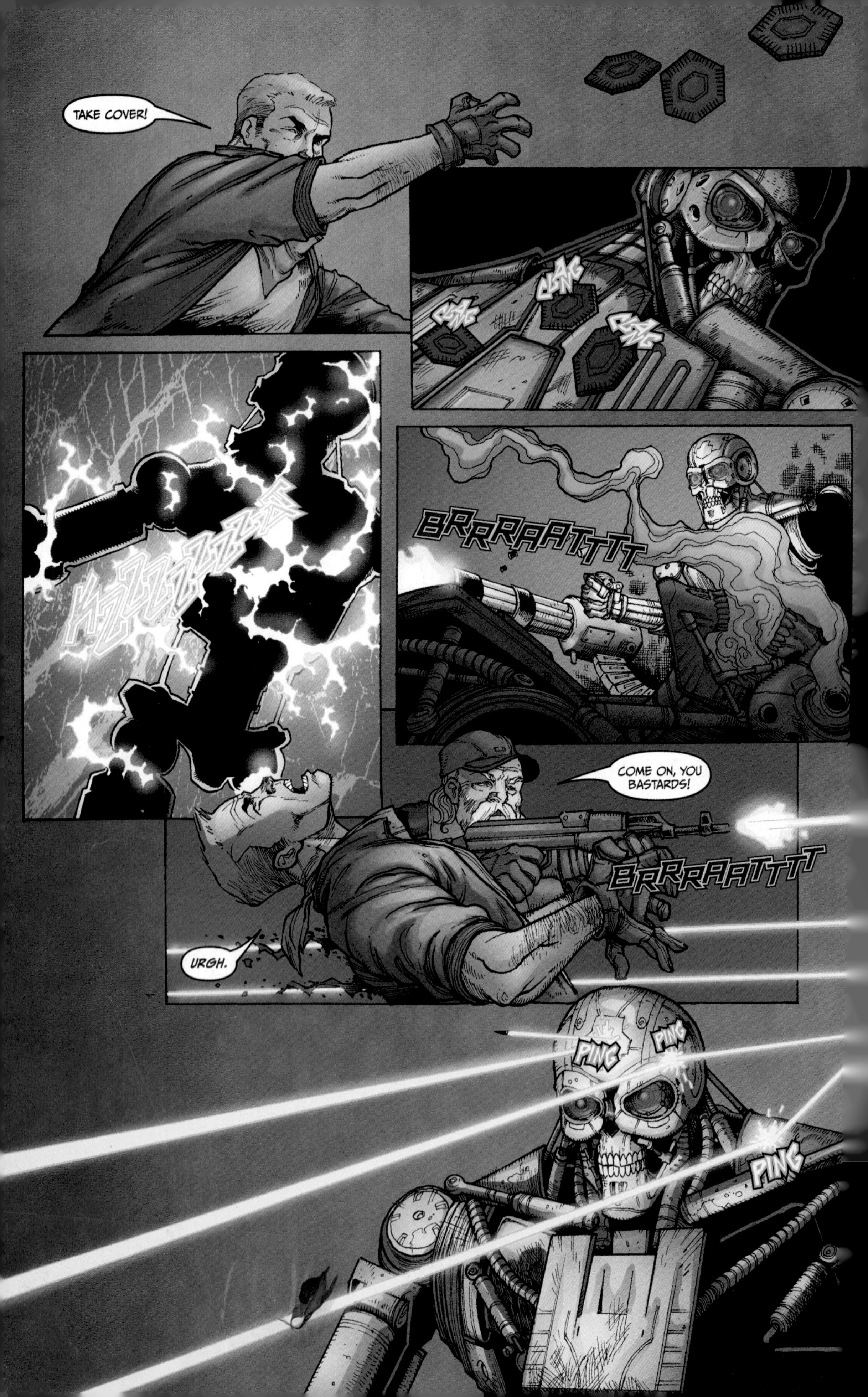
TAKE COVER!
CLANG
CLANG
CLANG
BRRRAATTTT
COME ON, YOU BASTARDS!
BRRRAATTTT
URGH.
PING
PING
PING

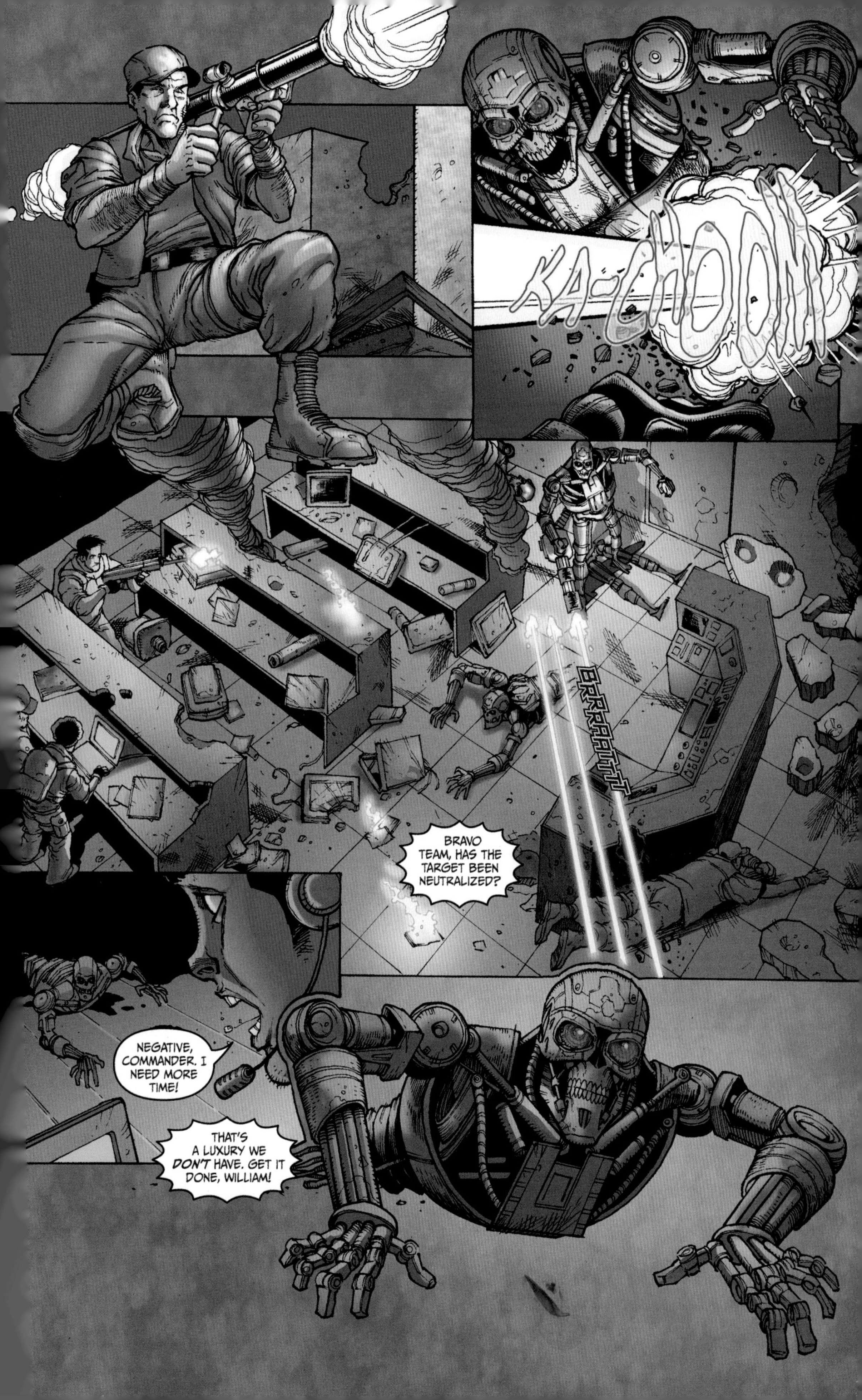
KA-CHOOM!
BRRRAAKTT
BRAVO TEAM, HAS THE TARGET BEEN NEUTRALIZED?
NEGATIVE, COMMANDER. I NEED MORE TIME!
THAT'S A LUXURY WE DON'T HAVE. GET IT DONE, WILLIAM!

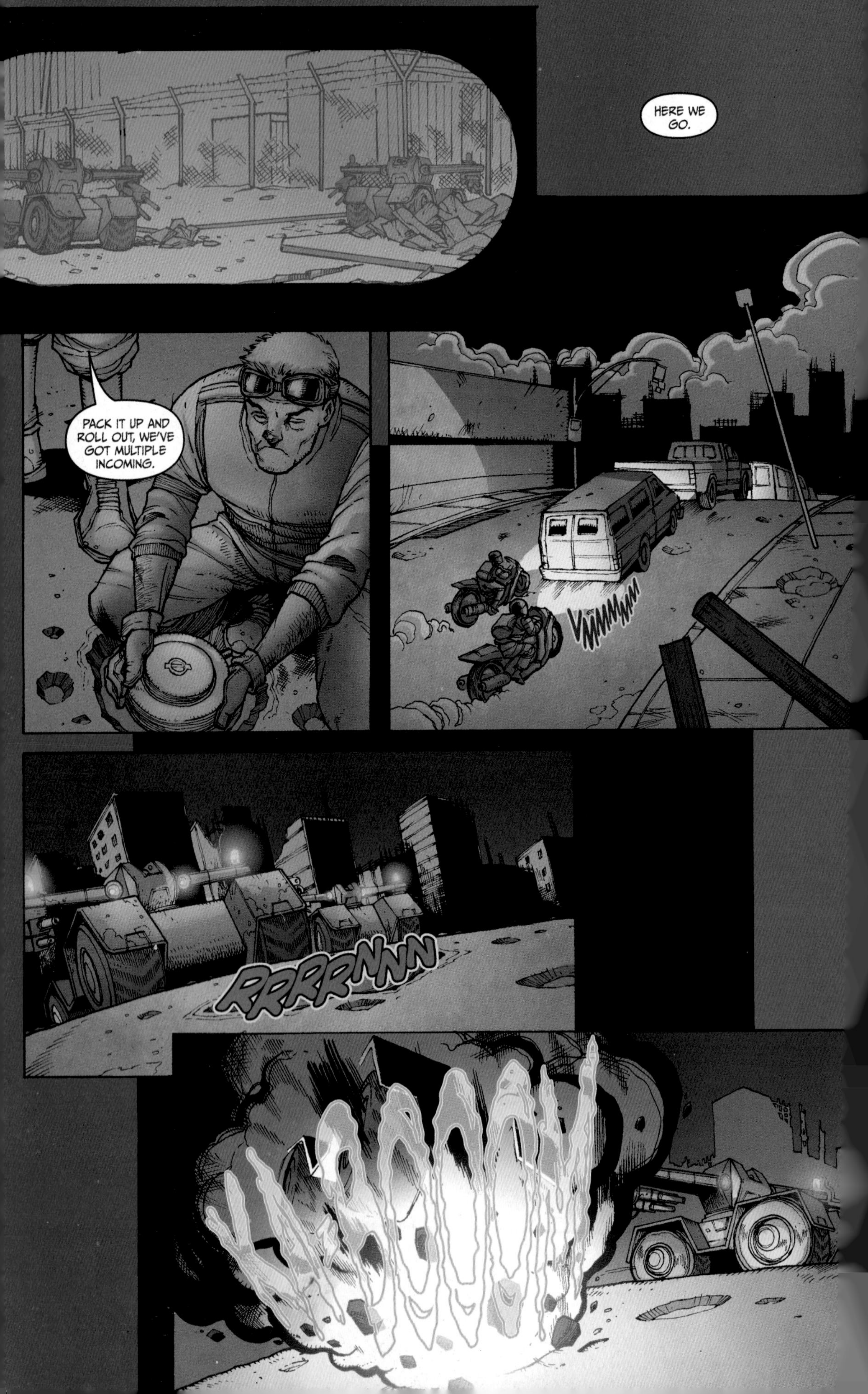
HERE WE GO.
PACK IT UP AND ROLL OUT, WE'VE GOT MULTIPLE INCOMING.
VMMMMM
RRRRNNN
KABOOOM

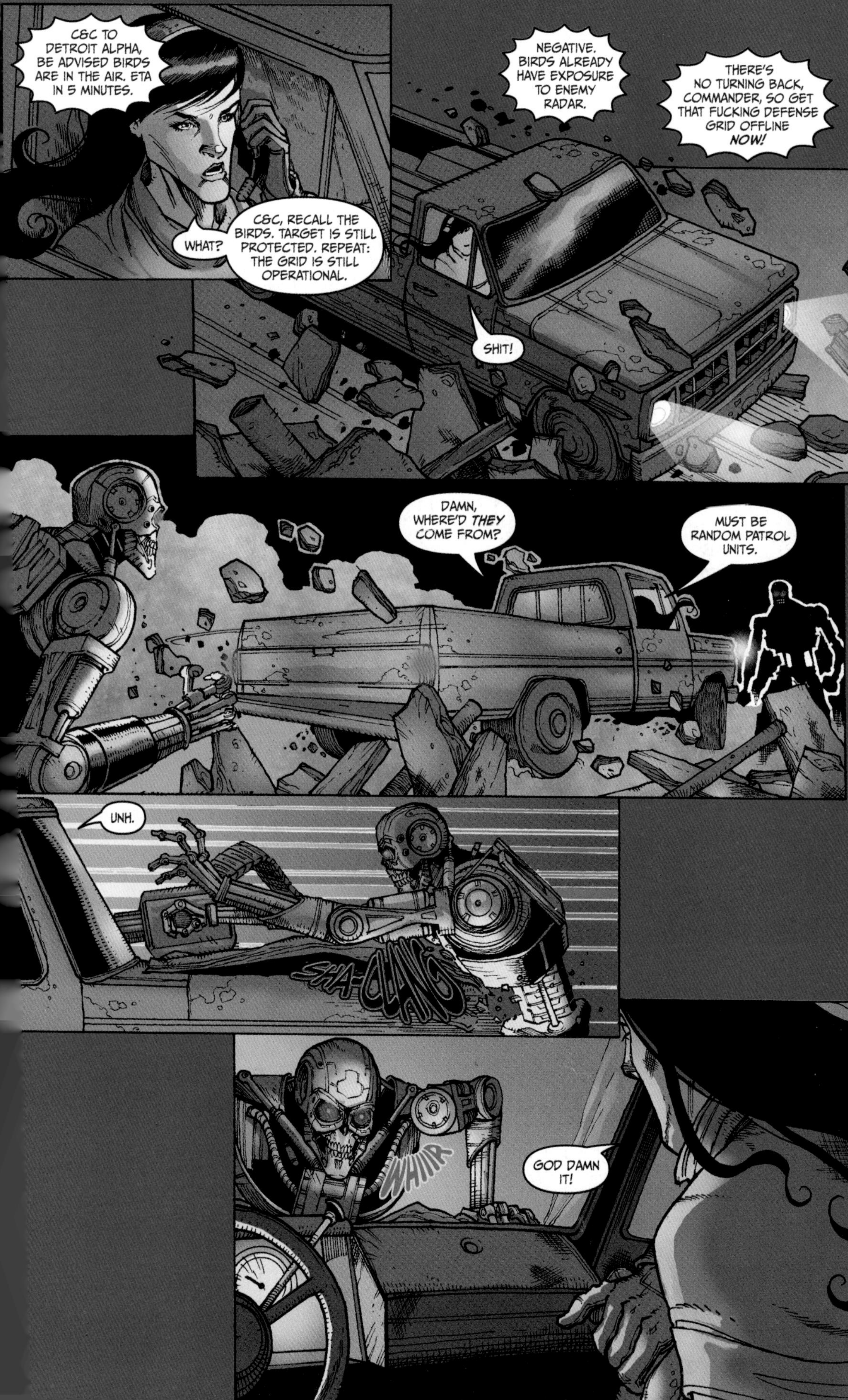
C&C TO DETROIT ALPHA, BE ADVISED BIRDS ARE IN THE AIR. ETA IN 5 MINUTES.
NEGATIVE. BIRDS ALREADY HAVE EXPOSURE TO ENEMY RADAR.
THERE'S NO TURNING BACK, COMMANDER, SO GET THAT FUCKING DEFENSE GRID OFFLINE *NOW!*
WHAT?
C&C, RECALL THE BIRDS. TARGET IS STILL PROTECTED. REPEAT: THE GRID IS STILL OPERATIONAL.
SHIT!
DAMN, WHERE'D *THEY* COME FROM?
MUST BE RANDOM PATROL UNITS.
UNH.
SHA-CLANG
WHIIIR
GOD DAMN IT!

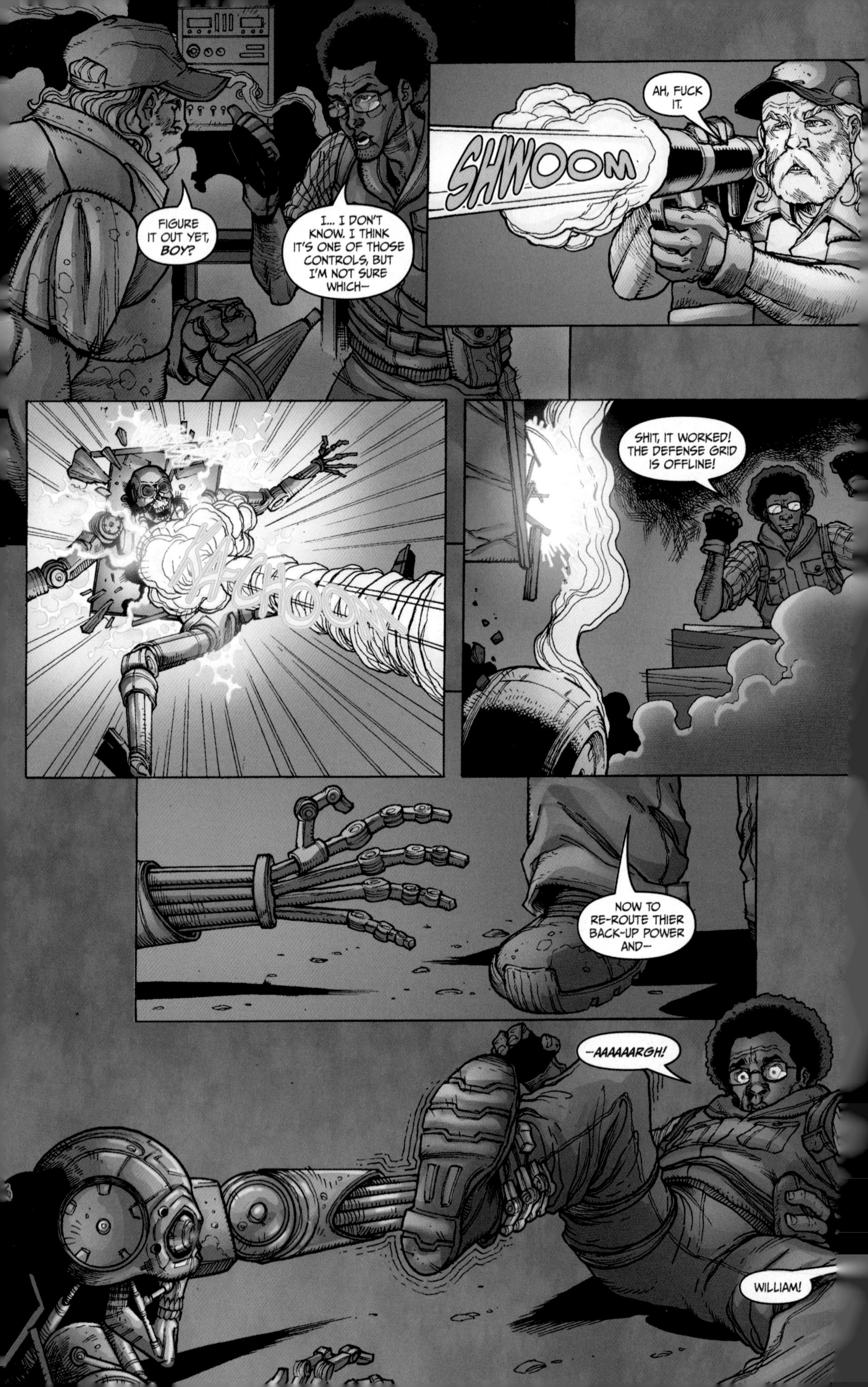
FIGURE IT OUT YET, *BOY?*
I... I DON'T KNOW. I THINK IT'S ONE OF THOSE CONTROLS, BUT I'M NOT SURE WHICH--
AH, FUCK IT.
SHWOOM
KA-CHOOM
SHIT, IT WORKED! THE DEFENSE GRID IS OFFLINE!
NOW TO RE-ROUTE THIER BACK-UP POWER AND--
--*AAAAAARGH!*
WILLIAM!

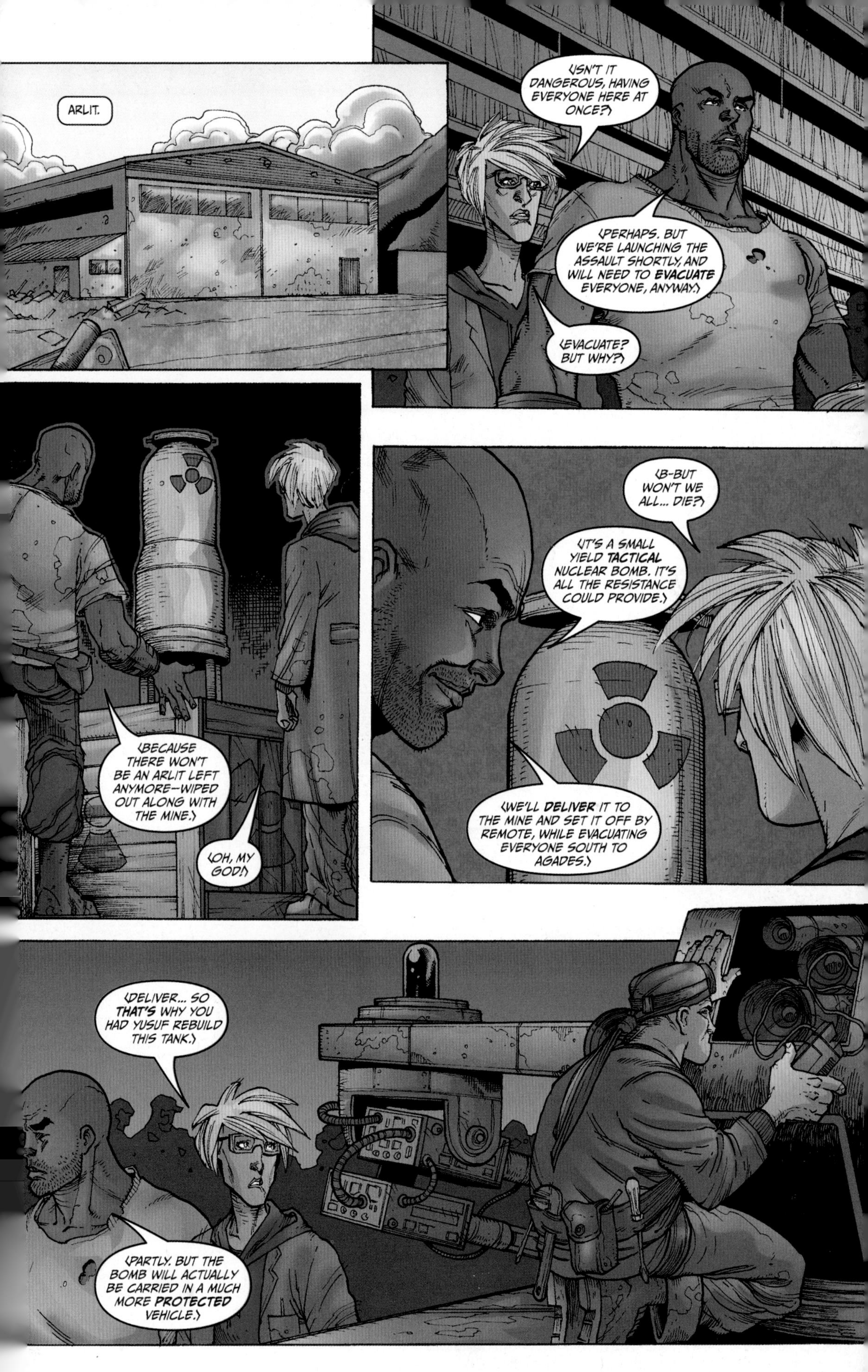
ARLIT.
‹ISN'T IT DANGEROUS, HAVING EVERYONE HERE AT ONCE?›
‹PERHAPS. BUT WE'RE LAUNCHING THE ASSAULT SHORTLY, AND WILL NEED TO **EVACUATE** EVERYONE, ANYWAY.›
‹EVACUATE? BUT WHY?›
‹BECAUSE THERE WON'T BE AN ARLIT LEFT ANYMORE--WIPED OUT ALONG WITH THE MINE.›
‹OH, MY GOD!›
‹B-BUT WON'T WE ALL... DIE?›
‹IT'S A SMALL YIELD **TACTICAL** NUCLEAR BOMB. IT'S ALL THE RESISTANCE COULD PROVIDE.›
‹WE'LL **DELIVER** IT TO THE MINE AND SET IT OFF BY REMOTE, WHILE EVACUATING EVERYONE SOUTH TO AGADES.›
‹DELIVER... SO **THAT'S** WHY YOU HAD YUSUF REBUILD THIS TANK.›
‹PARTLY. BUT THE BOMB WILL ACTUALLY BE CARRIED IN A MUCH MORE **PROTECTED** VEHICLE.›

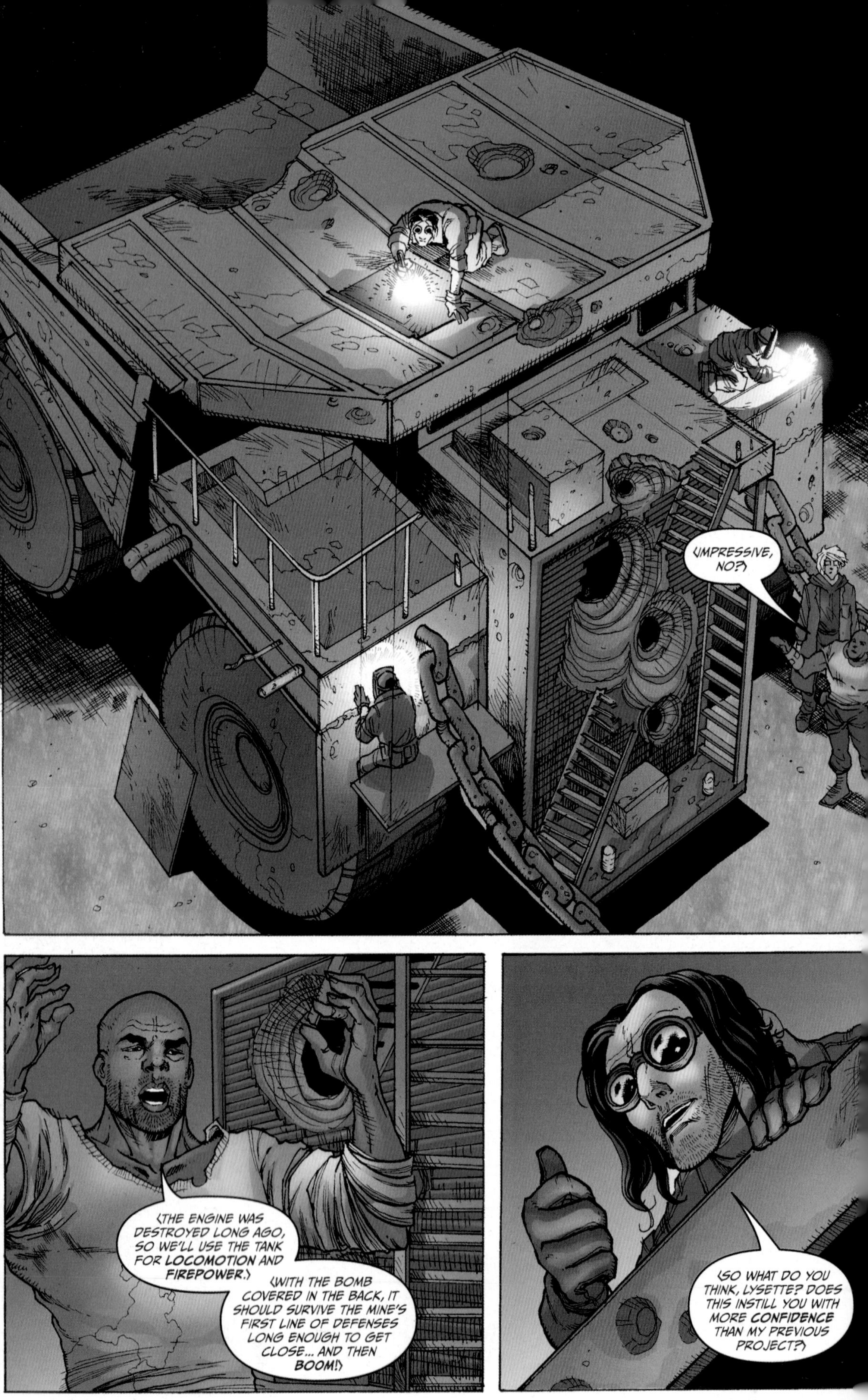
‹IMPRESSIVE, NO?›
‹THE ENGINE WAS DESTROYED LONG AGO, SO WE'LL USE THE TANK FOR **LOCOMOTION** AND **FIREPOWER**.›
‹WITH THE BOMB COVERED IN THE BACK, IT SHOULD SURVIVE THE MINE'S FIRST LINE OF DEFENSES LONG ENOUGH TO GET CLOSE... AND THEN **BOOM**!›
‹SO WHAT DO YOU THINK, LYSETTE? DOES THIS INSTILL YOU WITH MORE **CONFIDENCE** THAN MY PREVIOUS PROJECT?›

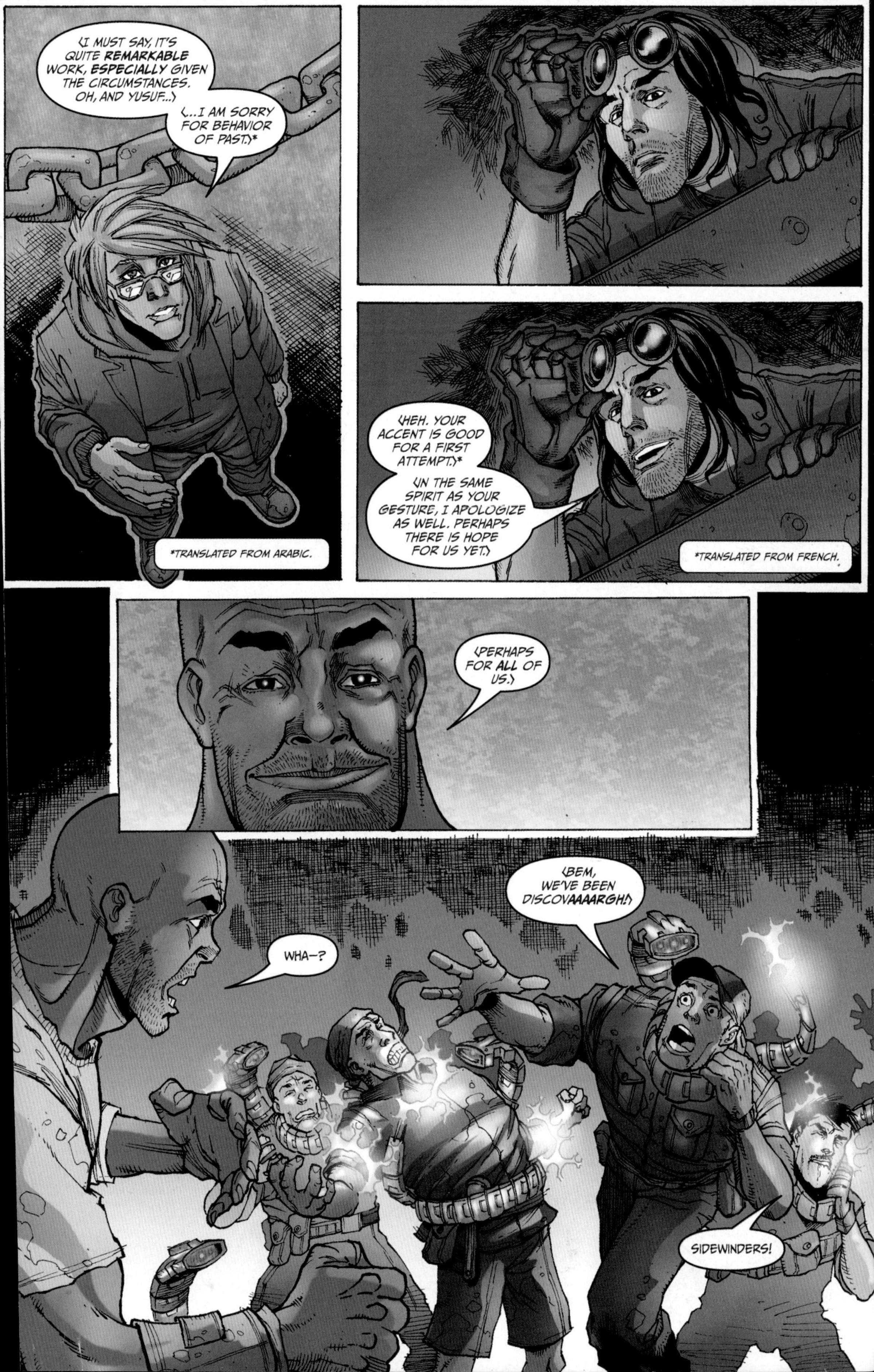

‹I MUST SAY, IT'S QUITE **REMARKABLE** WORK, **ESPECIALLY** GIVEN THE CIRCUMSTANCES. OH, AND YUSUF...›
‹...I AM SORRY FOR BEHAVIOR OF PAST.›*
*TRANSLATED FROM ARABIC.
‹HEH. YOUR ACCENT IS GOOD FOR A FIRST ATTEMPT.›*
‹IN THE SAME SPIRIT AS YOUR GESTURE, I APOLOGIZE AS WELL. PERHAPS THERE IS HOPE FOR US YET.›
*TRANSLATED FROM FRENCH.
‹PERHAPS FOR **ALL** OF US.›
WHA–?
‹BEM, WE'VE BEEN DISCOV**AAAARGH!**›
SIDEWINDERS!

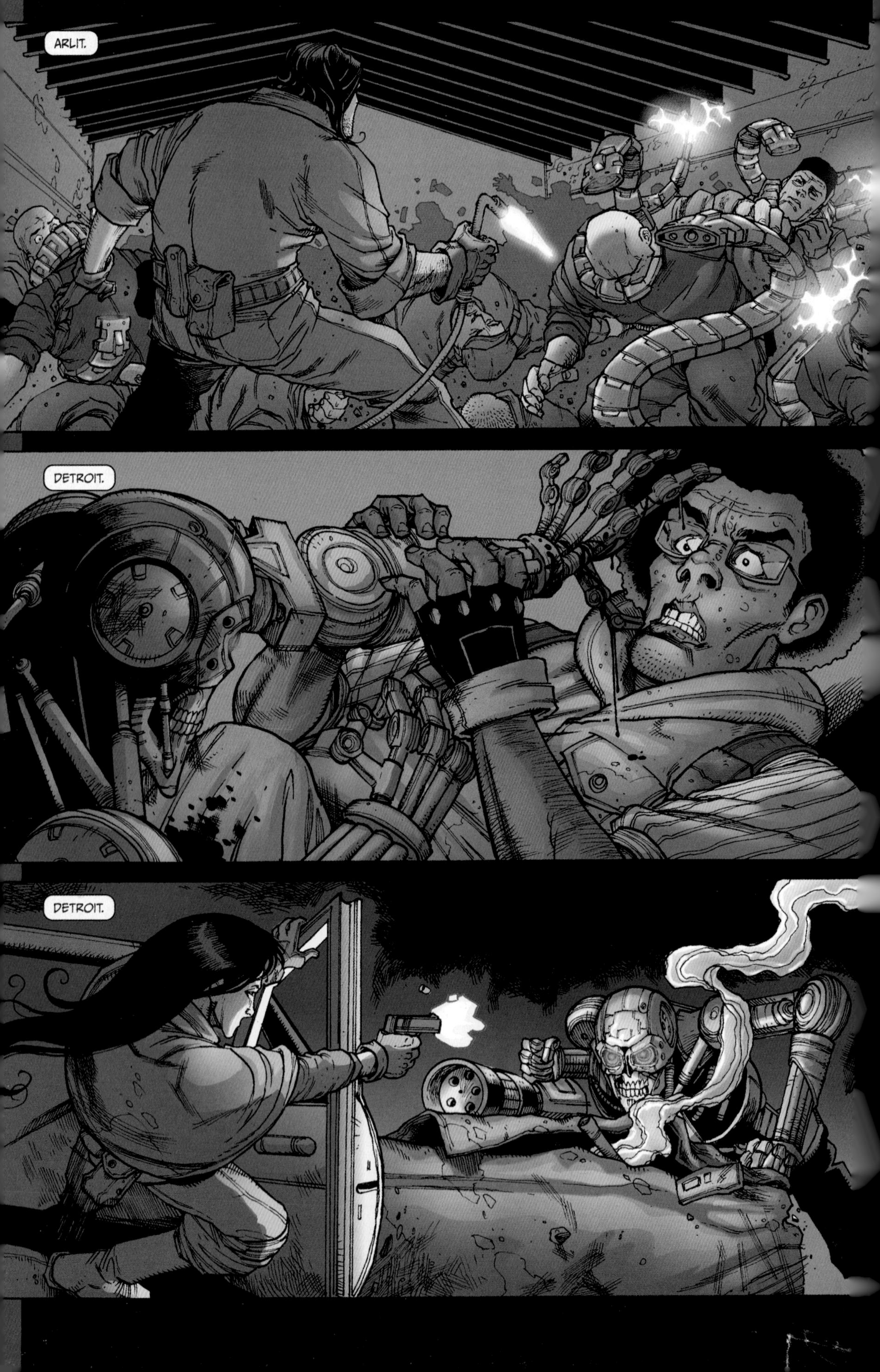
ARLIT.
DETROIT.
DETROIT.

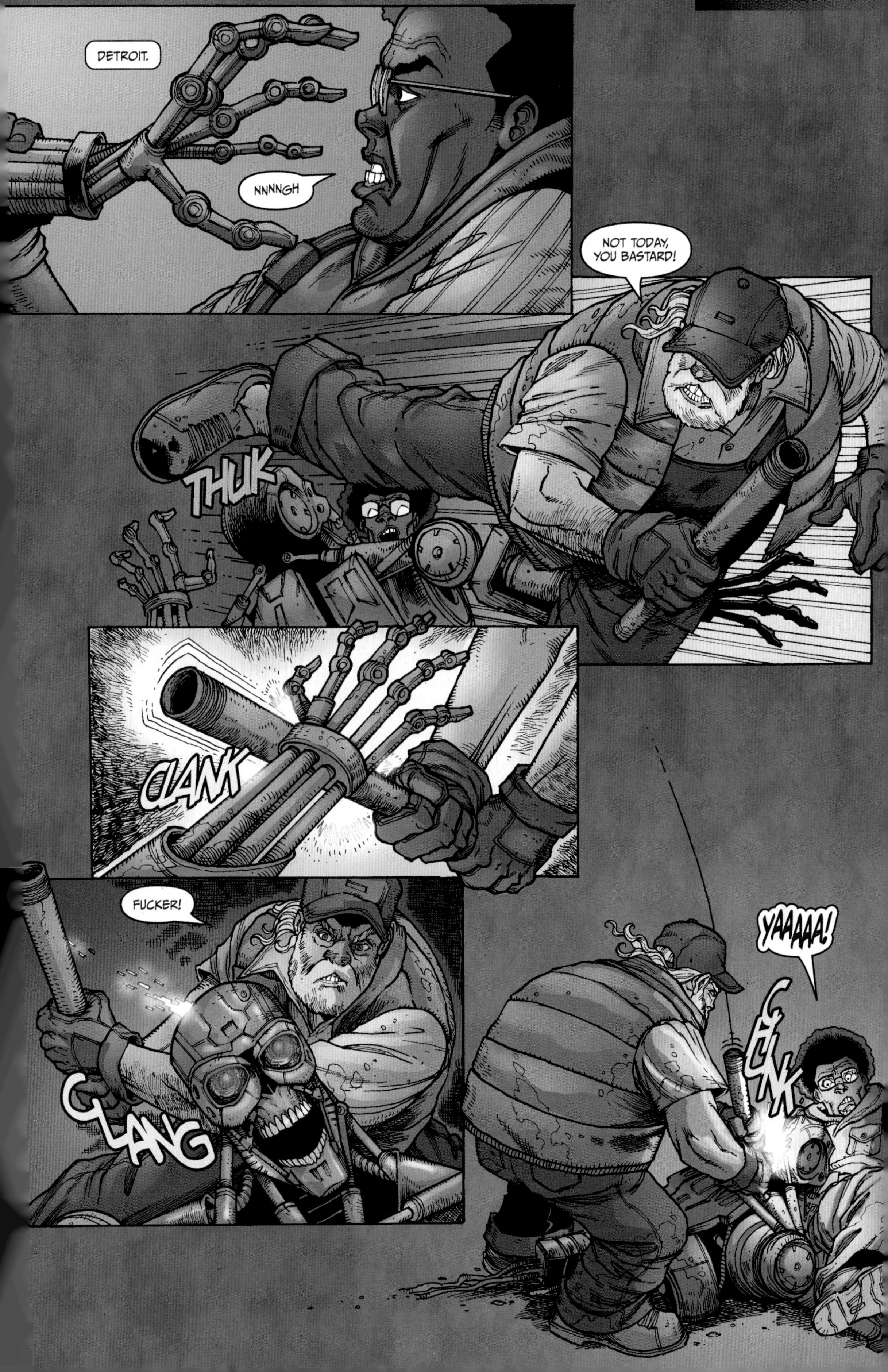
DETROIT.
NNNNGH
NOT TODAY, YOU BASTARD!
THUK
CLANK
FUCKER!
CLANG
YAAAAA!
CLUNK

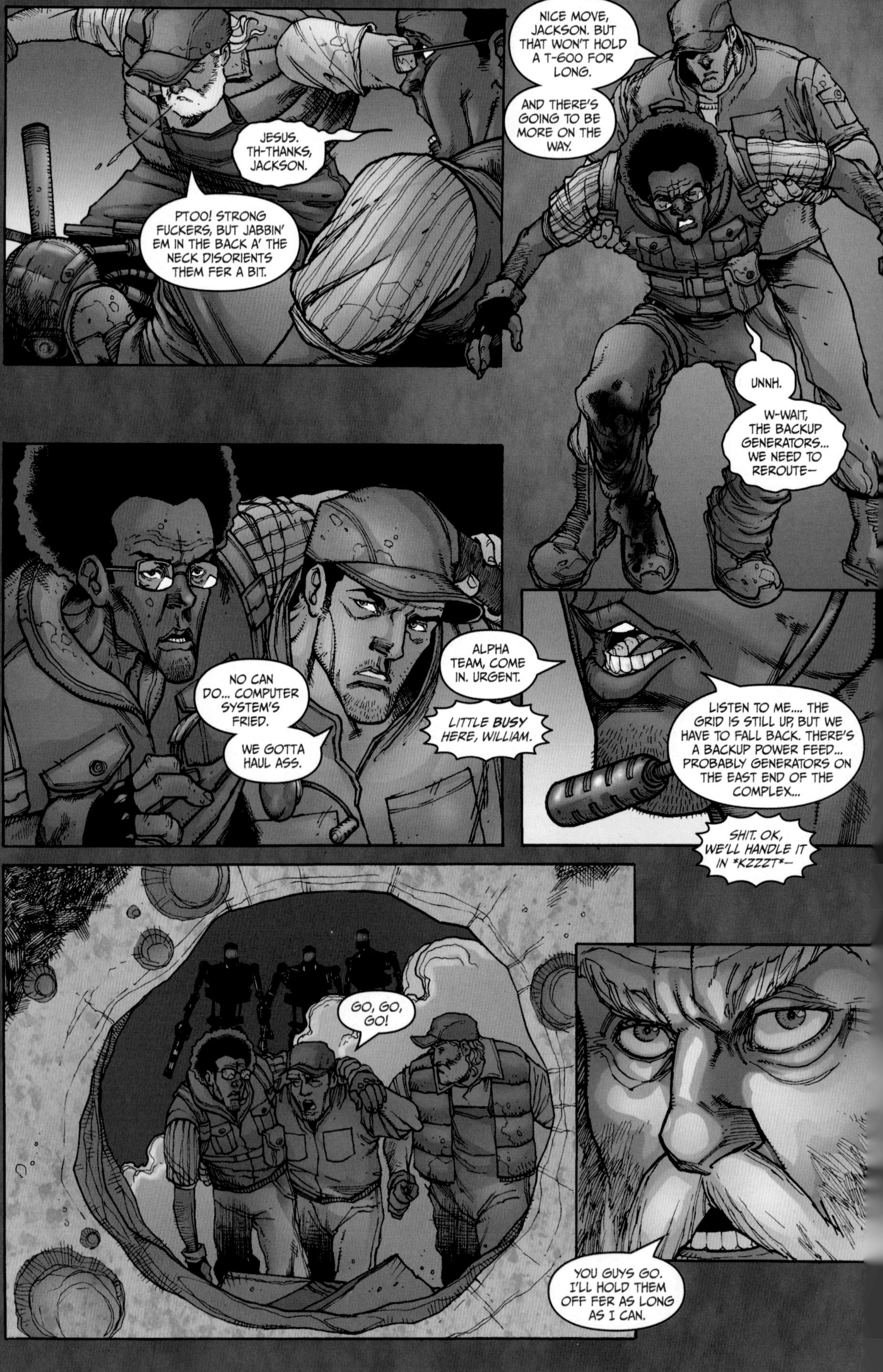
JESUS. TH-THANKS, JACKSON.
PTOO! STRONG FUCKERS, BUT JABBIN' EM IN THE BACK A' THE NECK DISORIENTS THEM FER A BIT.
NICE MOVE, JACKSON. BUT THAT WON'T HOLD A T-600 FOR LONG.
AND THERE'S GOING TO BE MORE ON THE WAY.
UNNH.
W-WAIT, THE BACKUP GENERATORS... WE NEED TO REROUTE–
NO CAN DO... COMPUTER SYSTEM'S FRIED.
WE GOTTA HAUL ASS.
ALPHA TEAM, COME IN. URGENT.
LITTLE BUSY HERE, WILLIAM.
LISTEN TO ME.... THE GRID IS STILL UP, BUT WE HAVE TO FALL BACK. THERE'S A BACKUP POWER FEED... PROBABLY GENERATORS ON THE EAST END OF THE COMPLEX...
SHIT. OK, WE'LL HANDLE IT IN *KZZZT*–
GO, GO, GO!
YOU GUYS GO. I'LL HOLD THEM OFF FER AS LONG AS I CAN.

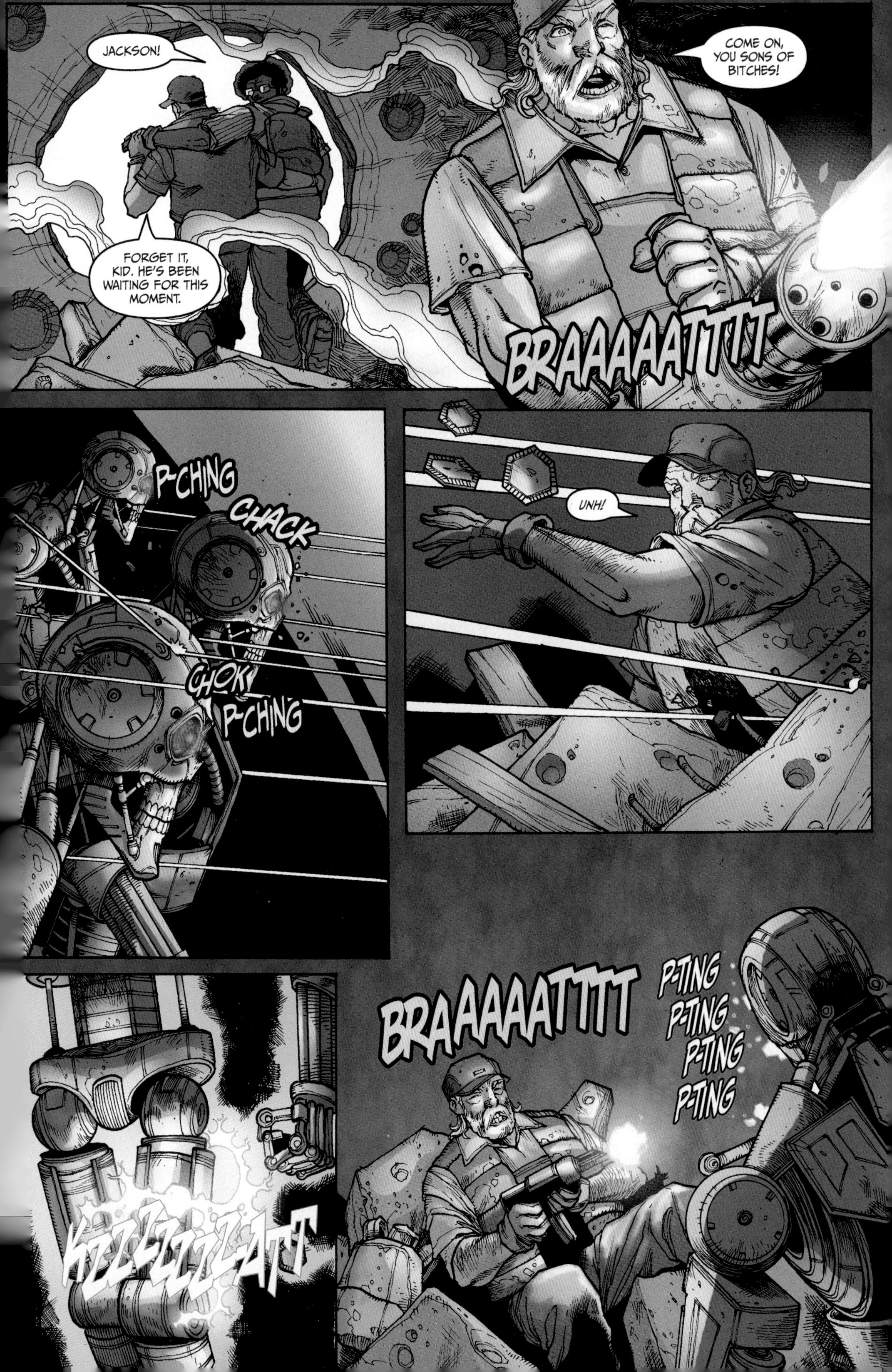

JACKSON!
FORGET IT, KID. HE'S BEEN WAITING FOR THIS MOMENT.
COME ON, YOU SONS OF BITCHES!
BRAAAAATTTT
P-CHING
CHACK
CHOK
P-CHING
UNH!
KZZZZZZZAττ
BRAAAAATTTT
P-TING
P-TING
P-TING
P-TING

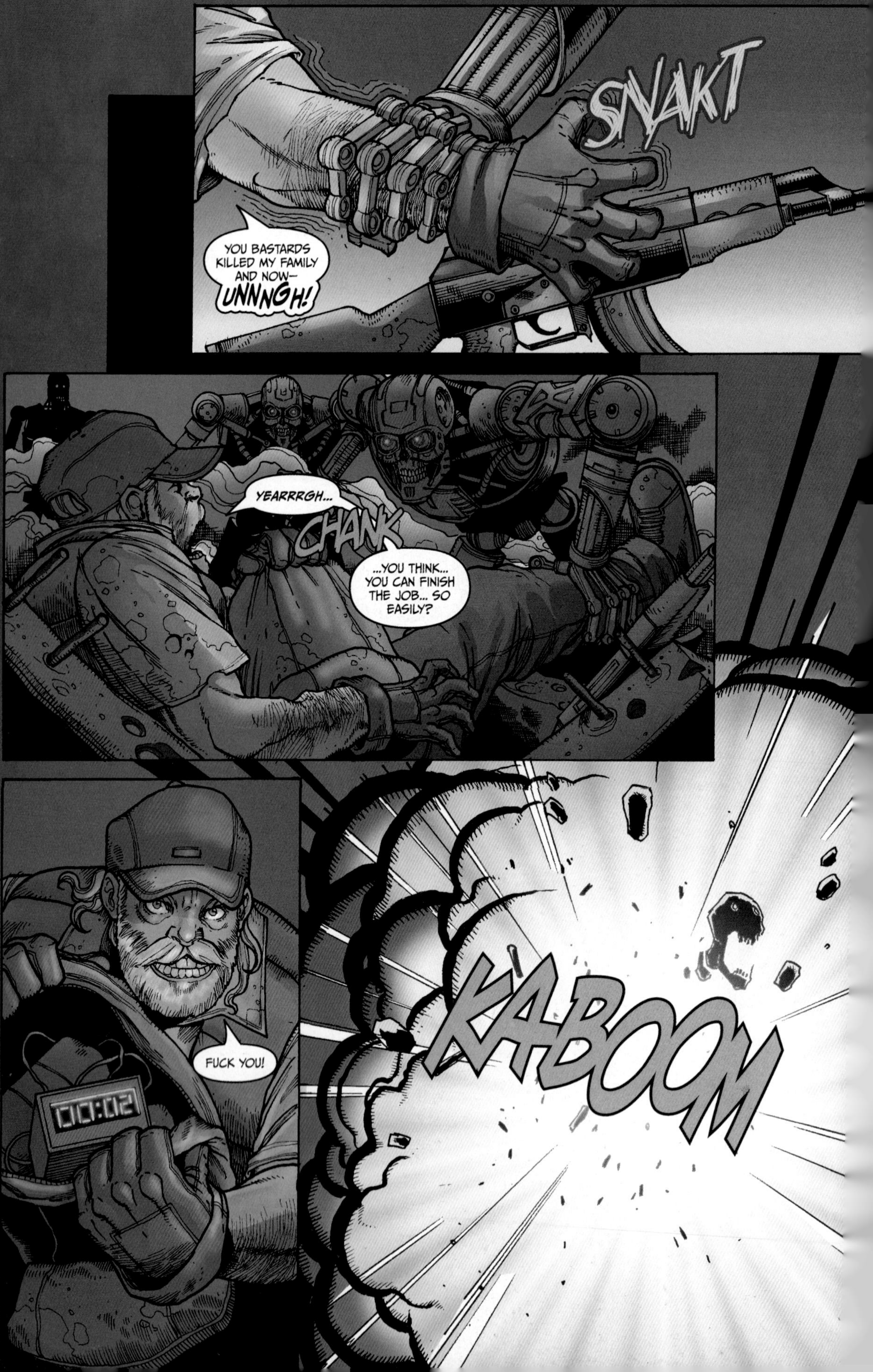
SNAKT
YOU BASTARDS KILLED MY FAMILY AND NOW— UNNNGH!
YEARRRGH...
CHANK
...YOU THINK... YOU CAN FINISH THE JOB... SO EASILY?
FUCK YOU!
00:02
KABOOM

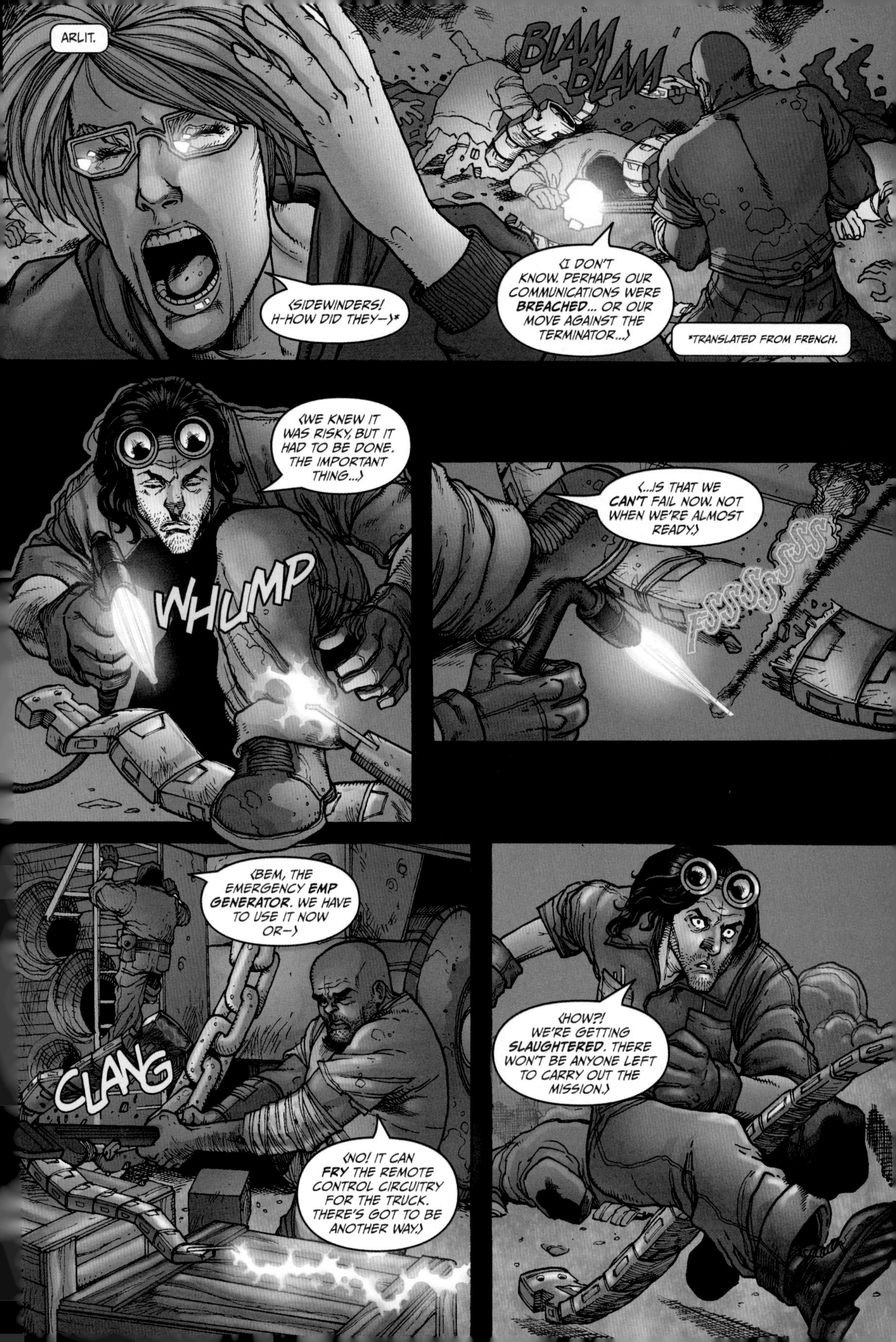
ARLIT.
BLAM BLAM
‹SIDEWINDERS! H-HOW DID THEY—›*
‹I DON'T KNOW. PERHAPS OUR COMMUNICATIONS WERE BREACHED... OR OUR MOVE AGAINST THE TERMINATOR...›
*TRANSLATED FROM FRENCH.
‹WE KNEW IT WAS RISKY, BUT IT HAD TO BE DONE. THE IMPORTANT THING...›
WHUMP
‹...IS THAT WE CAN'T FAIL NOW. NOT WHEN WE'RE ALMOST READY.›
FSSSSSSS
‹BEM, THE EMERGENCY EMP GENERATOR. WE HAVE TO USE IT NOW OR—›
CLANG
‹NO! IT CAN FRY THE REMOTE CONTROL CIRCUITRY FOR THE TRUCK. THERE'S GOT TO BE ANOTHER WAY.›
‹HOW?! WE'RE GETTING SLAUGHTERED. THERE WON'T BE ANYONE LEFT TO CARRY OUT THE MISSION.›

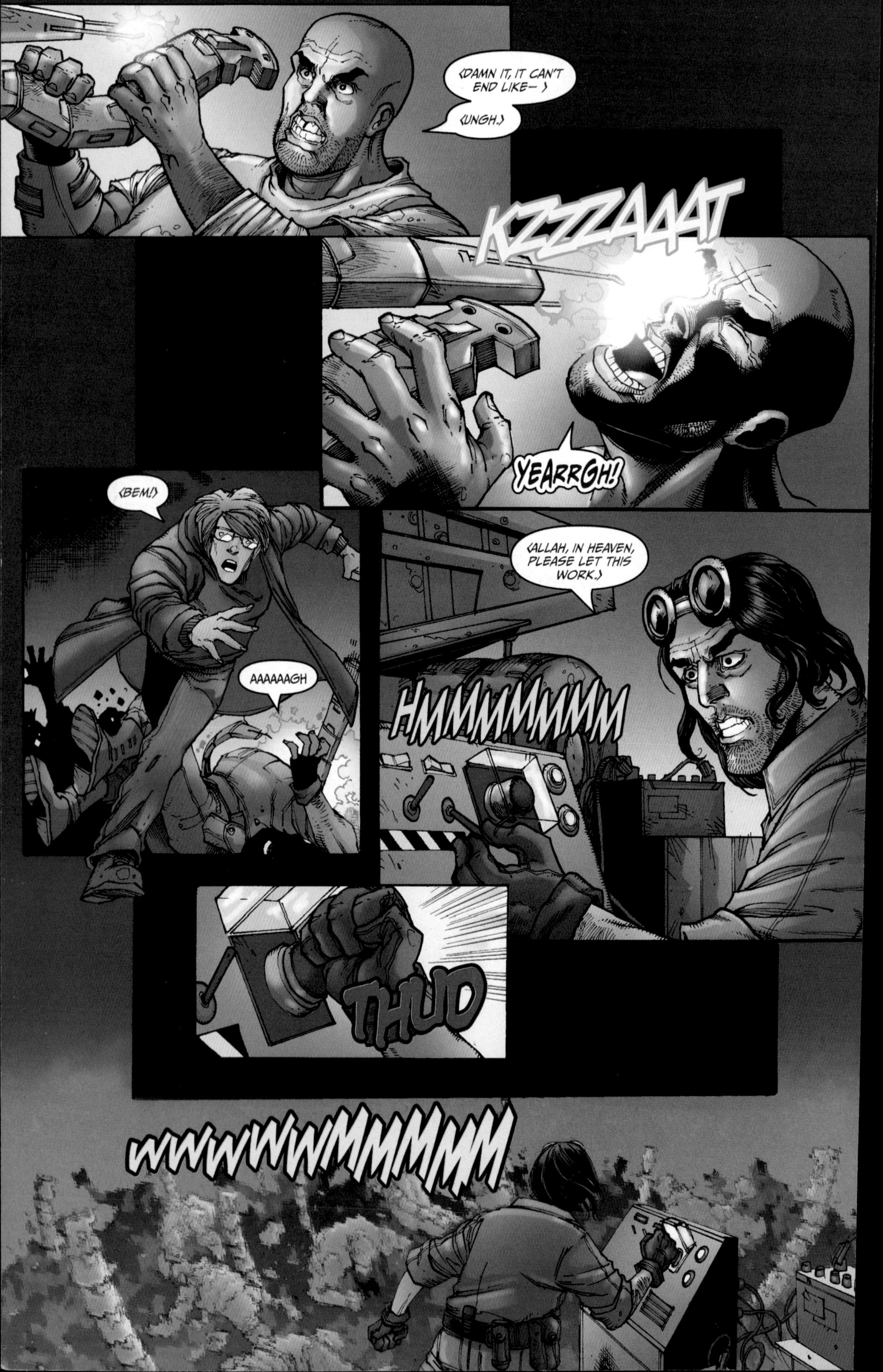

‹DAMN IT, IT CAN'T END LIKE— ›
‹UNGH.›
KZZZAAAT
YEARRGH!
‹BEM!›
AAAAAAGH
‹ALLAH, IN HEAVEN, PLEASE LET THIS WORK.›
HMMMMMMM
THUD
WWWWWMMMMM

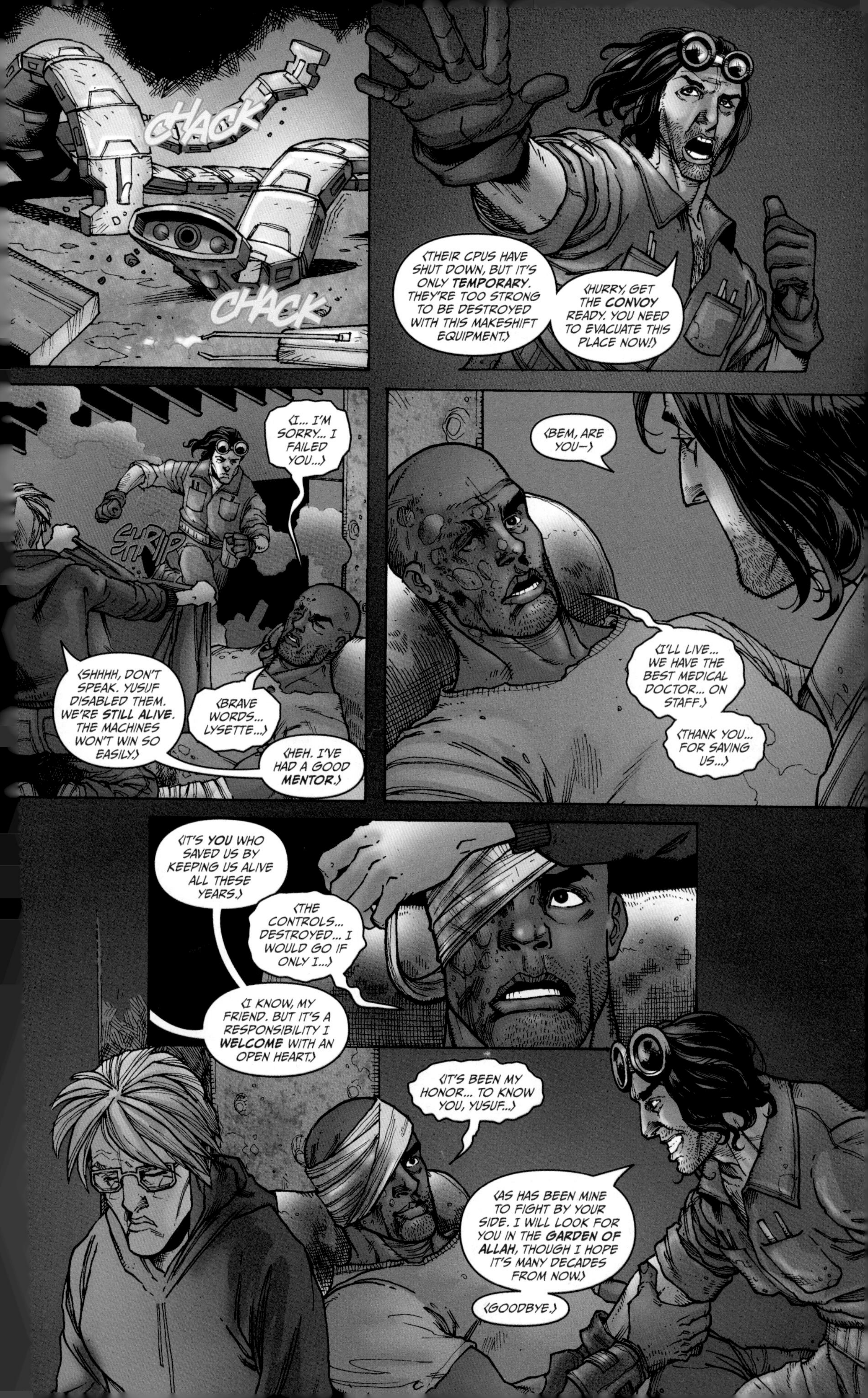
CHACK
CHACK
<THEIR CPUS HAVE SHUT DOWN, BUT IT'S ONLY TEMPORARY. THEY'RE TOO STRONG TO BE DESTROYED WITH THIS MAKESHIFT EQUIPMENT.>
<HURRY, GET THE CONVOY READY. YOU NEED TO EVACUATE THIS PLACE NOW!>
<I... I'M SORRY... I FAILED YOU...>
SHRIP
<SHHHH, DON'T SPEAK. YUSUF DISABLED THEM. WE'RE STILL ALIVE. THE MACHINES WON'T WIN SO EASILY.>
<BRAVE WORDS... LYSETTE...>
<HEH. I'VE HAD A GOOD MENTOR.>
<BEM, ARE YOU-->
<I'LL LIVE... WE HAVE THE BEST MEDICAL DOCTOR... ON STAFF.>
<THANK YOU... FOR SAVING US...>
<IT'S YOU WHO SAVED US BY KEEPING US ALIVE ALL THESE YEARS.>
<THE CONTROLS... DESTROYED... I WOULD GO IF ONLY I...>
<I KNOW, MY FRIEND. BUT IT'S A RESPONSIBILITY I WELCOME WITH AN OPEN HEART.>
<IT'S BEEN MY HONOR... TO KNOW YOU, YUSUF...>
<AS HAS BEEN MINE TO FIGHT BY YOUR SIDE. I WILL LOOK FOR YOU IN THE GARDEN OF ALLAH, THOUGH I HOPE IT'S MANY DECADES FROM NOW.>
<GOODBYE.>

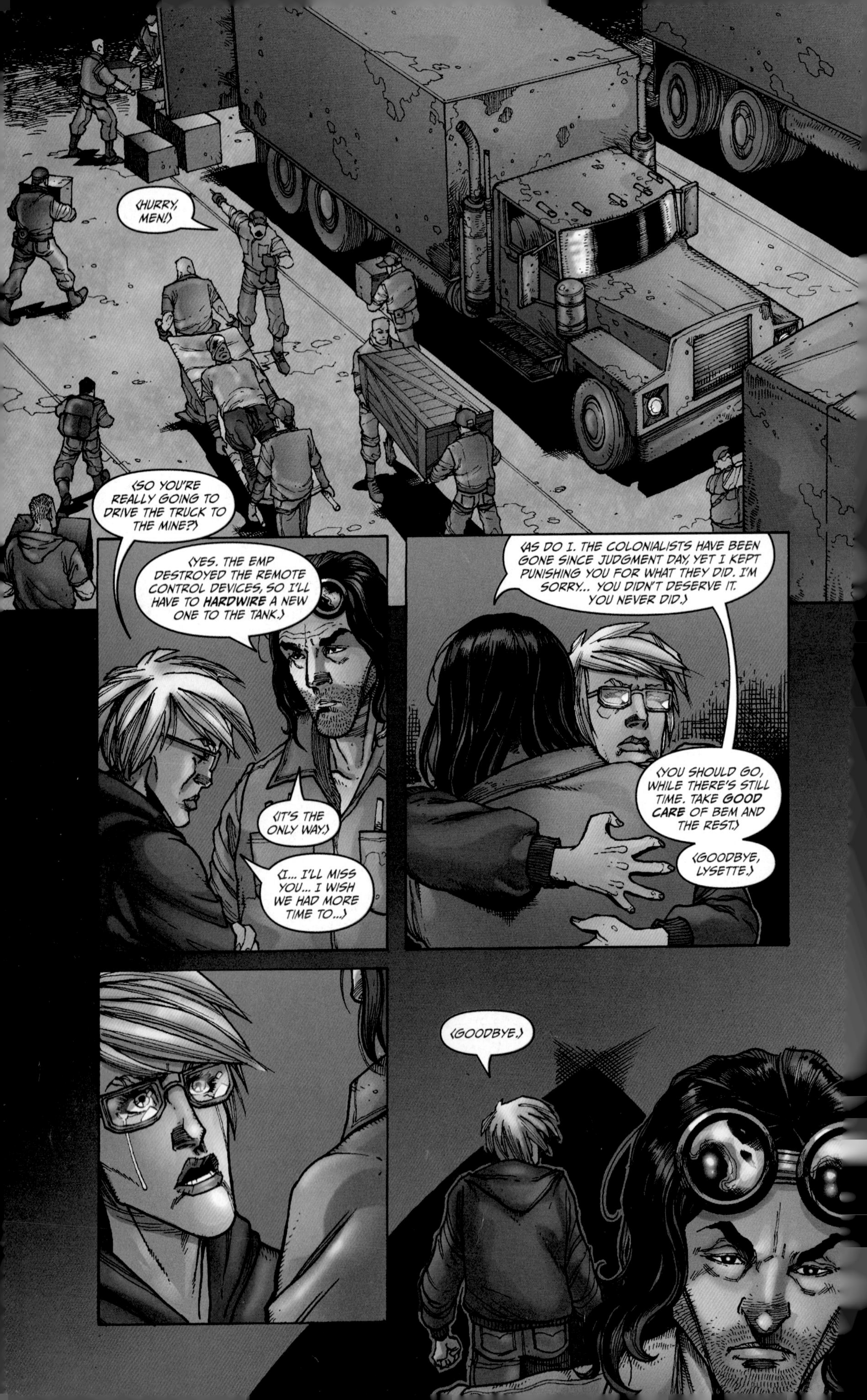

CHAPTER 4

‹HURRY, MEN!›
‹SO YOU'RE REALLY GOING TO DRIVE THE TRUCK TO THE MINE?›
‹YES. THE EMP DESTROYED THE REMOTE CONTROL DEVICES, SO I'LL HAVE TO HARDWIRE A NEW ONE TO THE TANK.›
‹IT'S THE ONLY WAY.›
‹I... I'LL MISS YOU... I WISH WE HAD MORE TIME TO...›
‹AS DO I. THE COLONIALISTS HAVE BEEN GONE SINCE JUDGMENT DAY, YET I KEPT PUNISHING YOU FOR WHAT THEY DID. I'M SORRY... YOU DIDN'T DESERVE IT. YOU NEVER DID.›
‹YOU SHOULD GO, WHILE THERE'S STILL TIME. TAKE GOOD CARE OF BEM AND THE REST.›
‹GOODBYE, LYSETTE.›
‹GOODBYE.›

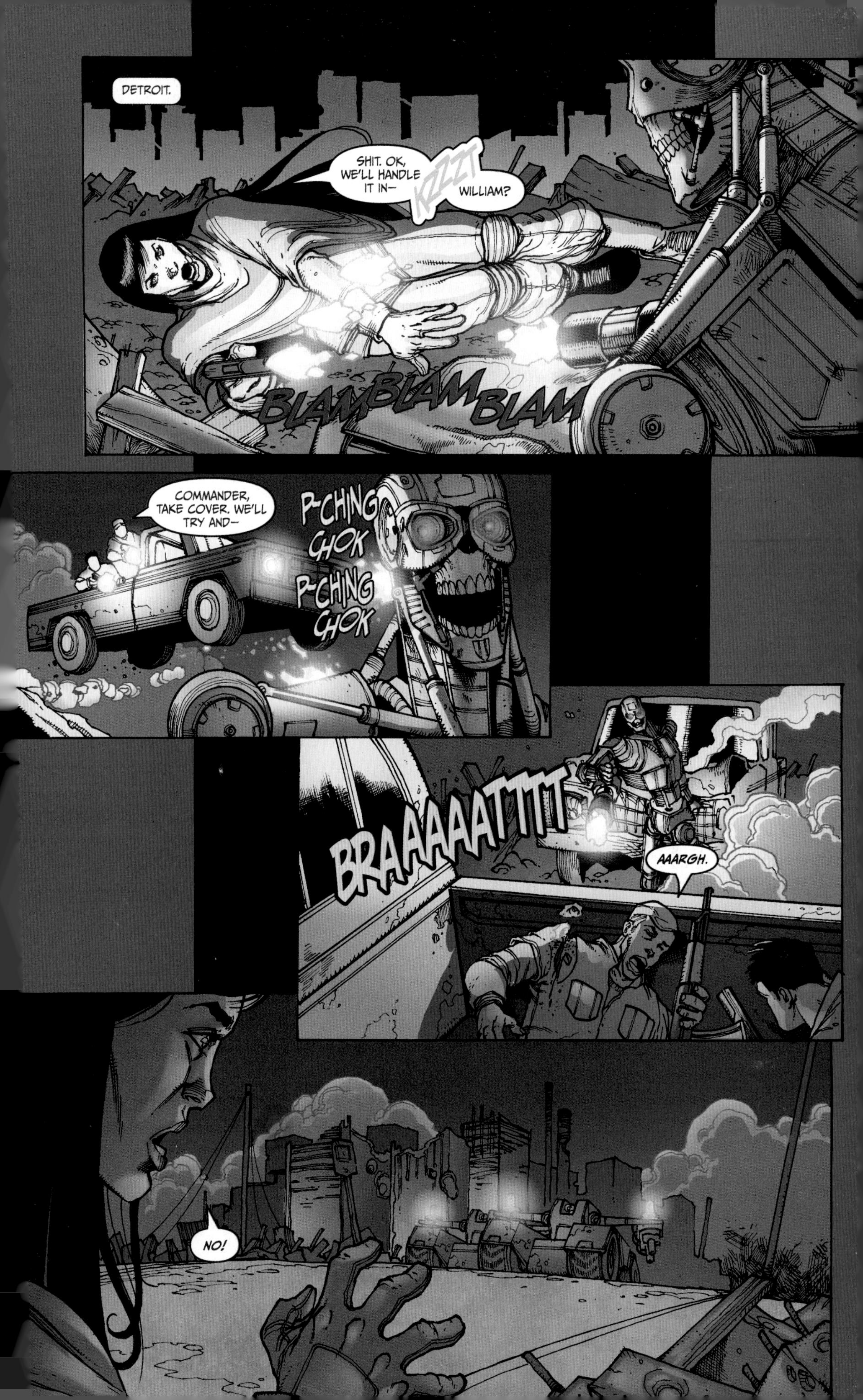
DETROIT.
SHIT. OK, WE'LL HANDLE IT IN—
KZZZT
WILLIAM?
BLAM BLAM BLAM
COMMANDER, TAKE COVER. WE'LL TRY AND—
P-CHING
CHOK
P-CHING
CHOK
BRAAAAATTTT
AAARGH.
NO!

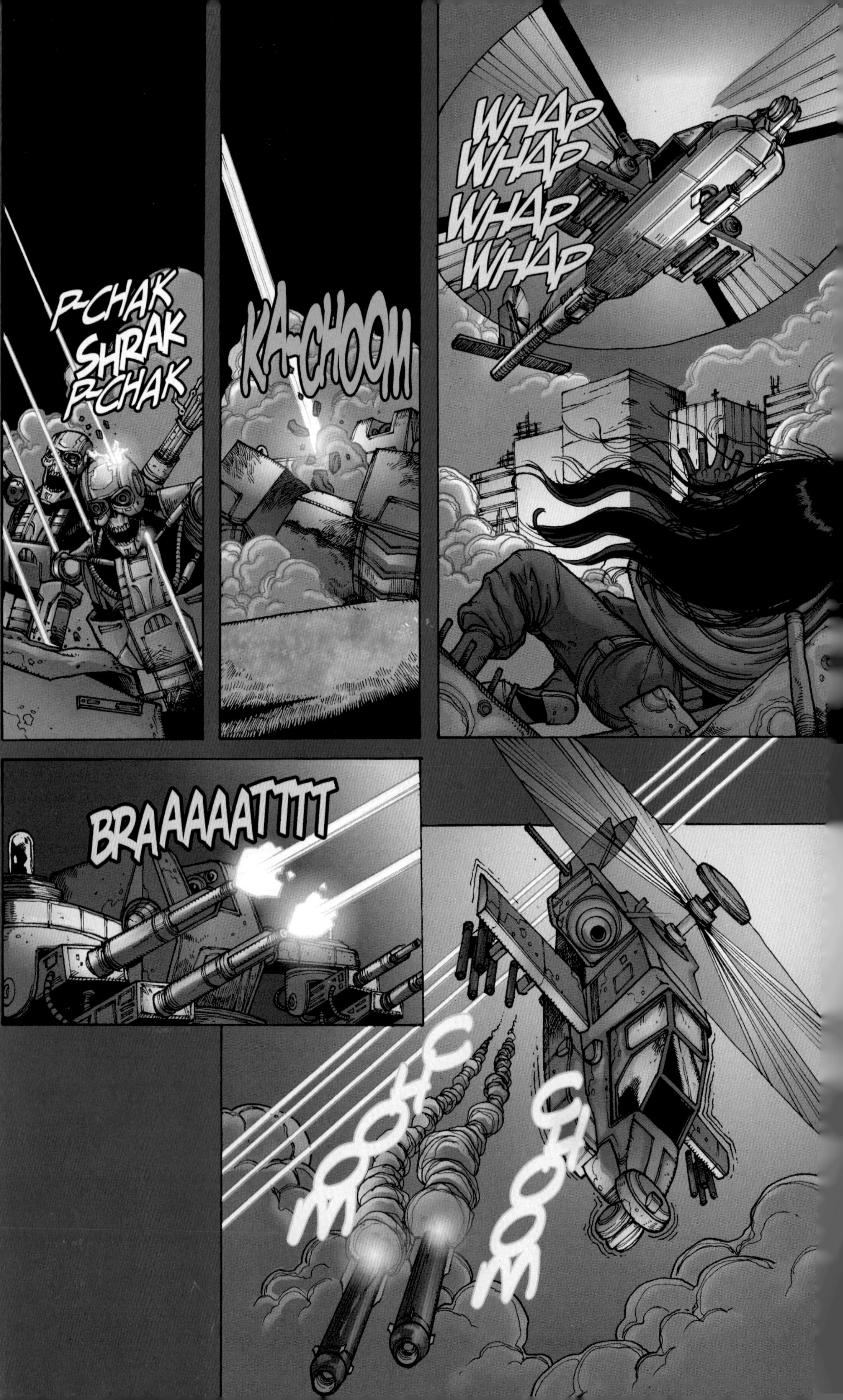
P-CHAK
SHRAK
P-CHAK
KA-CHOOM
WHAP
WHAP
WHAP
WHAP
BRAAAATTTT
CHOOM
CHOOM

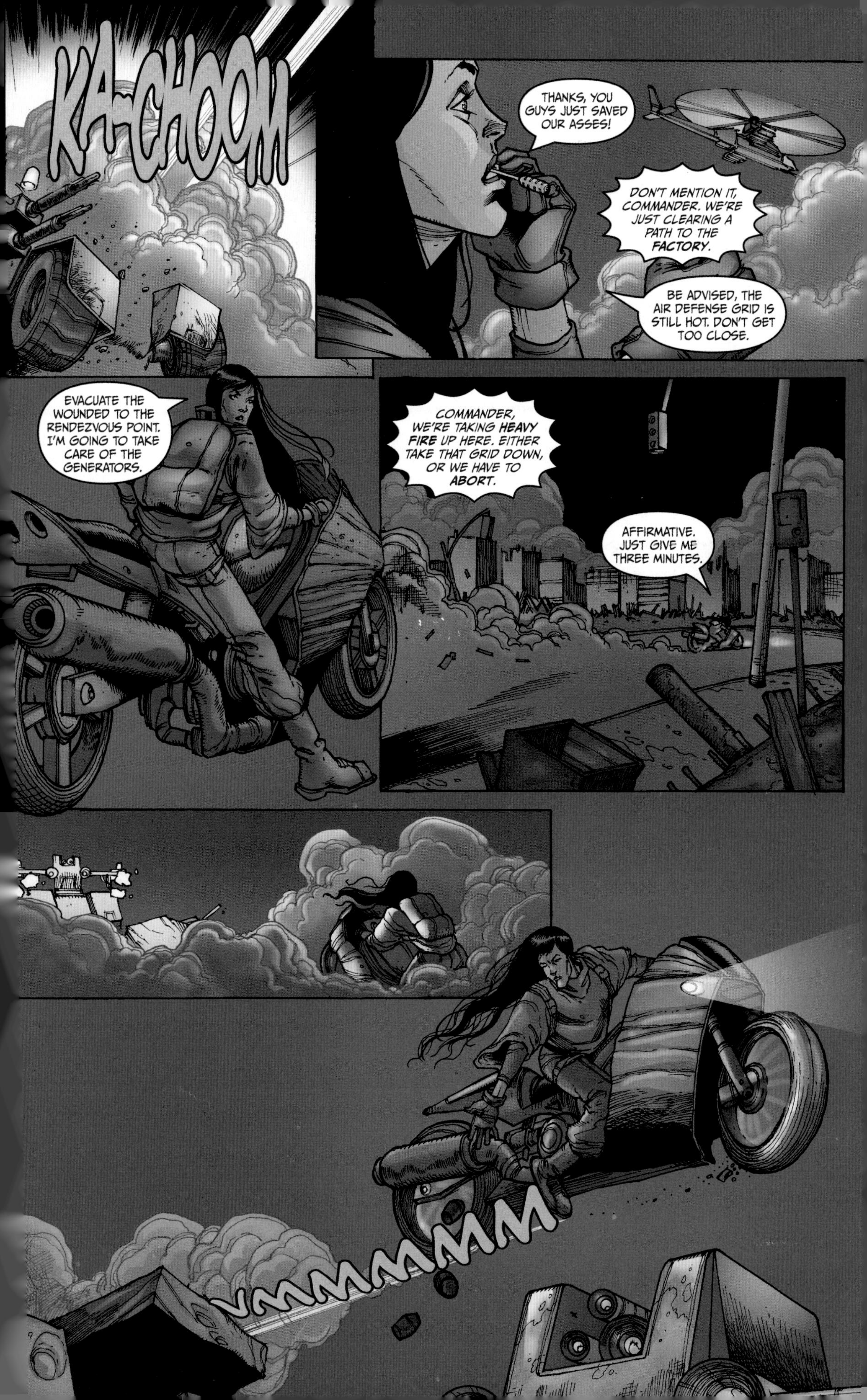
KA-CHOOM
THANKS, YOU GUYS JUST SAVED OUR ASSES!
DON'T MENTION IT, COMMANDER. WE'RE JUST CLEARING A PATH TO THE FACTORY.
BE ADVISED, THE AIR DEFENSE GRID IS STILL HOT. DON'T GET TOO CLOSE.
EVACUATE THE WOUNDED TO THE RENDEZVOUS POINT. I'M GOING TO TAKE CARE OF THE GENERATORS.
COMMANDER, WE'RE TAKING HEAVY FIRE UP HERE. EITHER TAKE THAT GRID DOWN, OR WE HAVE TO ABORT.
AFFIRMATIVE. JUST GIVE ME THREE MINUTES.
VMMMMMMM

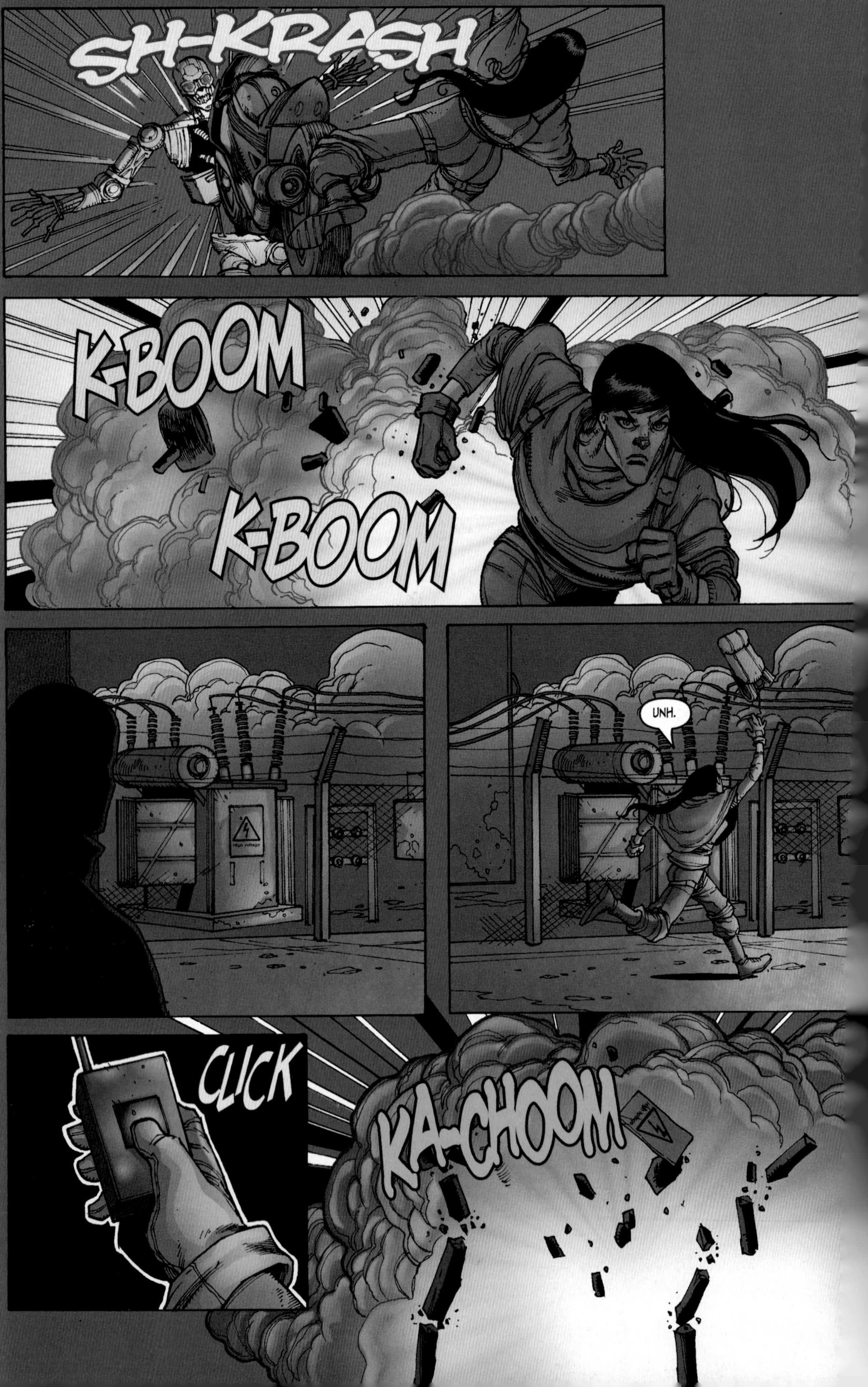
SH-KRASH
K-BOOM
K-BOOM
High voltage
UNH.
CLICK
KA-CHOOM

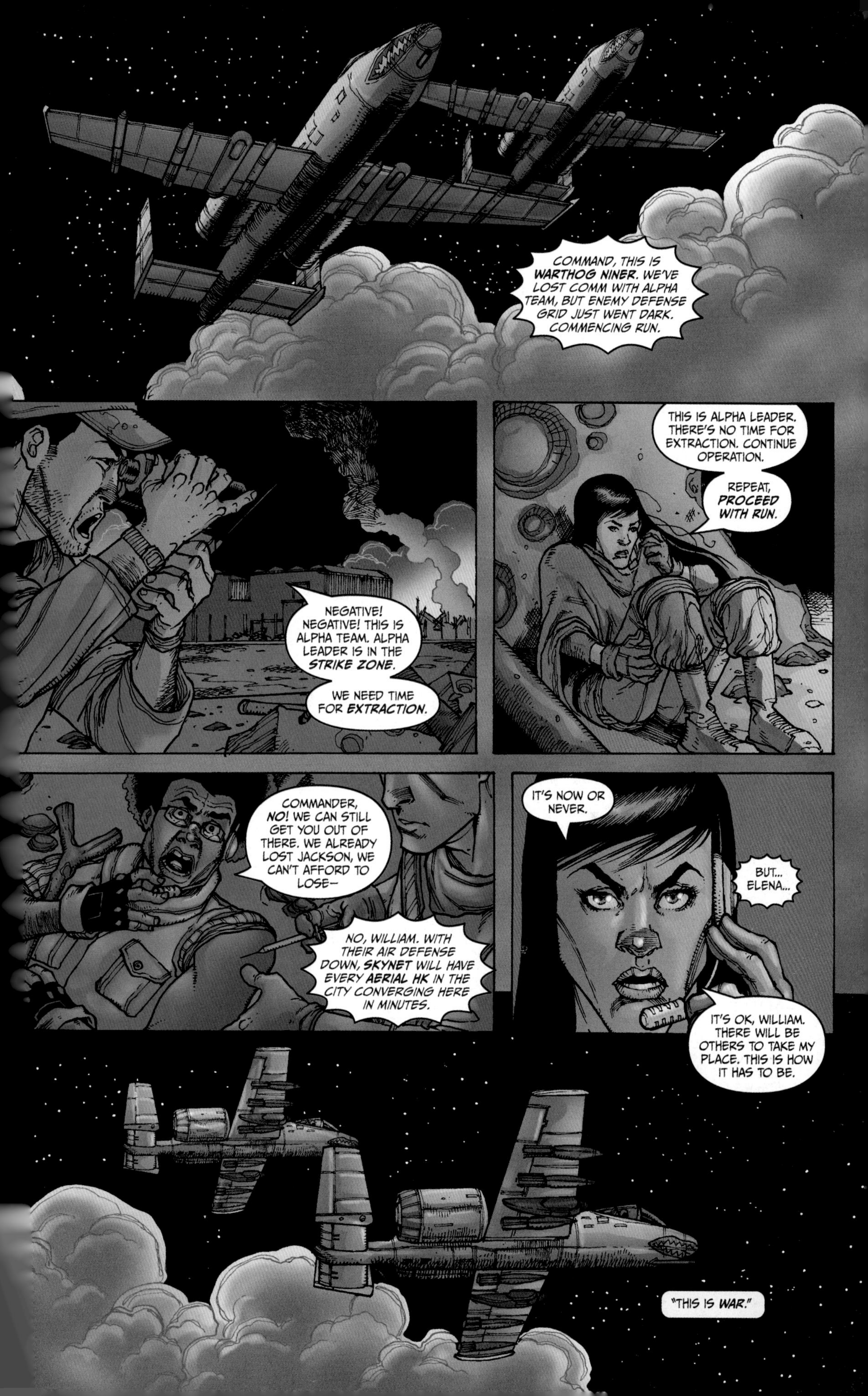
COMMAND, THIS IS WARTHOG NINER. WE'VE LOST COMM WITH ALPHA TEAM, BUT ENEMY DEFENSE GRID JUST WENT DARK. COMMENCING RUN.
NEGATIVE! NEGATIVE! THIS IS ALPHA TEAM. ALPHA LEADER IS IN THE STRIKE ZONE.
WE NEED TIME FOR EXTRACTION.
THIS IS ALPHA LEADER. THERE'S NO TIME FOR EXTRACTION. CONTINUE OPERATION.
REPEAT, PROCEED WITH RUN.
COMMANDER, NO! WE CAN STILL GET YOU OUT OF THERE. WE ALREADY LOST JACKSON, WE CAN'T AFFORD TO LOSE--
NO, WILLIAM. WITH THEIR AIR DEFENSE DOWN, SKYNET WILL HAVE EVERY AERIAL HK IN THE CITY CONVERGING HERE IN MINUTES.
IT'S NOW OR NEVER.
BUT... ELENA...
IT'S OK, WILLIAM. THERE WILL BE OTHERS TO TAKE MY PLACE. THIS IS HOW IT HAS TO BE.
"THIS IS WAR."

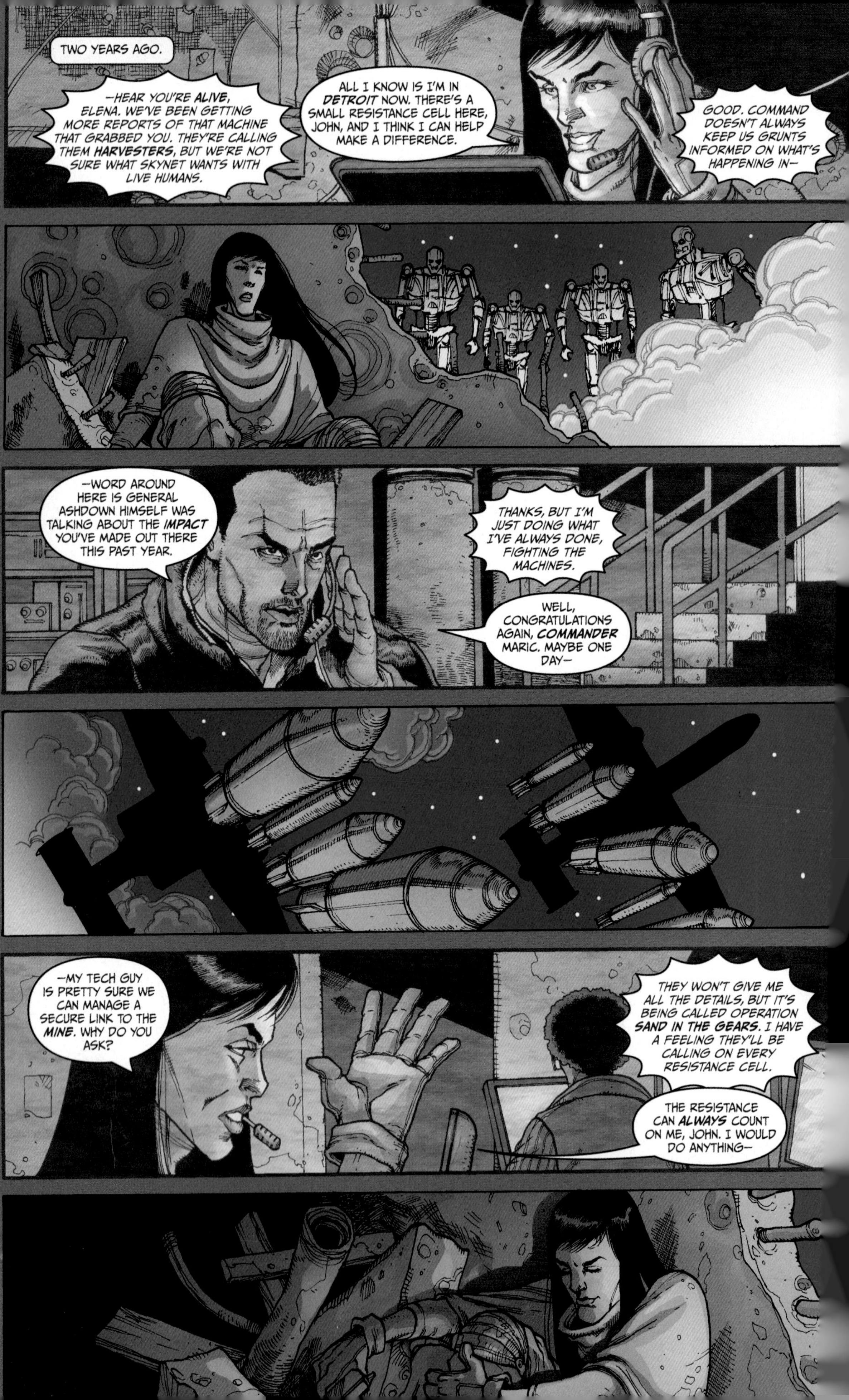
TWO YEARS AGO.
—HEAR YOU'RE ALIVE, ELENA. WE'VE BEEN GETTING MORE REPORTS OF THAT MACHINE THAT GRABBED YOU. THEY'RE CALLING THEM HARVESTERS, BUT WE'RE NOT SURE WHAT SKYNET WANTS WITH LIVE HUMANS.
ALL I KNOW IS I'M IN DETROIT NOW. THERE'S A SMALL RESISTANCE CELL HERE, JOHN, AND I THINK I CAN HELP MAKE A DIFFERENCE.
GOOD. COMMAND DOESN'T ALWAYS KEEP US GRUNTS INFORMED ON WHAT'S HAPPENING IN—
—WORD AROUND HERE IS GENERAL ASHDOWN HIMSELF WAS TALKING ABOUT THE IMPACT YOU'VE MADE OUT THERE THIS PAST YEAR.
THANKS, BUT I'M JUST DOING WHAT I'VE ALWAYS DONE, FIGHTING THE MACHINES.
WELL, CONGRATULATIONS AGAIN, COMMANDER MARIC. MAYBE ONE DAY—
—MY TECH GUY IS PRETTY SURE WE CAN MANAGE A SECURE LINK TO THE MINE. WHY DO YOU ASK?
THEY WON'T GIVE ME ALL THE DETAILS, BUT IT'S BEING CALLED OPERATION SAND IN THE GEARS. I HAVE A FEELING THEY'LL BE CALLING ON EVERY RESISTANCE CELL.
THE RESISTANCE CAN ALWAYS COUNT ON ME, JOHN. I WOULD DO ANYTHING—

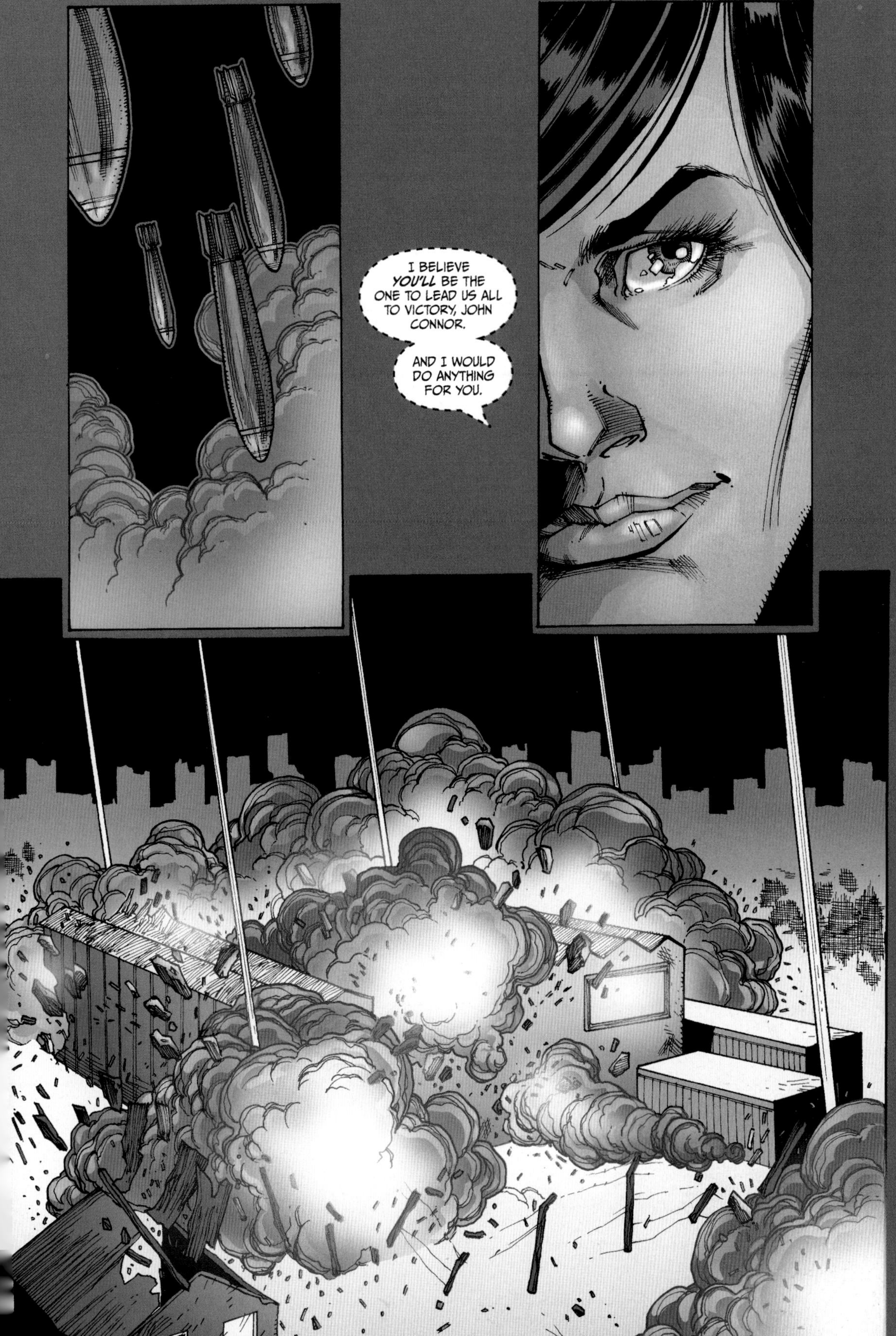
I BELIEVE *YOU'LL* BE THE ONE TO LEAD US ALL TO VICTORY, JOHN CONNOR.
AND I WOULD DO ANYTHING FOR YOU.

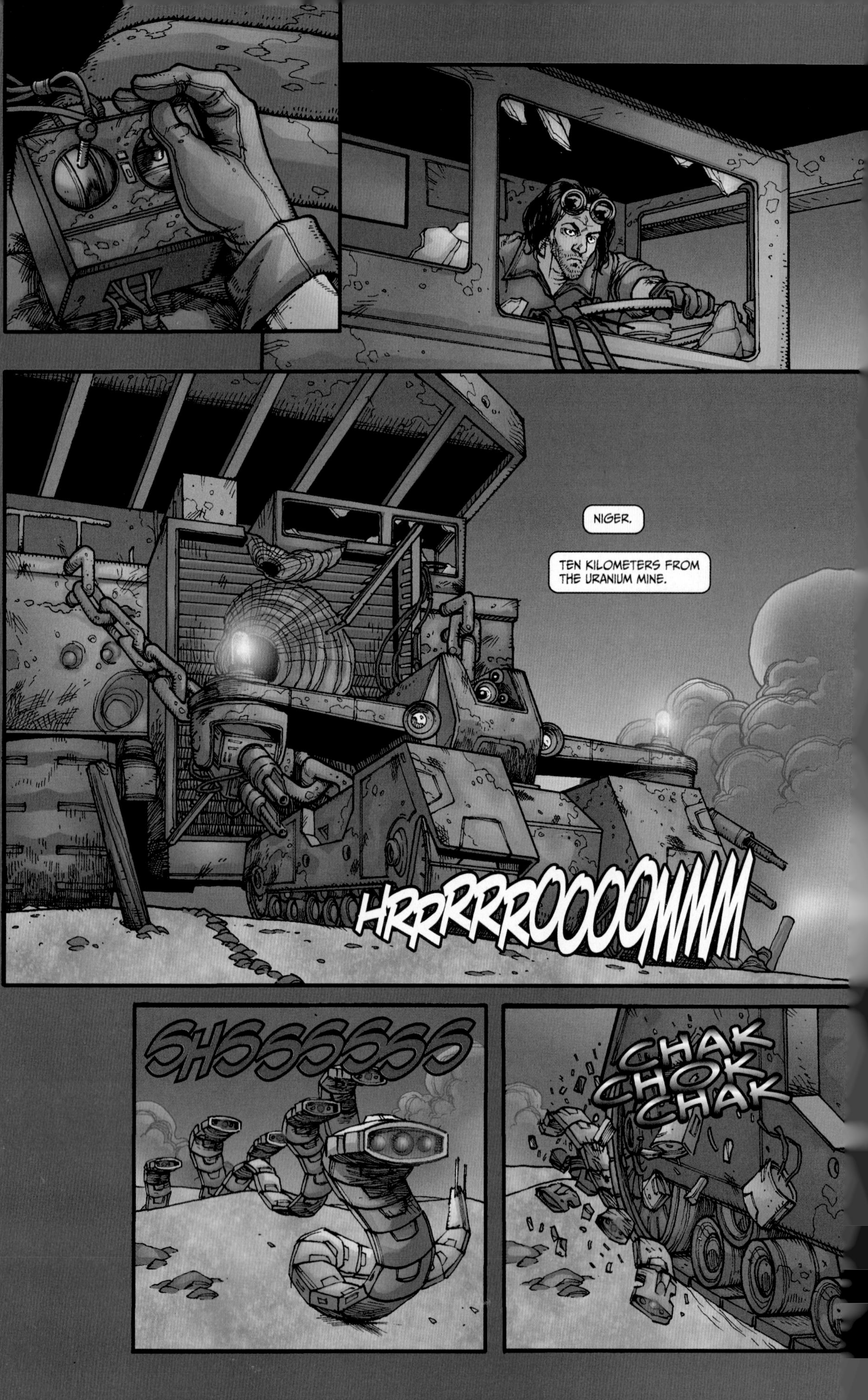
NIGER.
TEN KILOMETERS FROM THE URANIUM MINE.
HRRRRROOOOOMMM
SHSSSSSS
CHAK CHOK CHAK

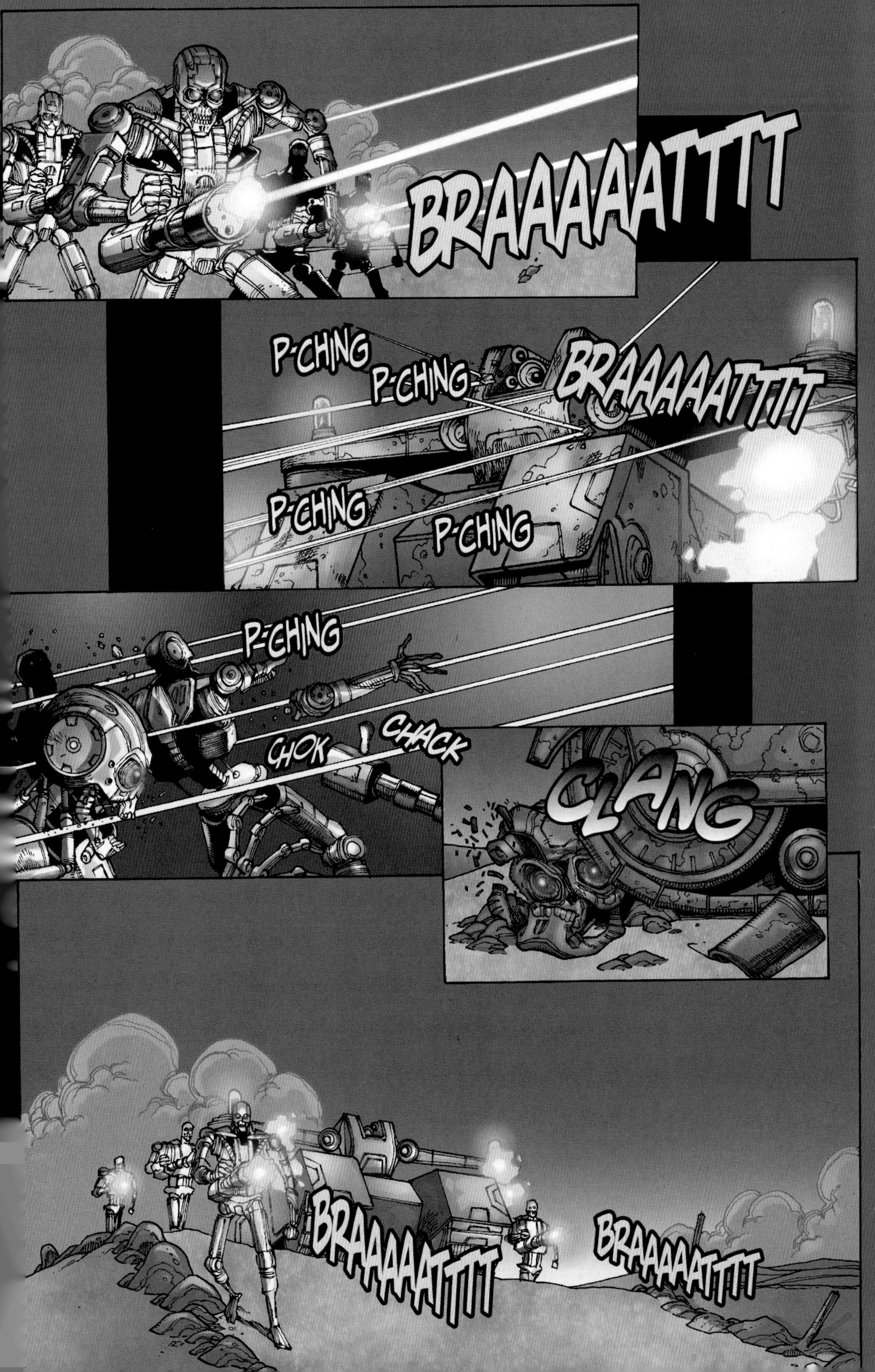
BRAAAAATTTT
P-CHING
P-CHING
BRAAAAATTTT
P-CHING
P-CHING
P-CHING
CHOK
CHACK
CLANG
BRAAAAATTTT
BRAAAAATTTT

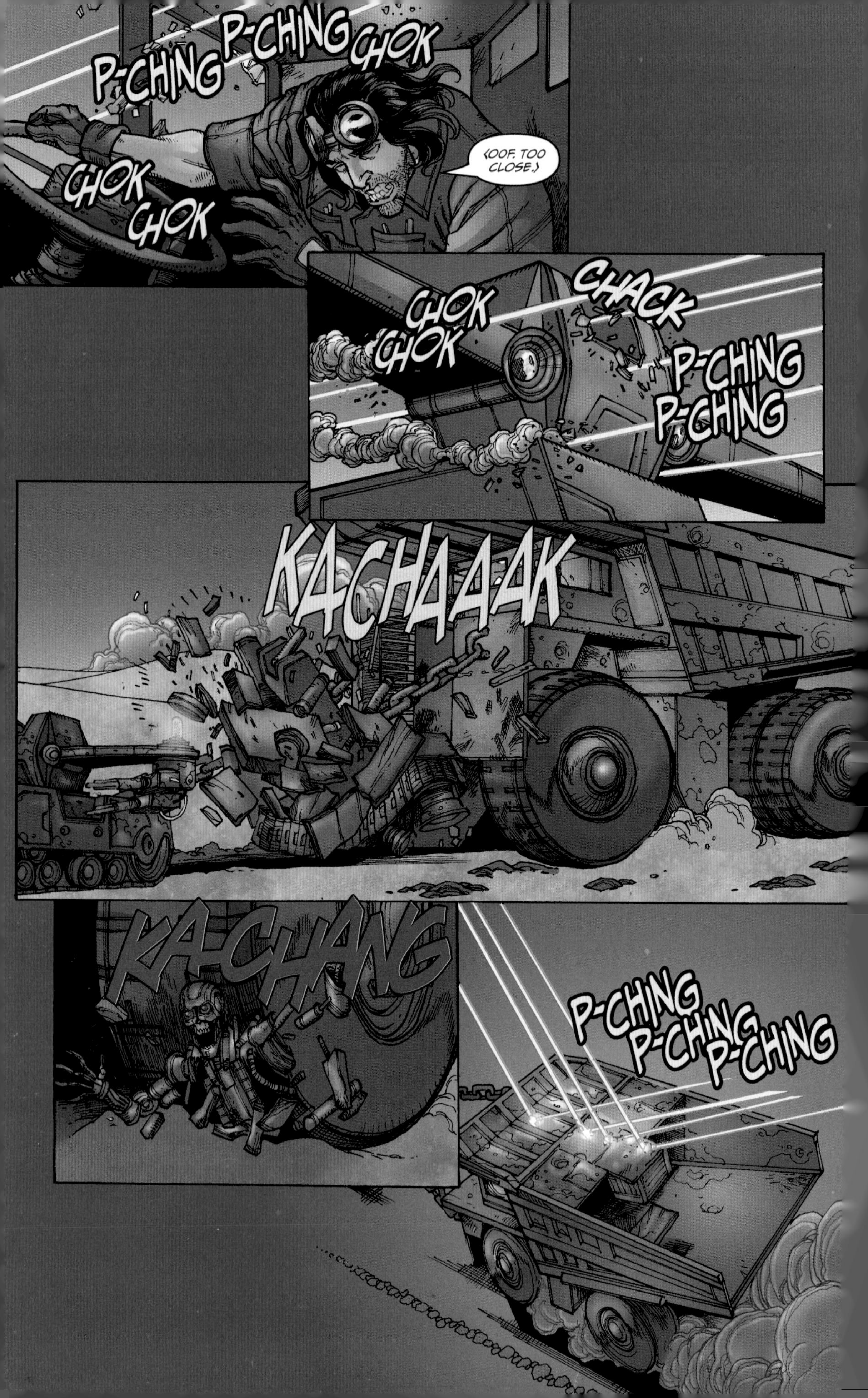
P-CHING
P-CHING
CHOK
CHOK
CHOK
‹OOF. TOO CLOSE.›
CHOK
CHOK
CHACK
P-CHING
P-CHING
KACHAAAK
KA-CHANG
P-CHING
P-CHING
P-CHING

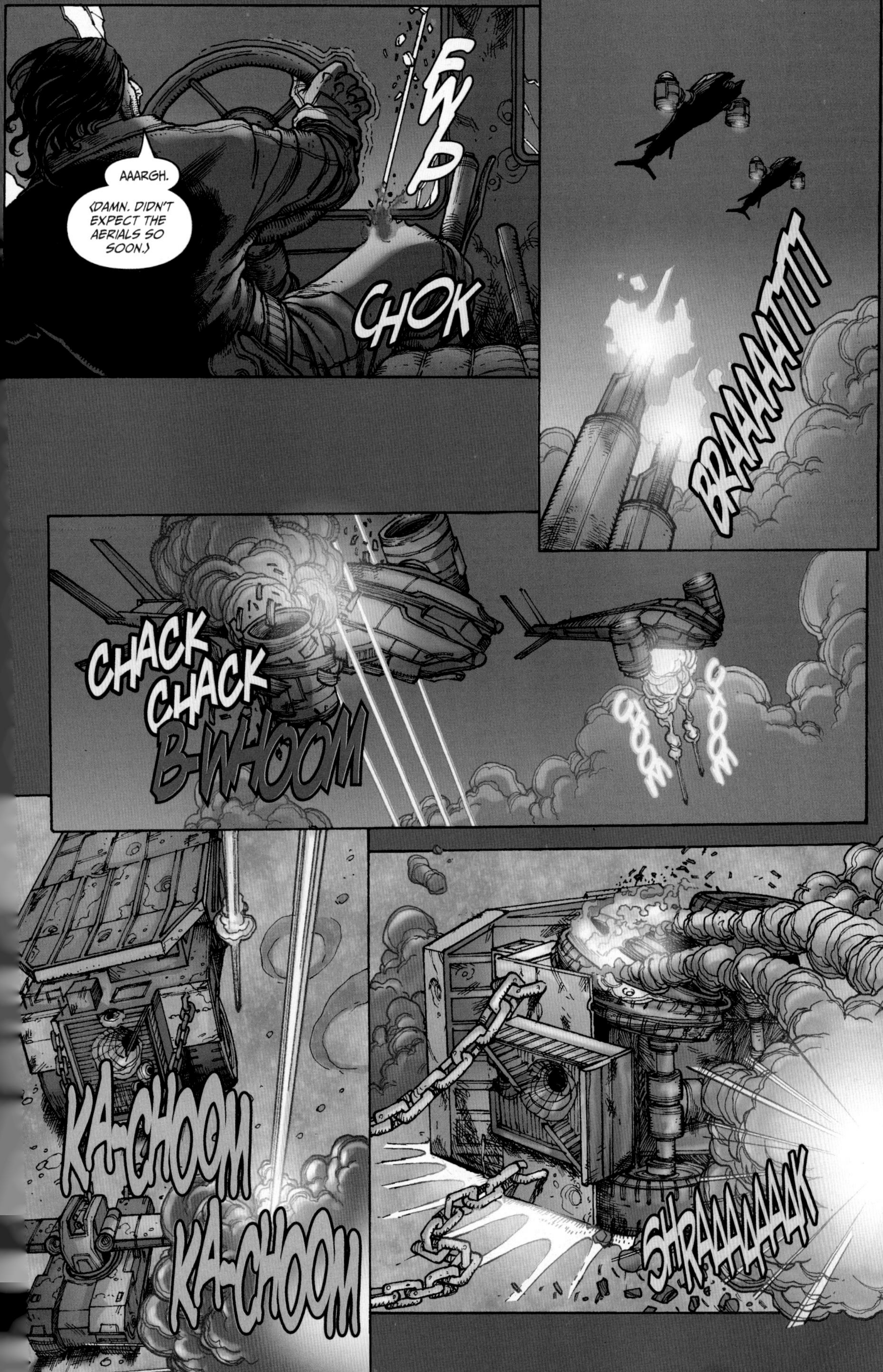

FWP
AAARGH.
‹DAMN. DIDN'T EXPECT THE AERIALS SO SOON.›
CHOK
BRAAAATTTT
CHACK CHACK
B-WHOOM
CHOOM
CHOOM
KA-CHOOM
KA-CHOOM
SHRAAAAAAK

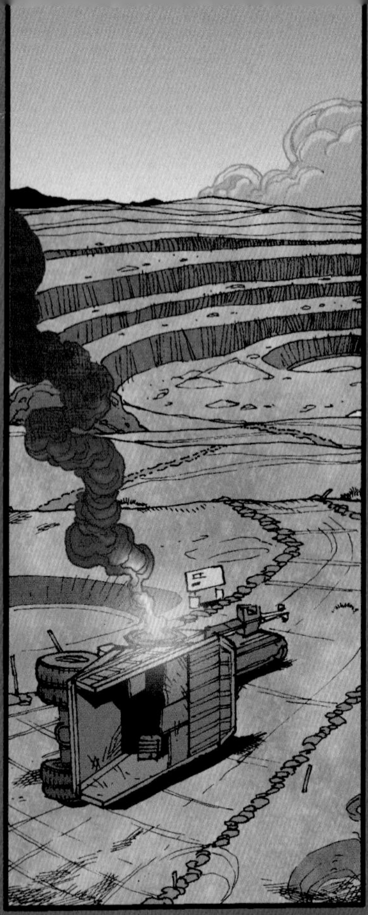

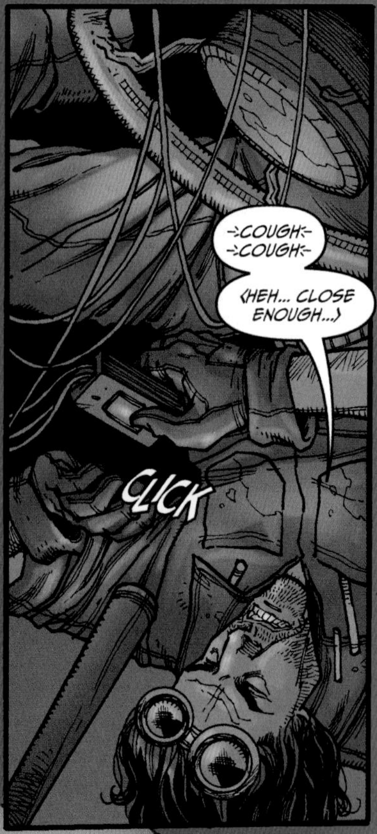
-COUGH-
-COUGH-
‹HEH... CLOSE ENOUGH...›
CLICK

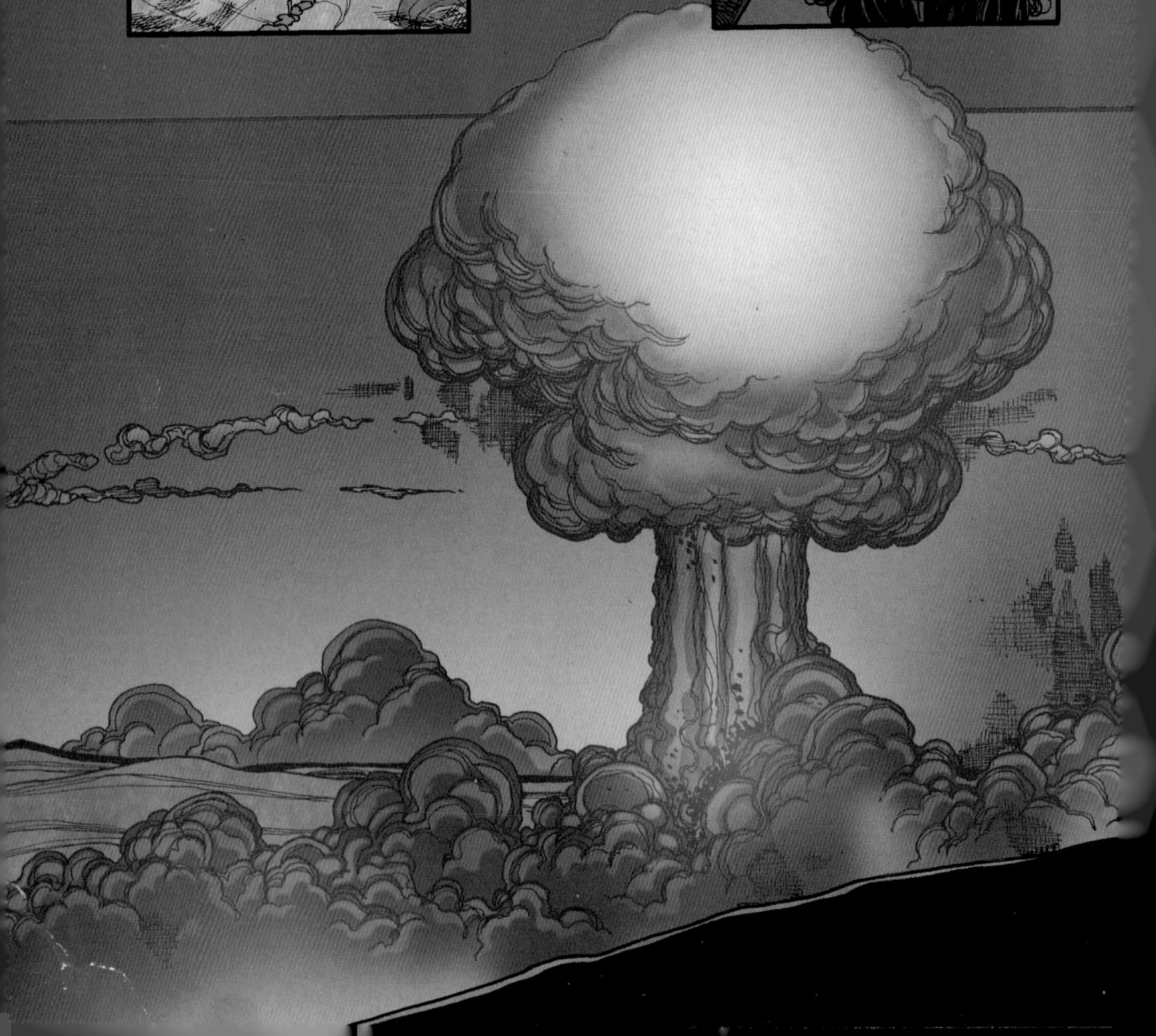

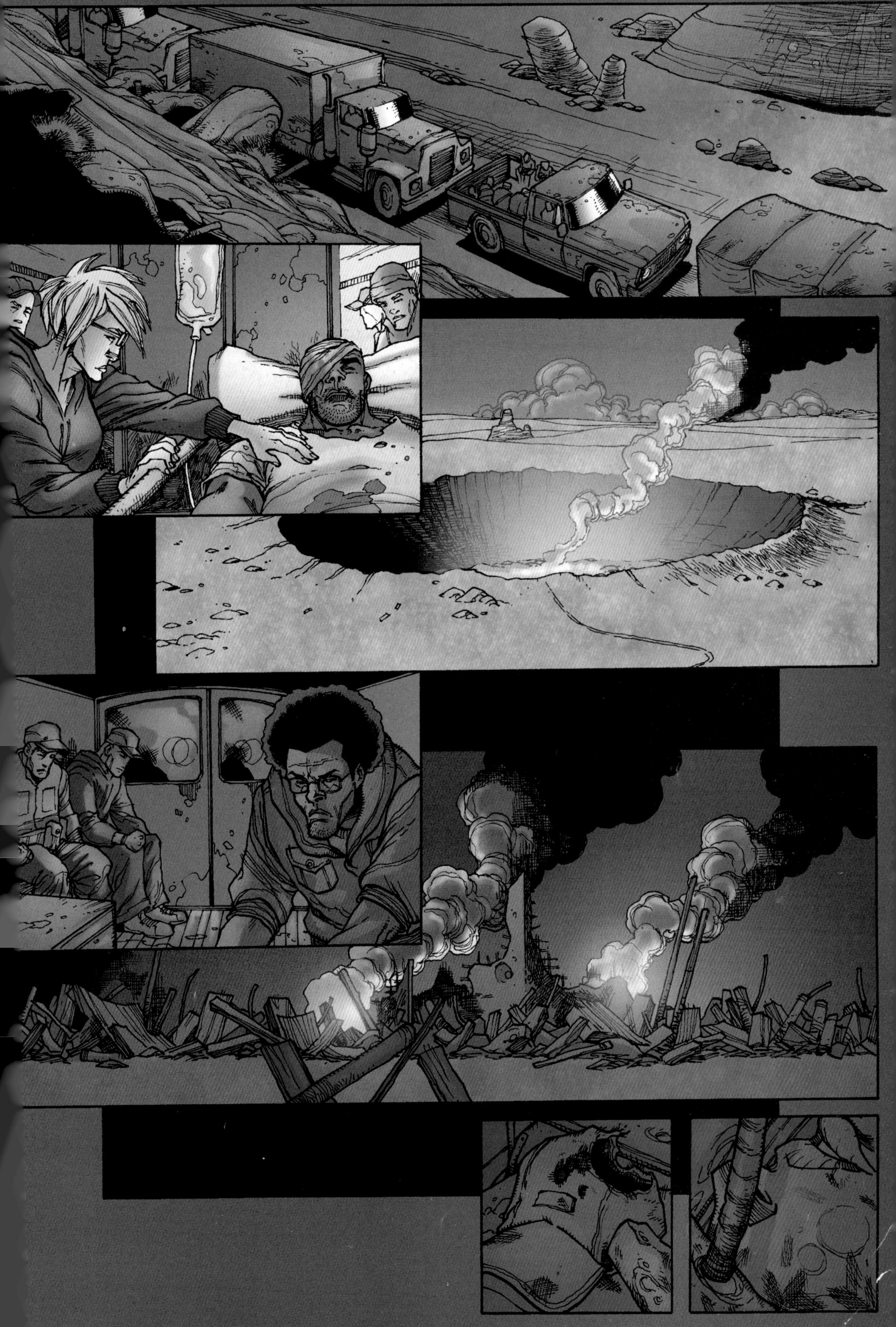

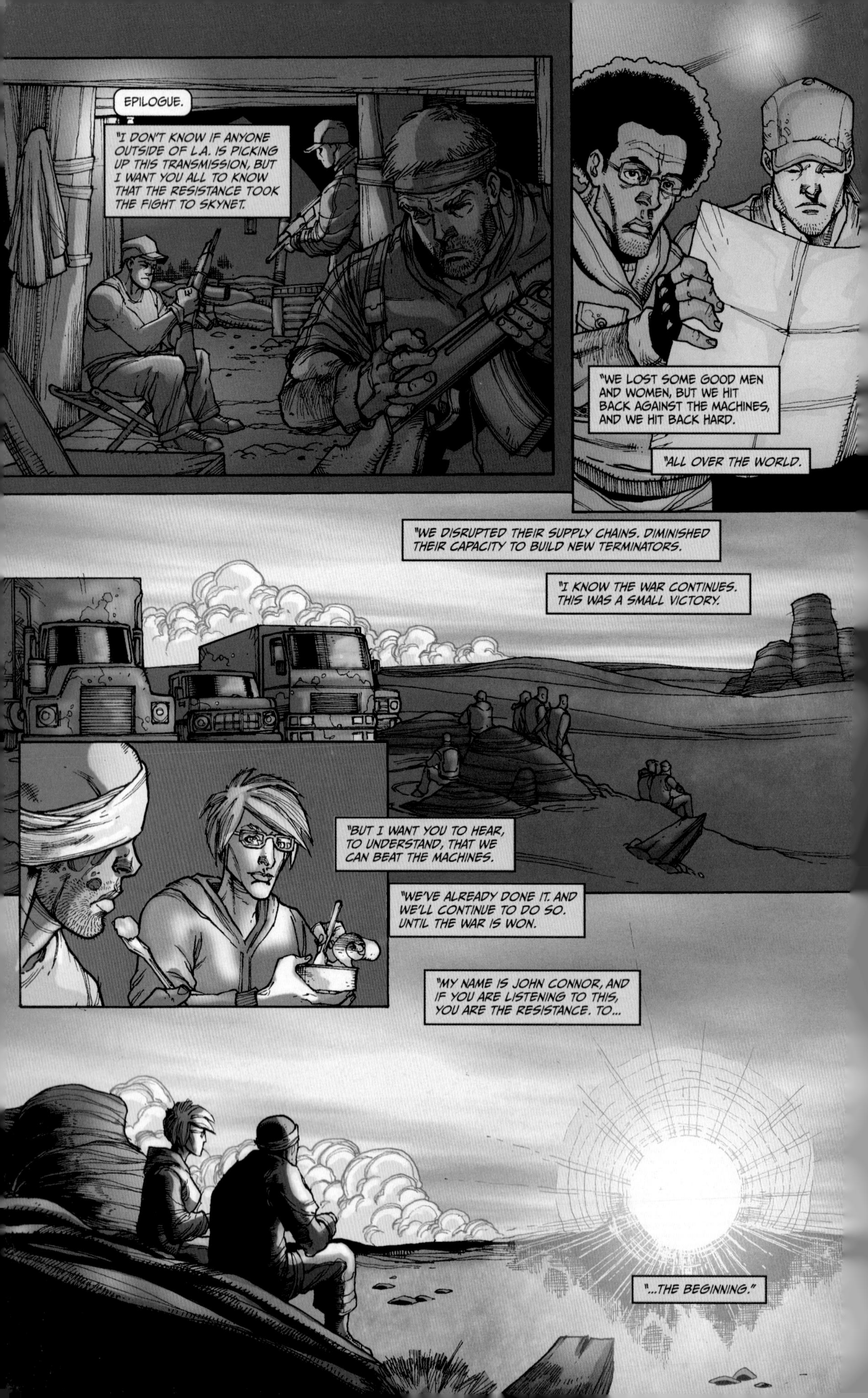
EPILOGUE.
"I DON'T KNOW IF ANYONE OUTSIDE OF L.A. IS PICKING UP THIS TRANSMISSION, BUT I WANT YOU ALL TO KNOW THAT THE RESISTANCE TOOK THE FIGHT TO SKYNET.
"WE LOST SOME GOOD MEN AND WOMEN, BUT WE HIT BACK AGAINST THE MACHINES, AND WE HIT BACK HARD.
"ALL OVER THE WORLD.
"WE DISRUPTED THEIR SUPPLY CHAINS. DIMINISHED THEIR CAPACITY TO BUILD NEW TERMINATORS.
"I KNOW THE WAR CONTINUES. THIS WAS A SMALL VICTORY.
"BUT I WANT YOU TO HEAR, TO UNDERSTAND, THAT WE CAN BEAT THE MACHINES.
"WE'VE ALREADY DONE IT. AND WE'LL CONTINUE TO DO SO. UNTIL THE WAR IS WON.
"MY NAME IS JOHN CONNOR, AND IF YOU ARE LISTENING TO THIS, YOU ARE THE RESISTANCE. TO...
"...THE BEGINNING."

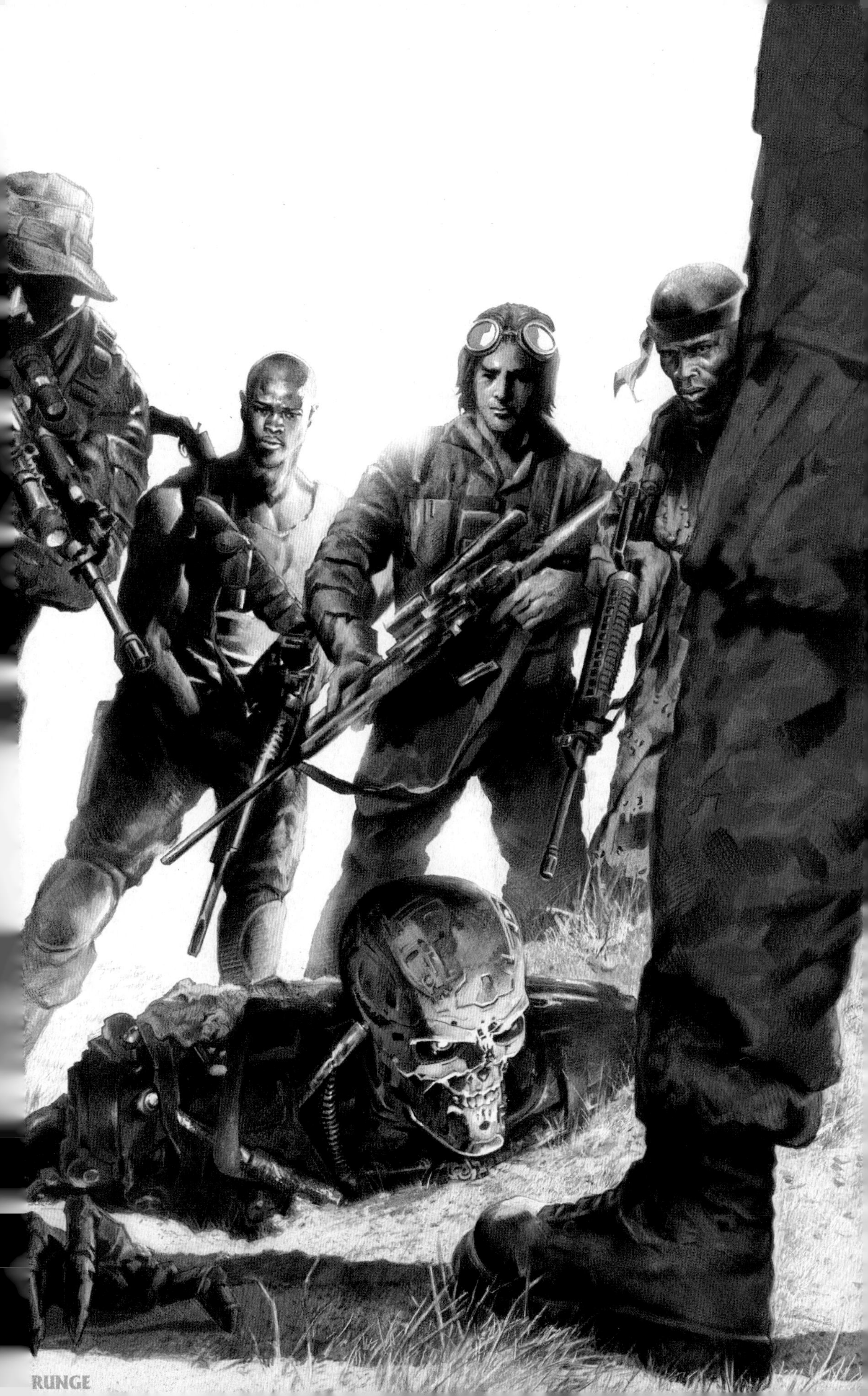
RUNGE

OFFICIAL MOVIE PREVIEW

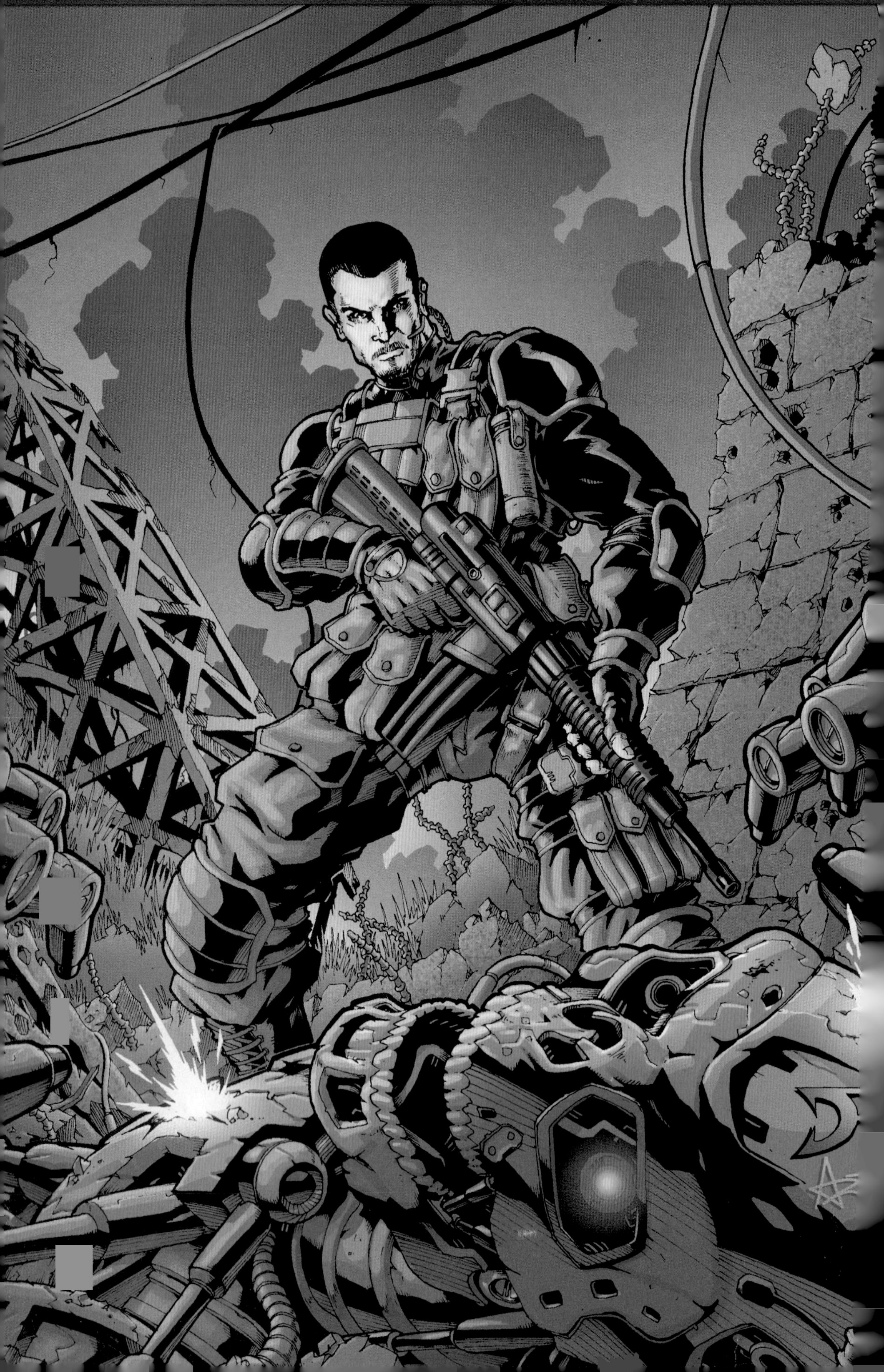

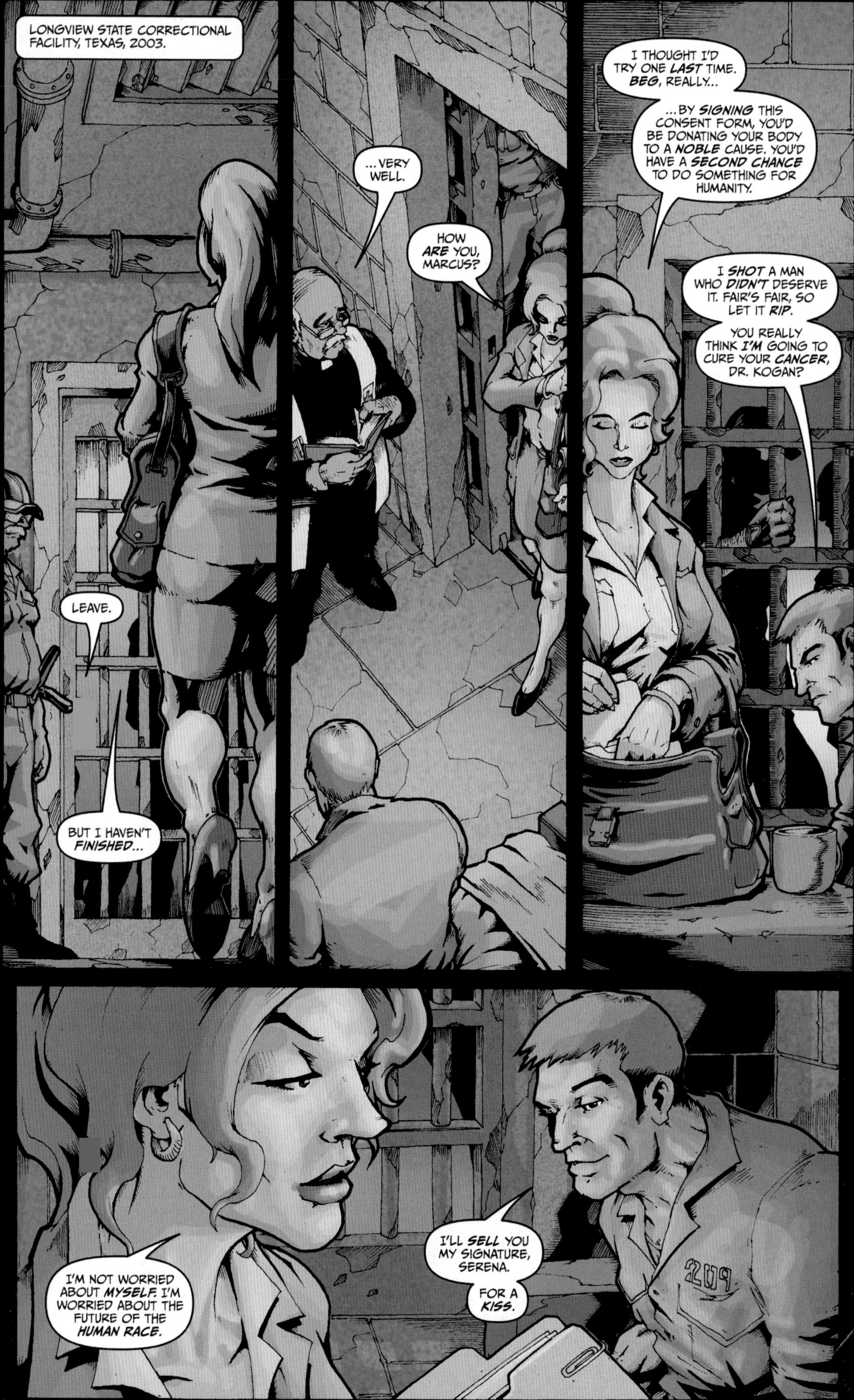
LONGVIEW STATE CORRECTIONAL FACILITY, TEXAS, 2003.
LEAVE.
BUT I HAVEN'T FINISHED...
...VERY WELL.
HOW ARE YOU, MARCUS?
I THOUGHT I'D TRY ONE LAST TIME. BEG, REALLY...
...BY SIGNING THIS CONSENT FORM, YOU'D BE DONATING YOUR BODY TO A NOBLE CAUSE. YOU'D HAVE A SECOND CHANCE TO DO SOMETHING FOR HUMANITY.
I SHOT A MAN WHO DIDN'T DESERVE IT. FAIR'S FAIR, SO LET IT RIP.
YOU REALLY THINK I'M GOING TO CURE YOUR CANCER, DR. KOGAN?
I'M NOT WORRIED ABOUT MYSELF. I'M WORRIED ABOUT THE FUTURE OF THE HUMAN RACE.
I'LL SELL YOU MY SIGNATURE, SERENA.
FOR A KISS.

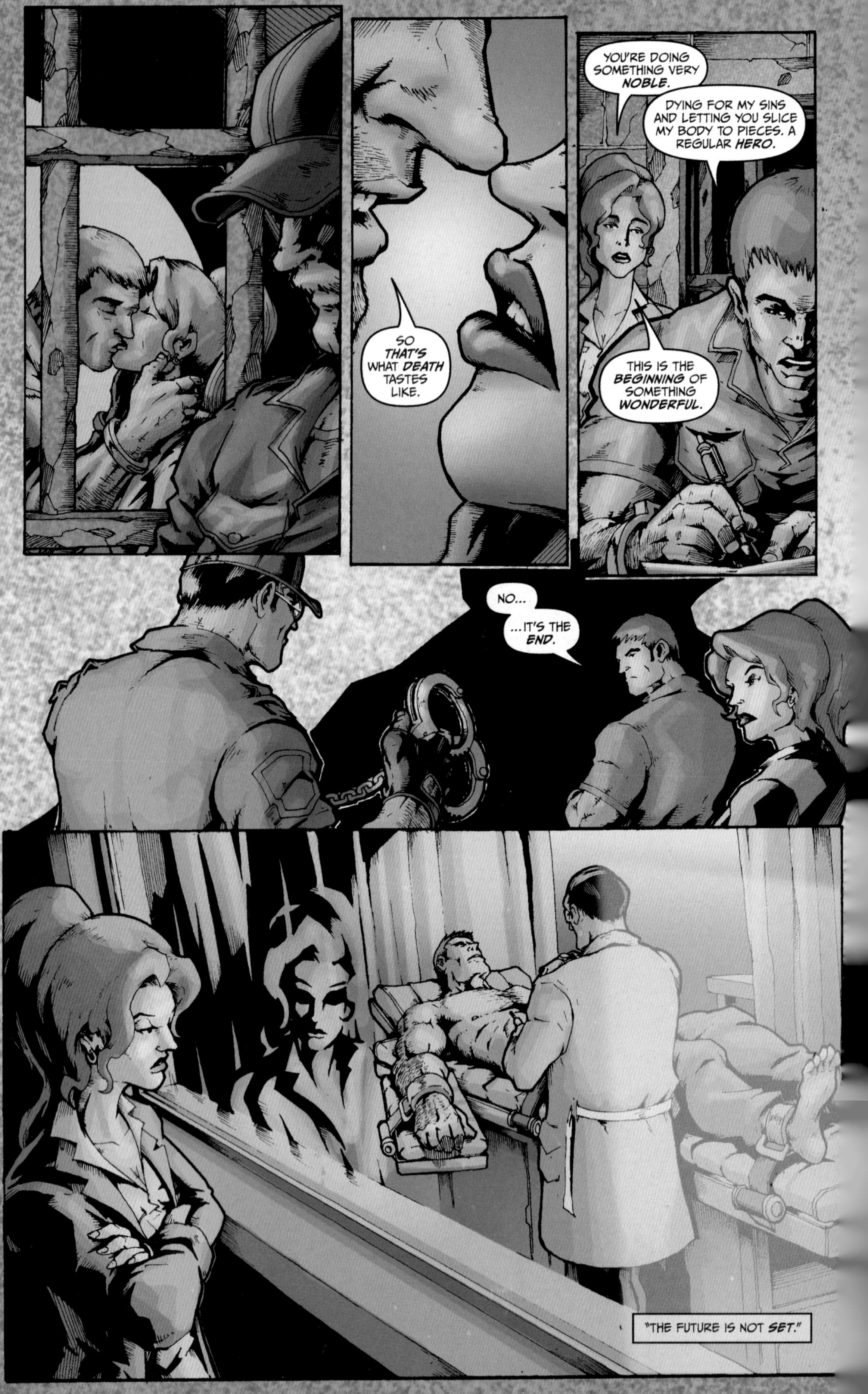
SO THAT'S WHAT DEATH TASTES LIKE.
YOU'RE DOING SOMETHING VERY NOBLE.
DYING FOR MY SINS AND LETTING YOU SLICE MY BODY TO PIECES. A REGULAR HERO.
THIS IS THE BEGINNING OF SOMETHING WONDERFUL.
NO...
...IT'S THE END.
"THE FUTURE IS NOT SET."

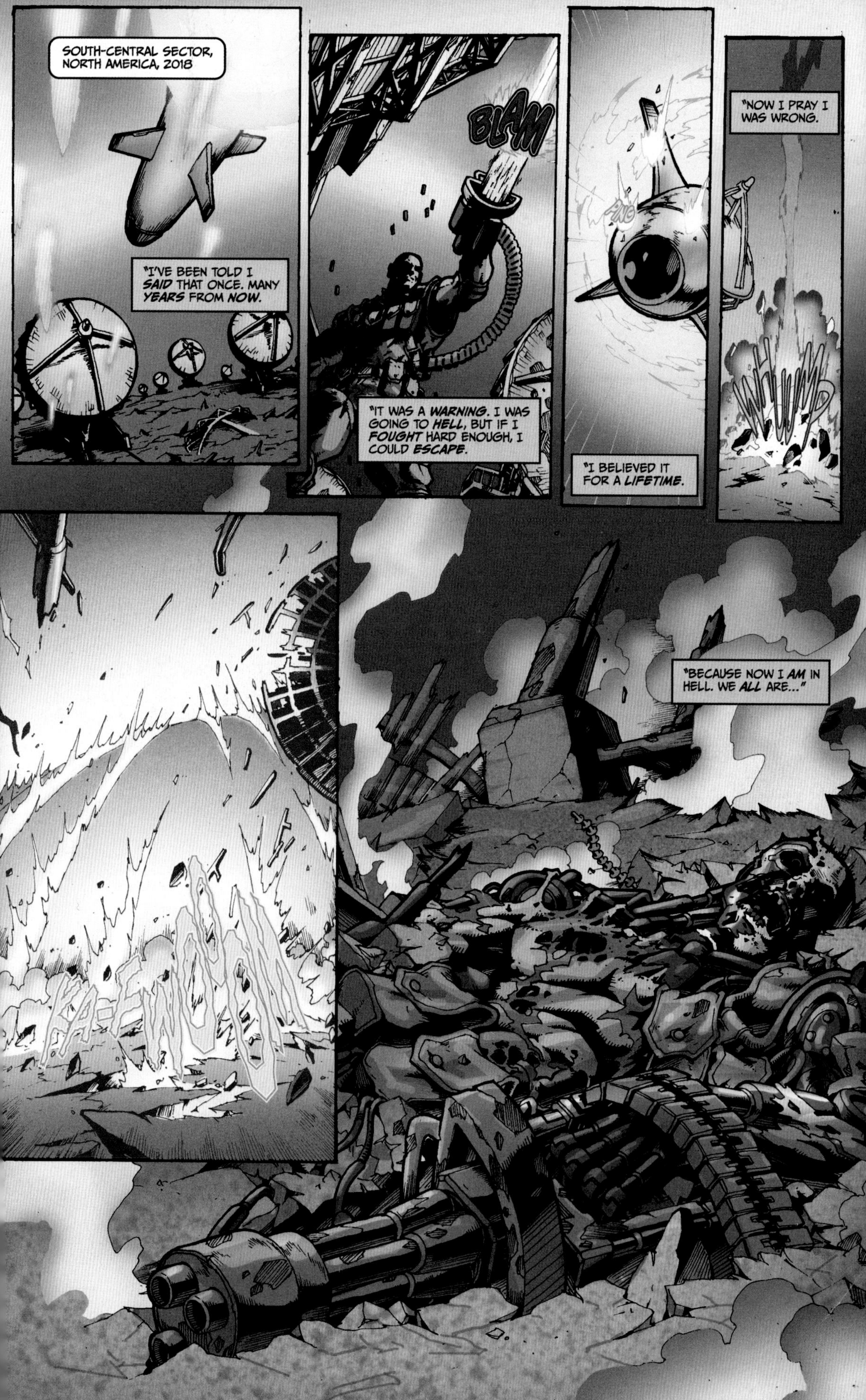
SOUTH-CENTRAL SECTOR, NORTH AMERICA, 2018
"I'VE BEEN TOLD I SAID THAT ONCE. MANY YEARS FROM NOW.
BLAM
"IT WAS A WARNING. I WAS GOING TO HELL, BUT IF I FOUGHT HARD ENOUGH, I COULD ESCAPE.
"I BELIEVED IT FOR A LIFETIME.
"NOW I PRAY I WAS WRONG.
"BECAUSE NOW I AM IN HELL. WE ALL ARE..."

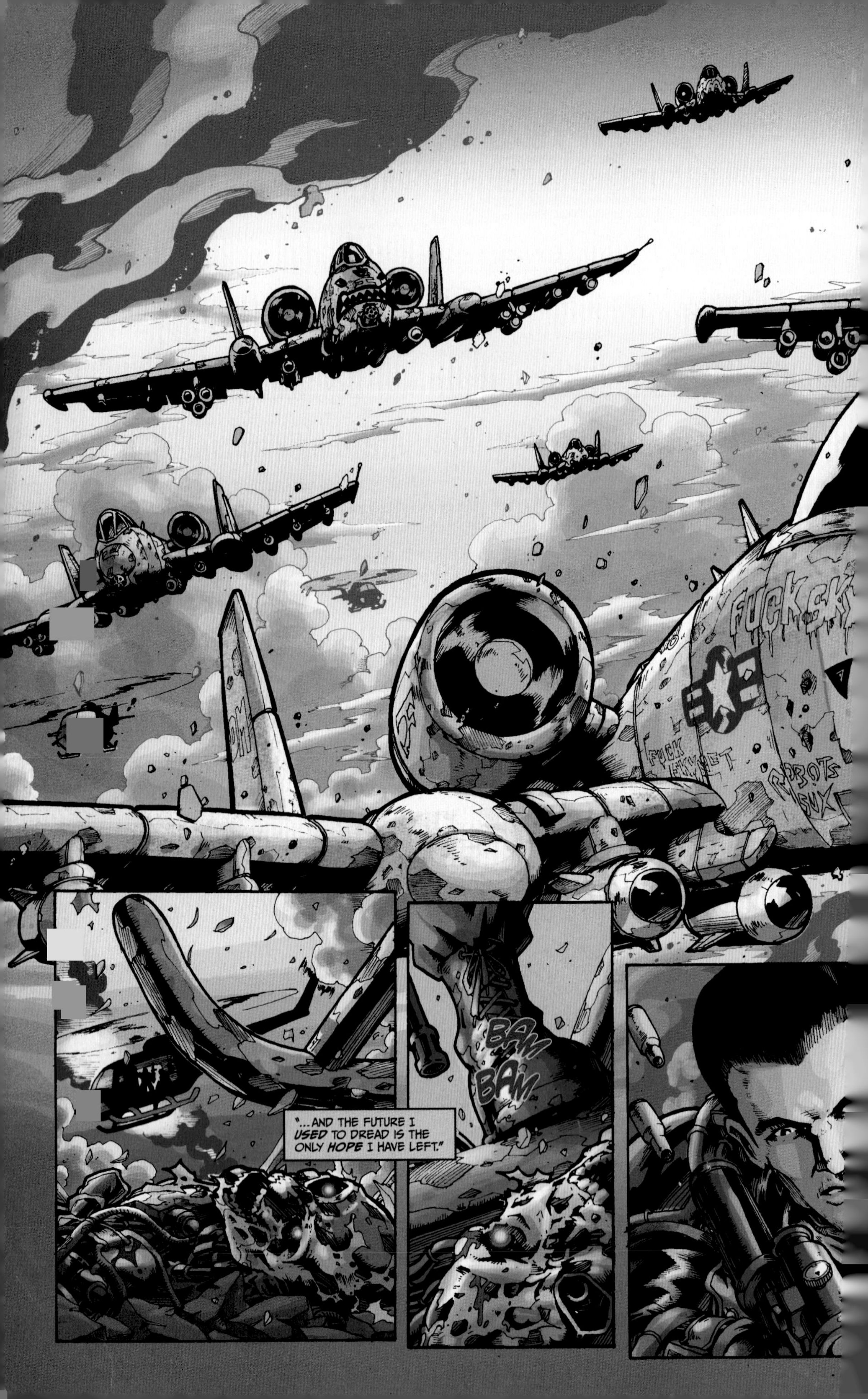
ROBOTS SUX
BAM
BAM
"...AND THE FUTURE I *USED* TO DREAD IS THE ONLY *HOPE* I HAVE LEFT."

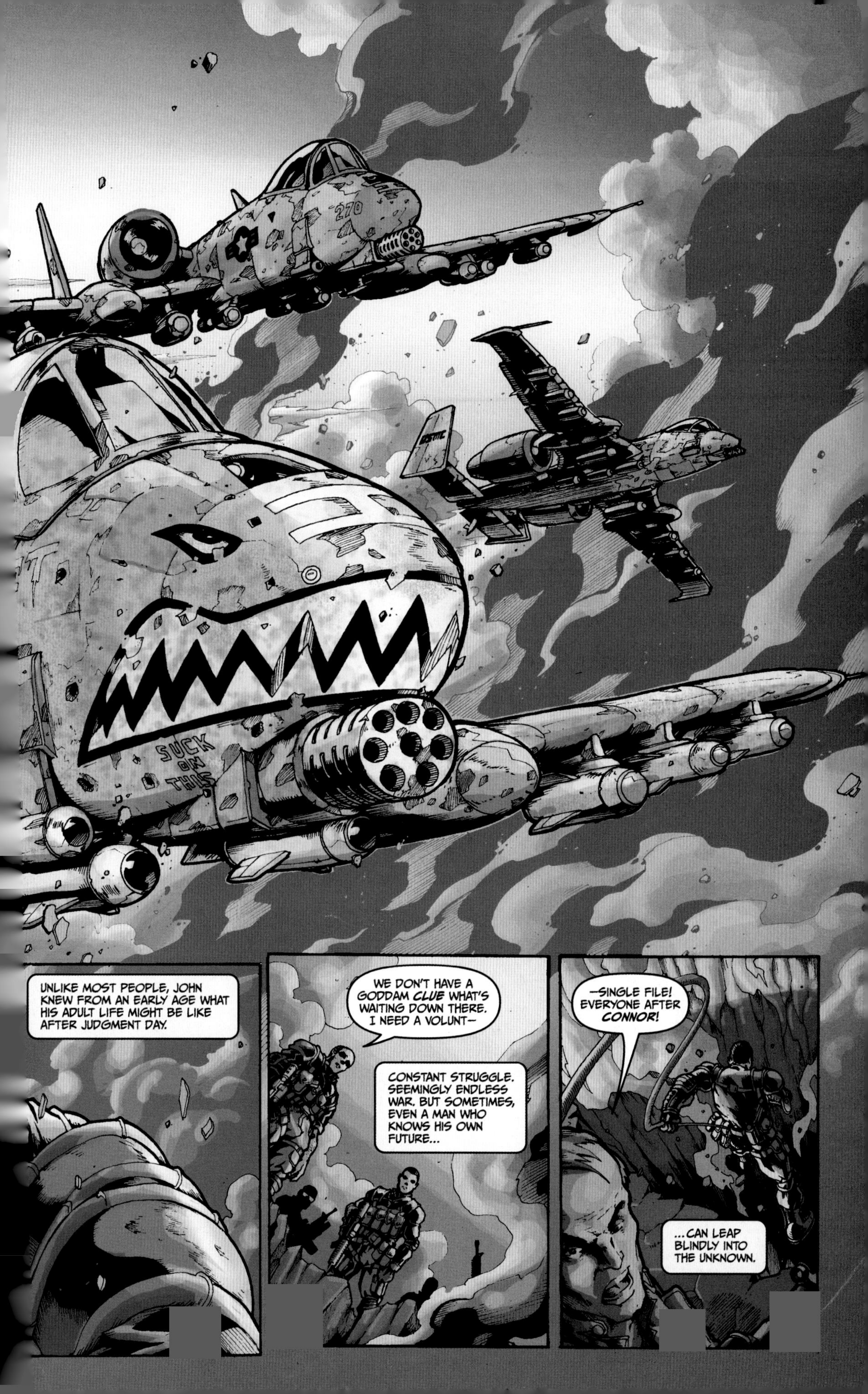

270
SUCK ON THIS
UNLIKE MOST PEOPLE, JOHN KNEW FROM AN EARLY AGE WHAT HIS ADULT LIFE MIGHT BE LIKE AFTER JUDGMENT DAY.
WE DON'T HAVE A GODDAM CLUE WHAT'S WAITING DOWN THERE. I NEED A VOLUNT—
CONSTANT STRUGGLE. SEEMINGLY ENDLESS WAR. BUT SOMETIMES, EVEN A MAN WHO KNOWS HIS OWN FUTURE...
—SINGLE FILE! EVERYONE AFTER CONNOR!
...CAN LEAP BLINDLY INTO THE UNKNOWN.

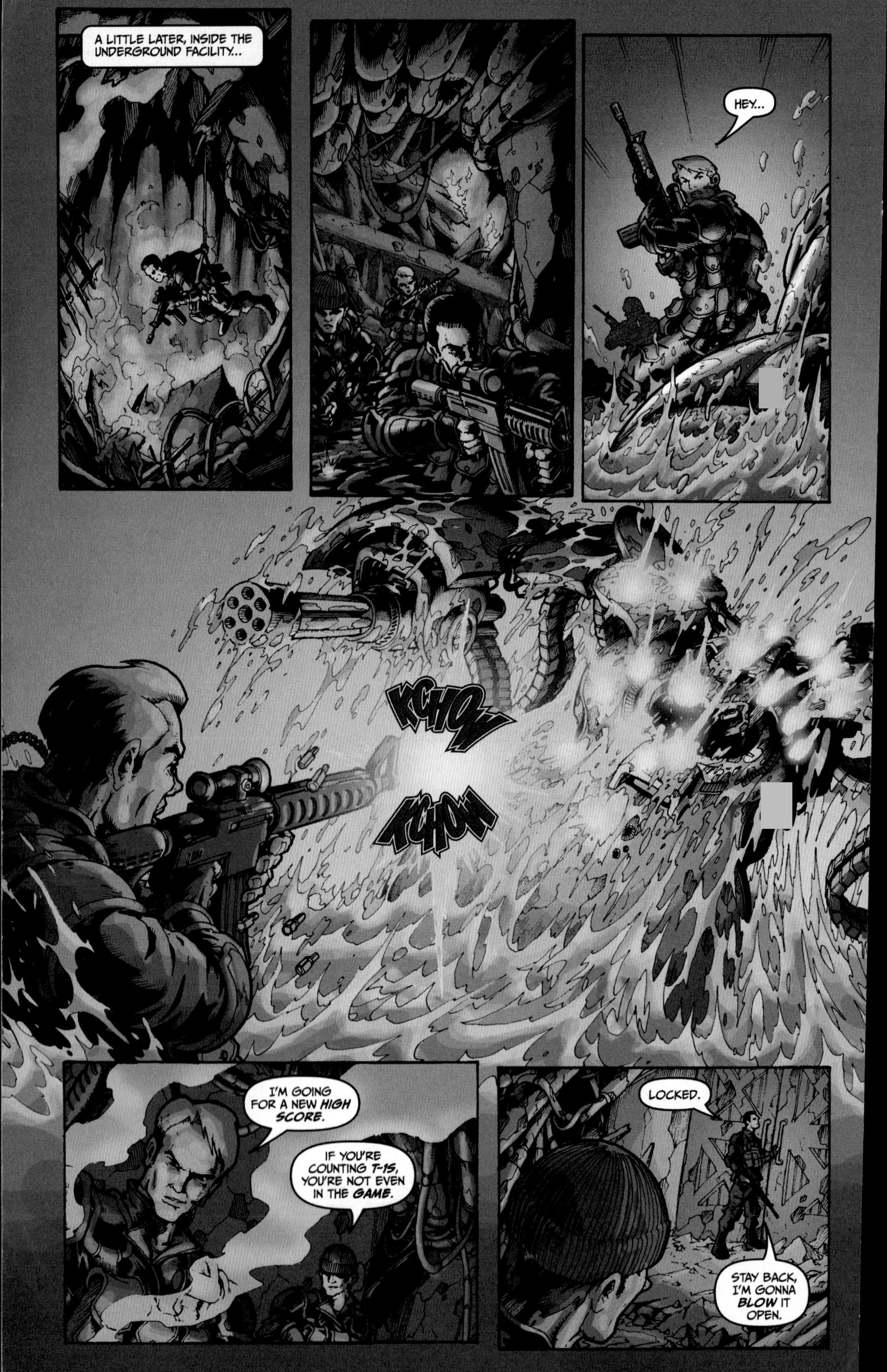
A LITTLE LATER, INSIDE THE UNDERGROUND FACILITY...
HEY...
KCHOW
KCHOW
I'M GOING FOR A NEW HIGH SCORE.
IF YOU'RE COUNTING T-1S, YOU'RE NOT EVEN IN THE GAME.
LOCKED.
STAY BACK, I'M GONNA BLOW IT OPEN.

THERE'S **BLOOD** HERE!

HELP US!

PLEASE, FOR THE LOVE OF...

SKYNET DOESN'T TAKE *PRISONERS*, SO WHY ARE THESE POOR BASTARDS STILL *ALIVE?*

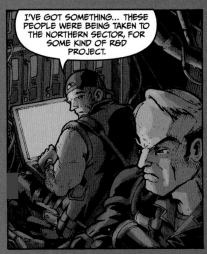

I'VE GOT SOMETHING... THESE PEOPLE WERE BEING TAKEN TO THE NORTHERN SECTOR, FOR SOME KIND OF R&D PROJECT.

I FOUND INTEL ON *OUR* PEOPLE HERE. LOOKS LIKE SKYNET'S DOING SOME *HOMEWORK.*

SEND IT ON TO COMMAND.

CONNOR, GET *TOPSIDE* AND REMIND THEM THAT THEY NEED TO *ANSWER* ME ON THE RADIO, EVEN IF THEY'RE *DEAD!*

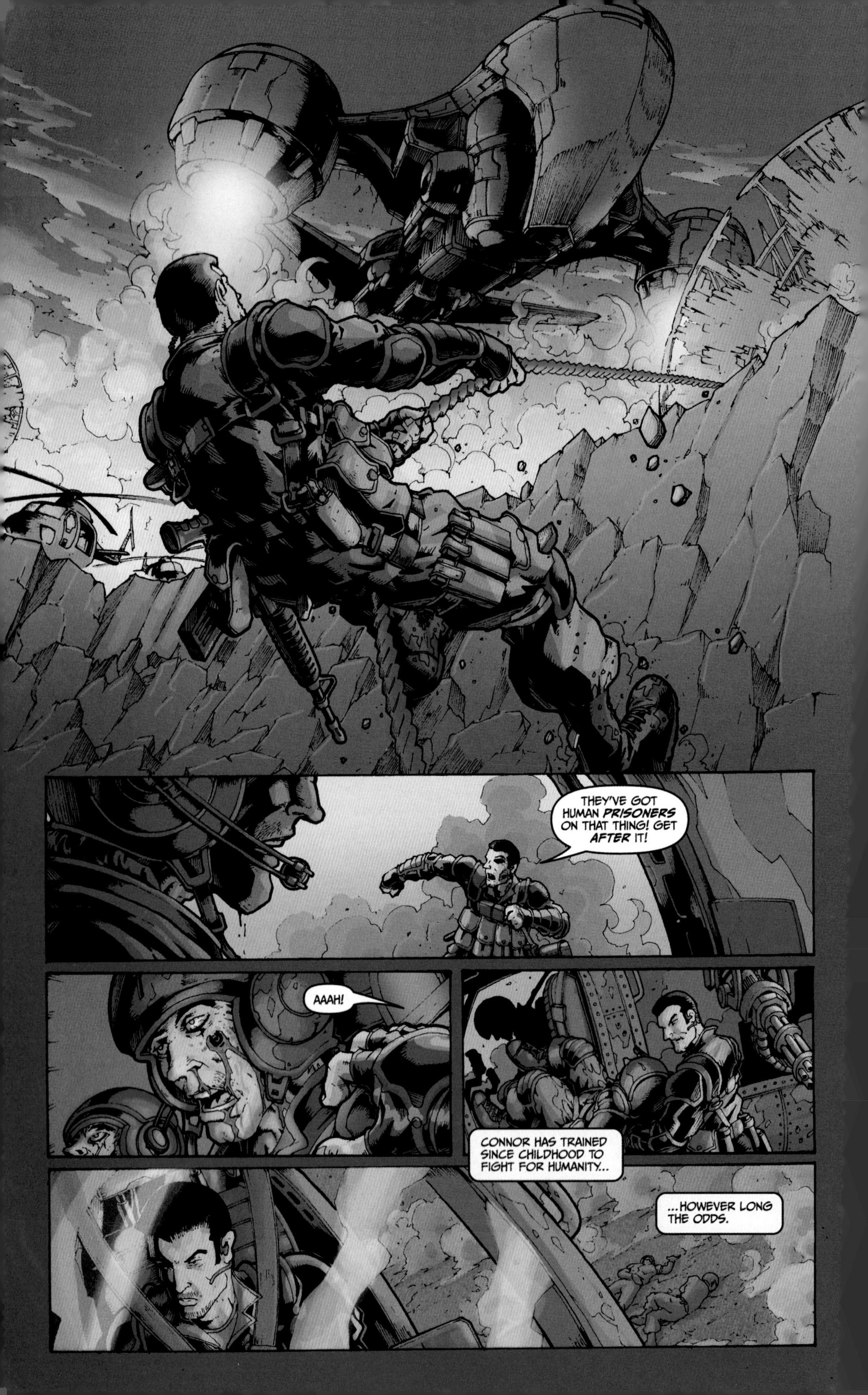
THEY'VE GOT HUMAN PRISONERS ON THAT THING! GET AFTER IT!
AAAH!
CONNOR HAS TRAINED SINCE CHILDHOOD TO FIGHT FOR HUMANITY...
...HOWEVER LONG THE ODDS.

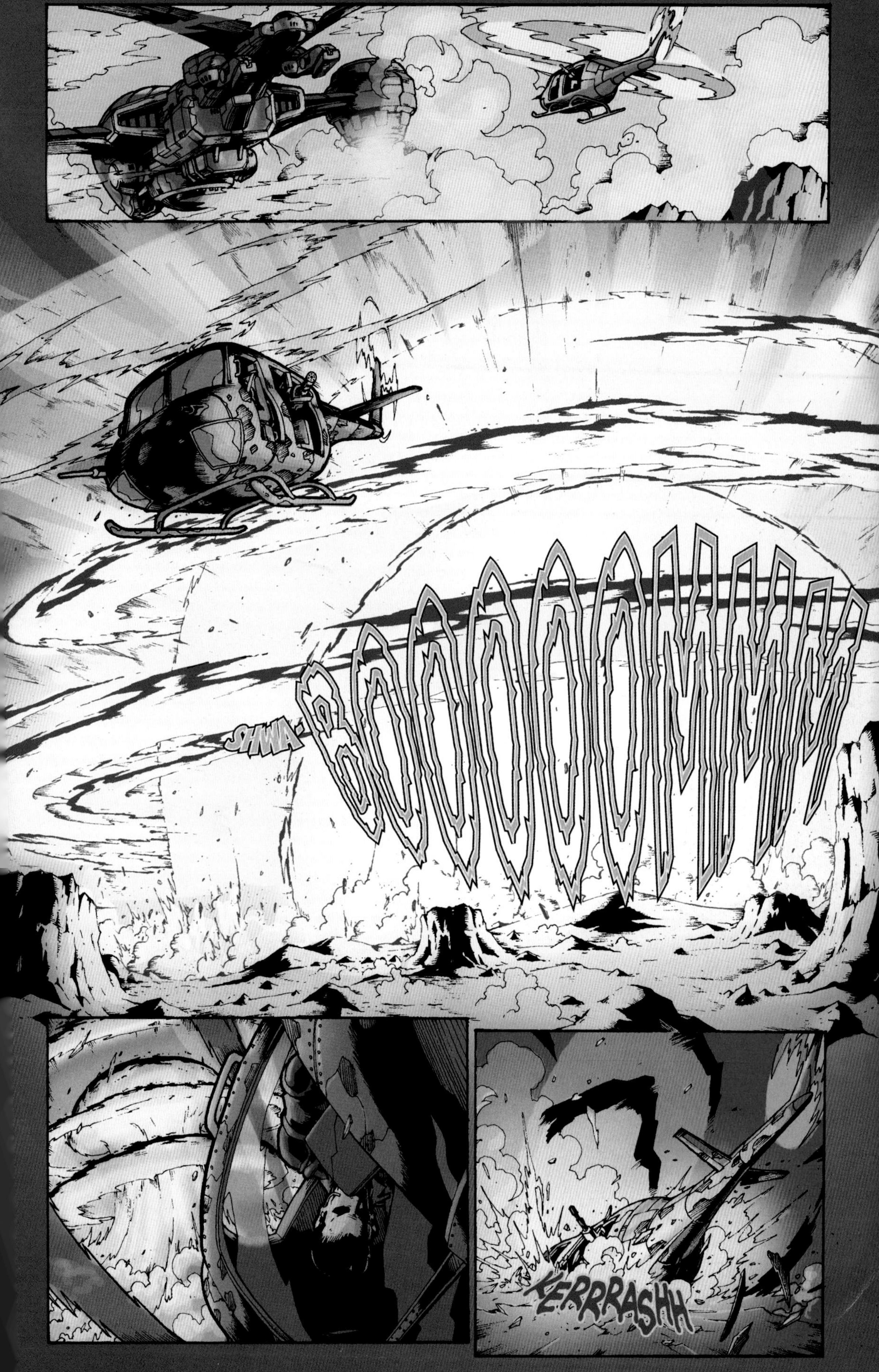
SHWA-BOOOOOMMM
KERRRASHH

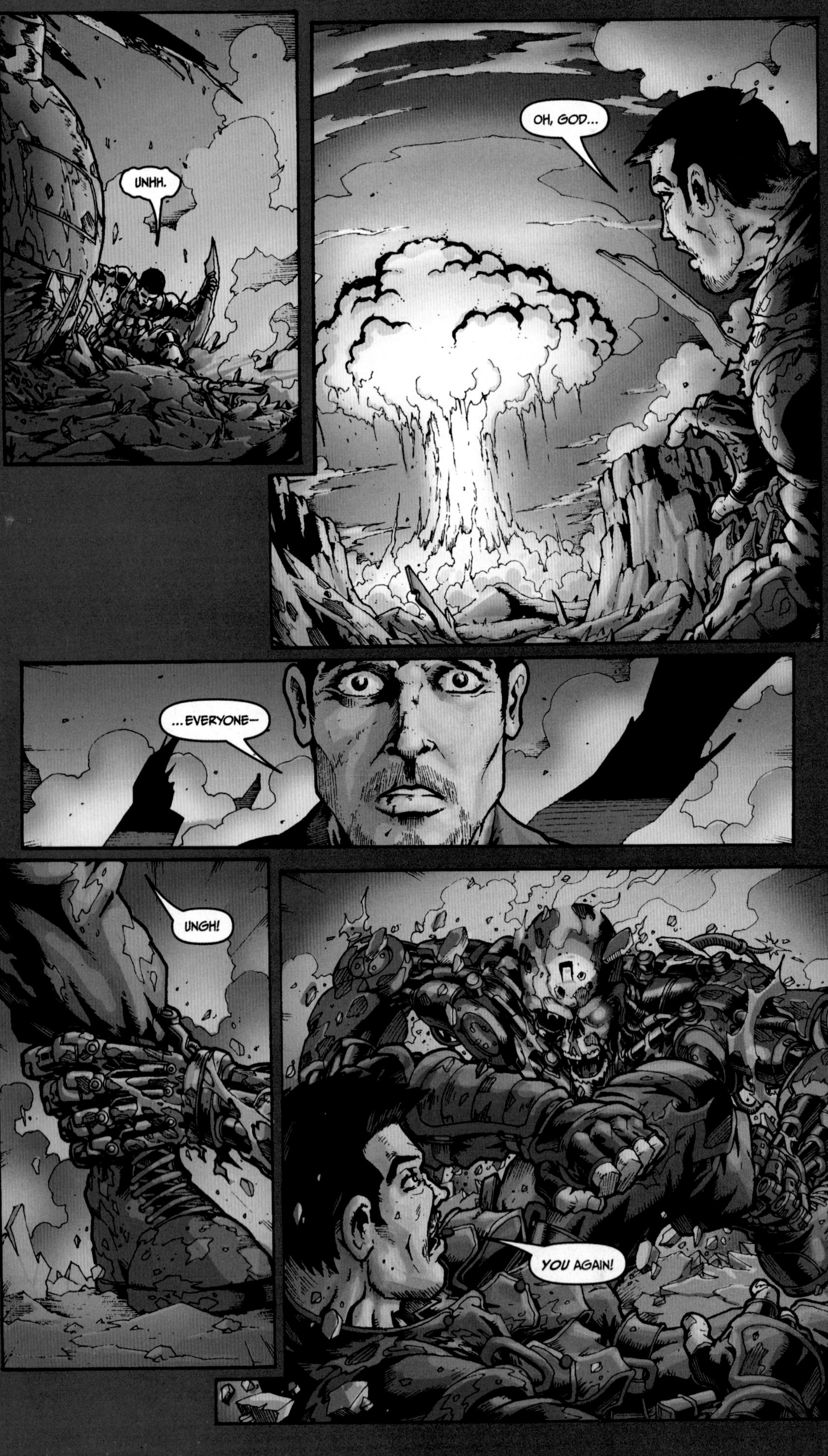
UNHH.
OH, GOD...
...EVERYONE--
UNGH!
YOU AGAIN!

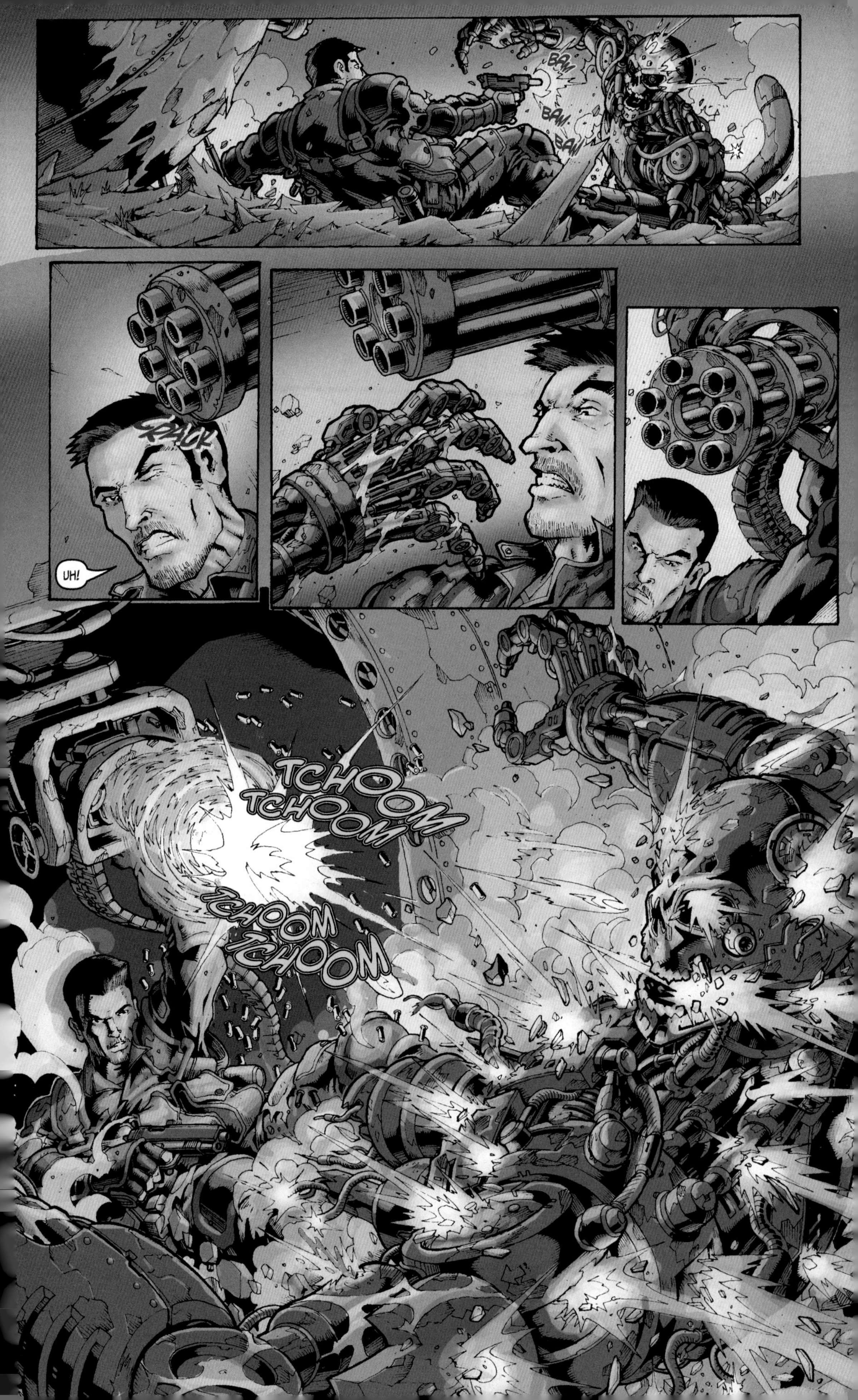
BAM
BAM
BAM
CRACK
UH!
TCHOOM
TCHOOM
TCHOOM
TCHOOM

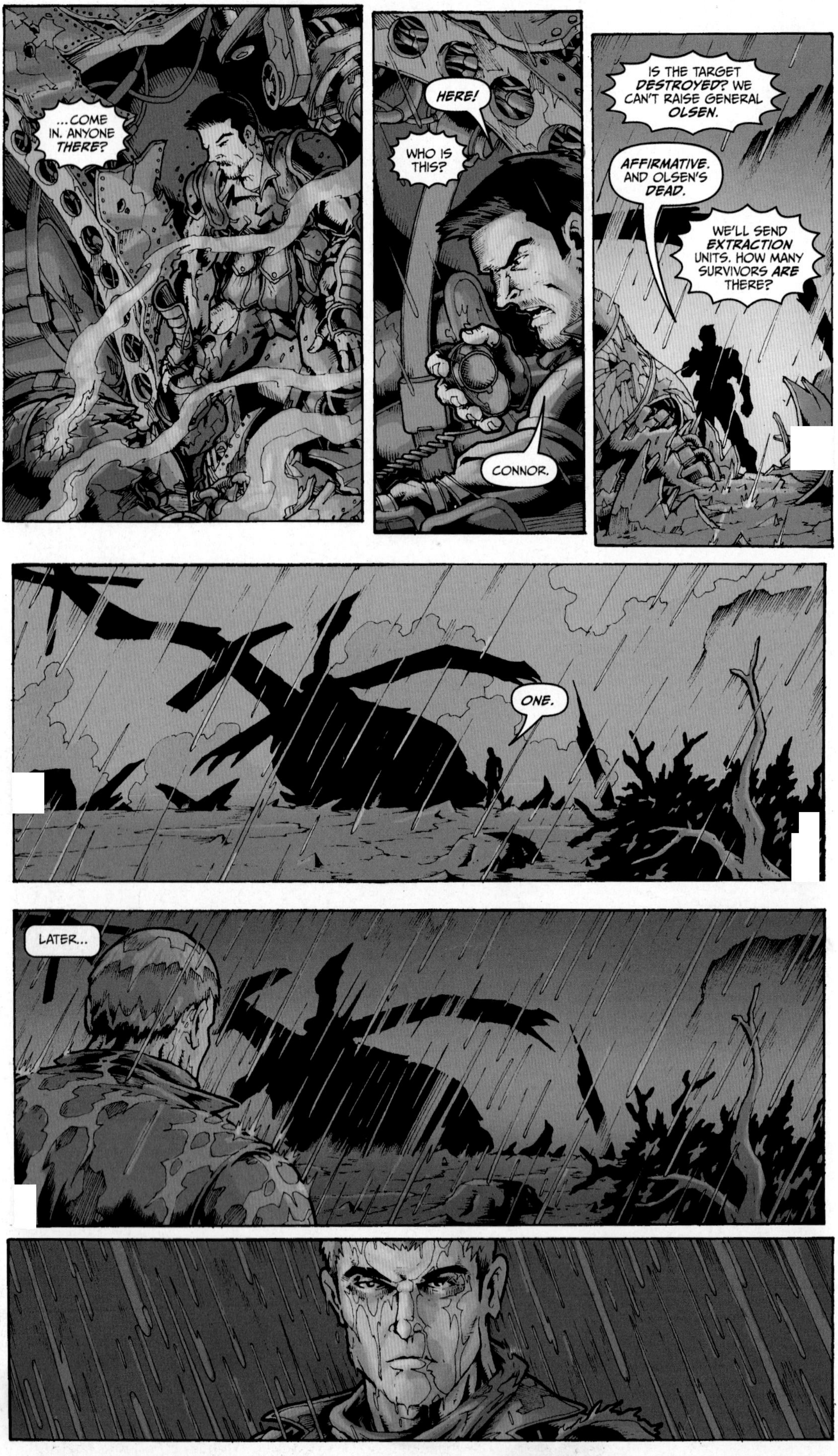
...COME IN. ANYONE THERE?
HERE!
WHO IS THIS?
CONNOR.
IS THE TARGET DESTROYED? WE CAN'T RAISE GENERAL OLSEN.
AFFIRMATIVE. AND OLSEN'S DEAD.
WE'LL SEND EXTRACTION UNITS. HOW MANY SURVIVORS ARE THERE?
ONE.
LATER...

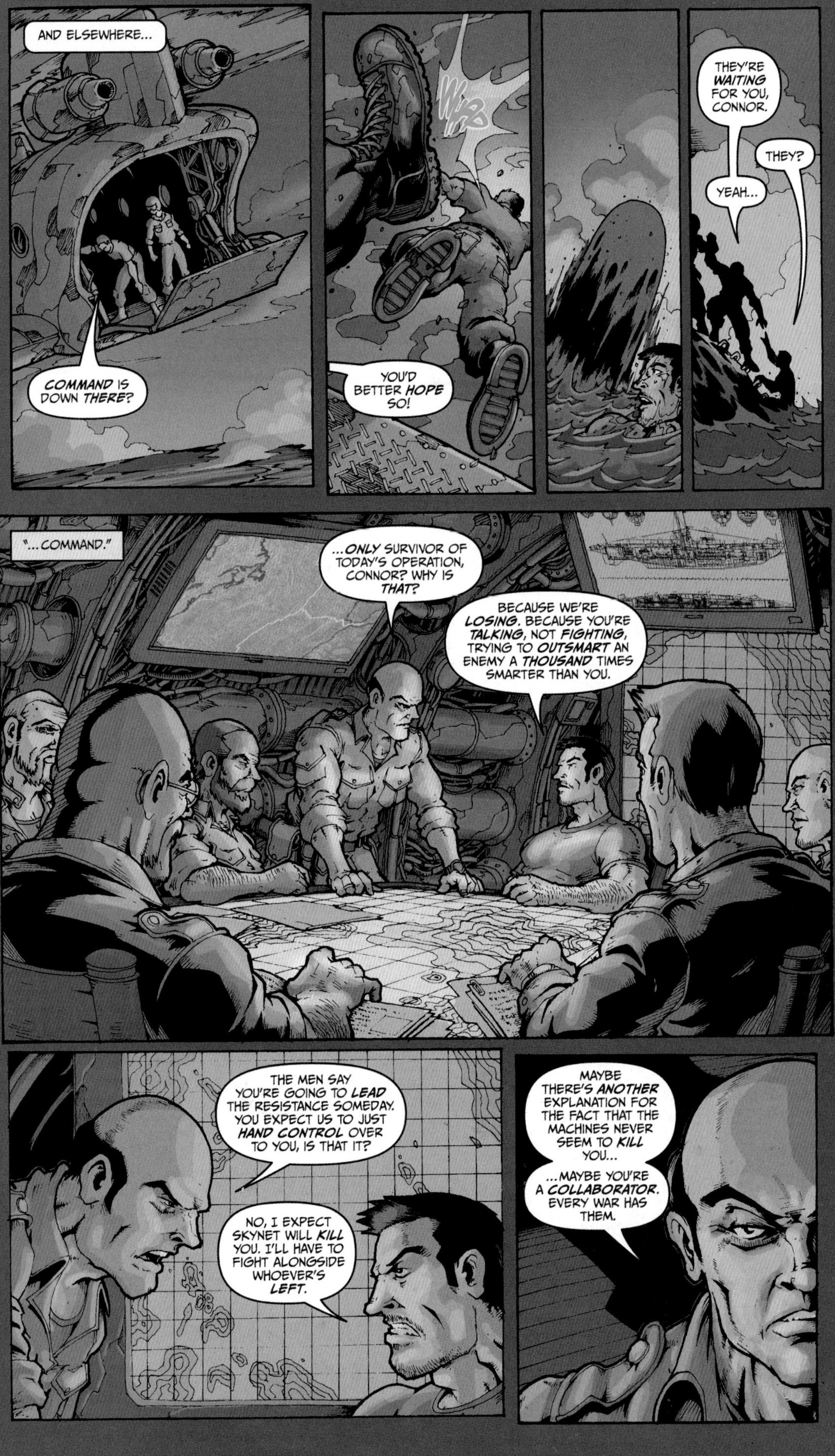
AND ELSEWHERE...
COMMAND IS DOWN THERE?
YOU'D BETTER HOPE SO!
THEY'RE WAITING FOR YOU, CONNOR.
THEY?
YEAH...
"...COMMAND."
...ONLY SURVIVOR OF TODAY'S OPERATION, CONNOR? WHY IS THAT?
BECAUSE WE'RE LOSING. BECAUSE YOU'RE TALKING, NOT FIGHTING, TRYING TO OUTSMART AN ENEMY A THOUSAND TIMES SMARTER THAN YOU.
THE MEN SAY YOU'RE GOING TO LEAD THE RESISTANCE SOMEDAY. YOU EXPECT US TO JUST HAND CONTROL OVER TO YOU, IS THAT IT?
NO, I EXPECT SKYNET WILL KILL YOU. I'LL HAVE TO FIGHT ALONGSIDE WHOEVER'S LEFT.
MAYBE THERE'S ANOTHER EXPLANATION FOR THE FACT THAT THE MACHINES NEVER SEEM TO KILL YOU...
...MAYBE YOU'RE A COLLABORATOR. EVERY WAR HAS THEM.

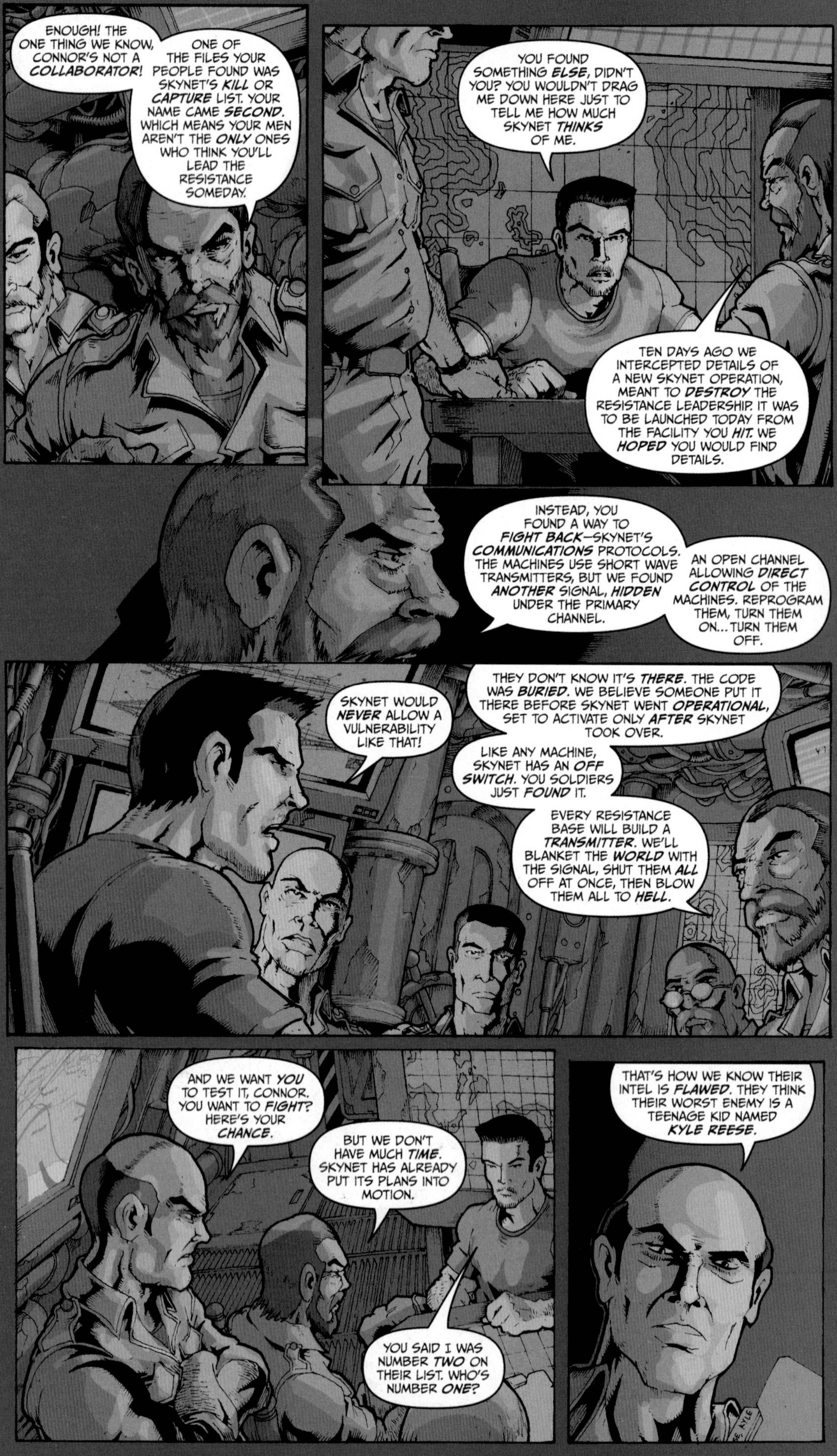
ENOUGH! THE ONE THING WE KNOW, CONNOR'S NOT A COLLABORATOR!
ONE OF THE FILES YOUR PEOPLE FOUND WAS SKYNET'S KILL OR CAPTURE LIST. YOUR NAME CAME SECOND. WHICH MEANS YOUR MEN AREN'T THE ONLY ONES WHO THINK YOU'LL LEAD THE RESISTANCE SOMEDAY.
YOU FOUND SOMETHING ELSE, DIDN'T YOU? YOU WOULDN'T DRAG ME DOWN HERE JUST TO TELL ME HOW MUCH SKYNET THINKS OF ME.
TEN DAYS AGO WE INTERCEPTED DETAILS OF A NEW SKYNET OPERATION, MEANT TO DESTROY THE RESISTANCE LEADERSHIP. IT WAS TO BE LAUNCHED TODAY FROM THE FACILITY YOU HIT. WE HOPED YOU WOULD FIND DETAILS.
INSTEAD, YOU FOUND A WAY TO FIGHT BACK—SKYNET'S COMMUNICATIONS PROTOCOLS. THE MACHINES USE SHORT WAVE TRANSMITTERS, BUT WE FOUND ANOTHER SIGNAL, HIDDEN UNDER THE PRIMARY CHANNEL.
AN OPEN CHANNEL ALLOWING DIRECT CONTROL OF THE MACHINES. REPROGRAM THEM, TURN THEM ON... TURN THEM OFF.
SKYNET WOULD NEVER ALLOW A VULNERABILITY LIKE THAT!
THEY DON'T KNOW IT'S THERE. THE CODE WAS BURIED. WE BELIEVE SOMEONE PUT IT THERE BEFORE SKYNET WENT OPERATIONAL, SET TO ACTIVATE ONLY AFTER SKYNET TOOK OVER.
LIKE ANY MACHINE, SKYNET HAS AN OFF SWITCH. YOU SOLDIERS JUST FOUND IT.
EVERY RESISTANCE BASE WILL BUILD A TRANSMITTER. WE'LL BLANKET THE WORLD WITH THE SIGNAL, SHUT THEM ALL OFF AT ONCE, THEN BLOW THEM ALL TO HELL.
AND WE WANT YOU TO TEST IT, CONNOR. YOU WANT TO FIGHT? HERE'S YOUR CHANCE.
BUT WE DON'T HAVE MUCH TIME. SKYNET HAS ALREADY PUT ITS PLANS INTO MOTION.
YOU SAID I WAS NUMBER TWO ON THEIR LIST. WHO'S NUMBER ONE?
THAT'S HOW WE KNOW THEIR INTEL IS FLAWED. THEY THINK THEIR WORST ENEMY IS A TEENAGE KID NAMED KYLE REESE.

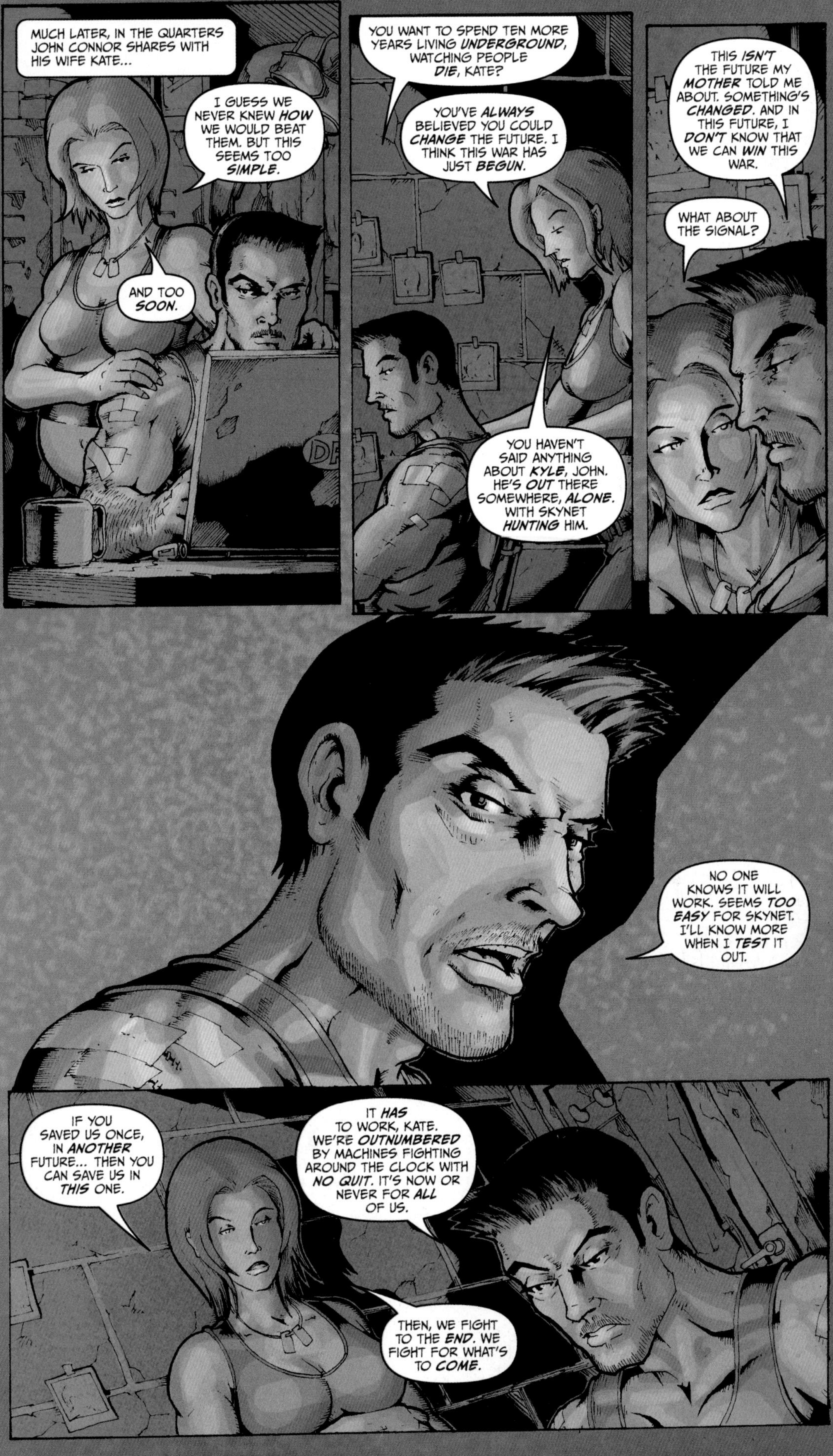
MUCH LATER, IN THE QUARTERS JOHN CONNOR SHARES WITH HIS WIFE KATE...
I GUESS WE NEVER KNEW HOW WE WOULD BEAT THEM. BUT THIS SEEMS TOO SIMPLE.
AND TOO SOON.
YOU WANT TO SPEND TEN MORE YEARS LIVING UNDERGROUND, WATCHING PEOPLE DIE, KATE?
YOU'VE ALWAYS BELIEVED YOU COULD CHANGE THE FUTURE. I THINK THIS WAR HAS JUST BEGUN.
YOU HAVEN'T SAID ANYTHING ABOUT KYLE, JOHN. HE'S OUT THERE SOMEWHERE, ALONE. WITH SKYNET HUNTING HIM.
THIS ISN'T THE FUTURE MY MOTHER TOLD ME ABOUT. SOMETHING'S CHANGED. AND IN THIS FUTURE, I DON'T KNOW THAT WE CAN WIN THIS WAR.
WHAT ABOUT THE SIGNAL?
NO ONE KNOWS IT WILL WORK. SEEMS TOO EASY FOR SKYNET. I'LL KNOW MORE WHEN I TEST IT OUT.
IF YOU SAVED US ONCE, IN ANOTHER FUTURE... THEN YOU CAN SAVE US IN THIS ONE.
IT HAS TO WORK, KATE. WE'RE OUTNUMBERED BY MACHINES FIGHTING AROUND THE CLOCK WITH NO QUIT. IT'S NOW OR NEVER FOR ALL OF US.
THEN, WE FIGHT TO THE END. WE FIGHT FOR WHAT'S TO COME.

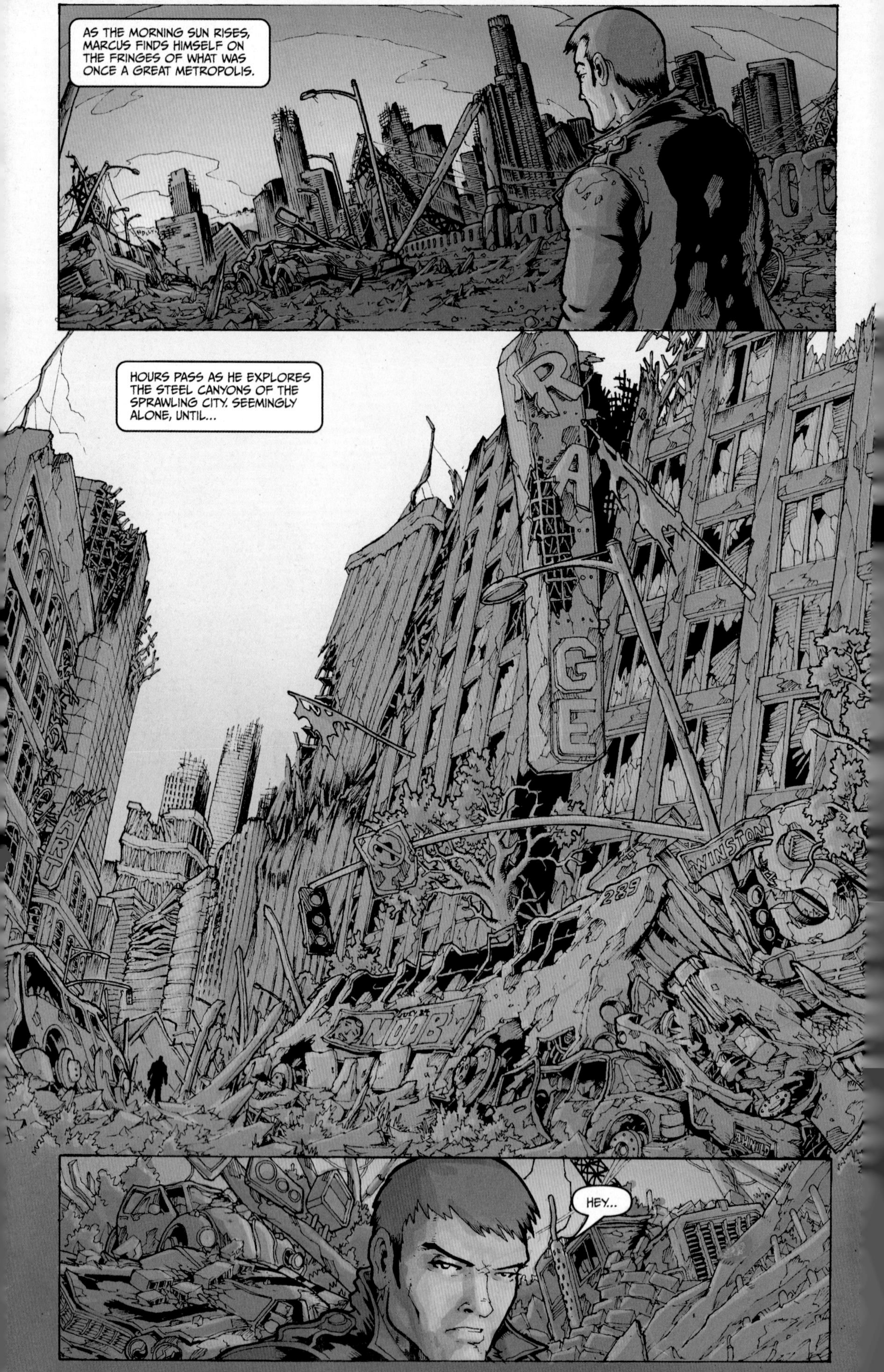
AS THE MORNING SUN RISES, MARCUS FINDS HIMSELF ON THE FRINGES OF WHAT WAS ONCE A GREAT METROPOLIS.
HOURS PASS AS HE EXPLORES THE STEEL CANYONS OF THE SPRAWLING CITY. SEEMINGLY ALONE, UNTIL...
WINSTON
NOOB
HEY...

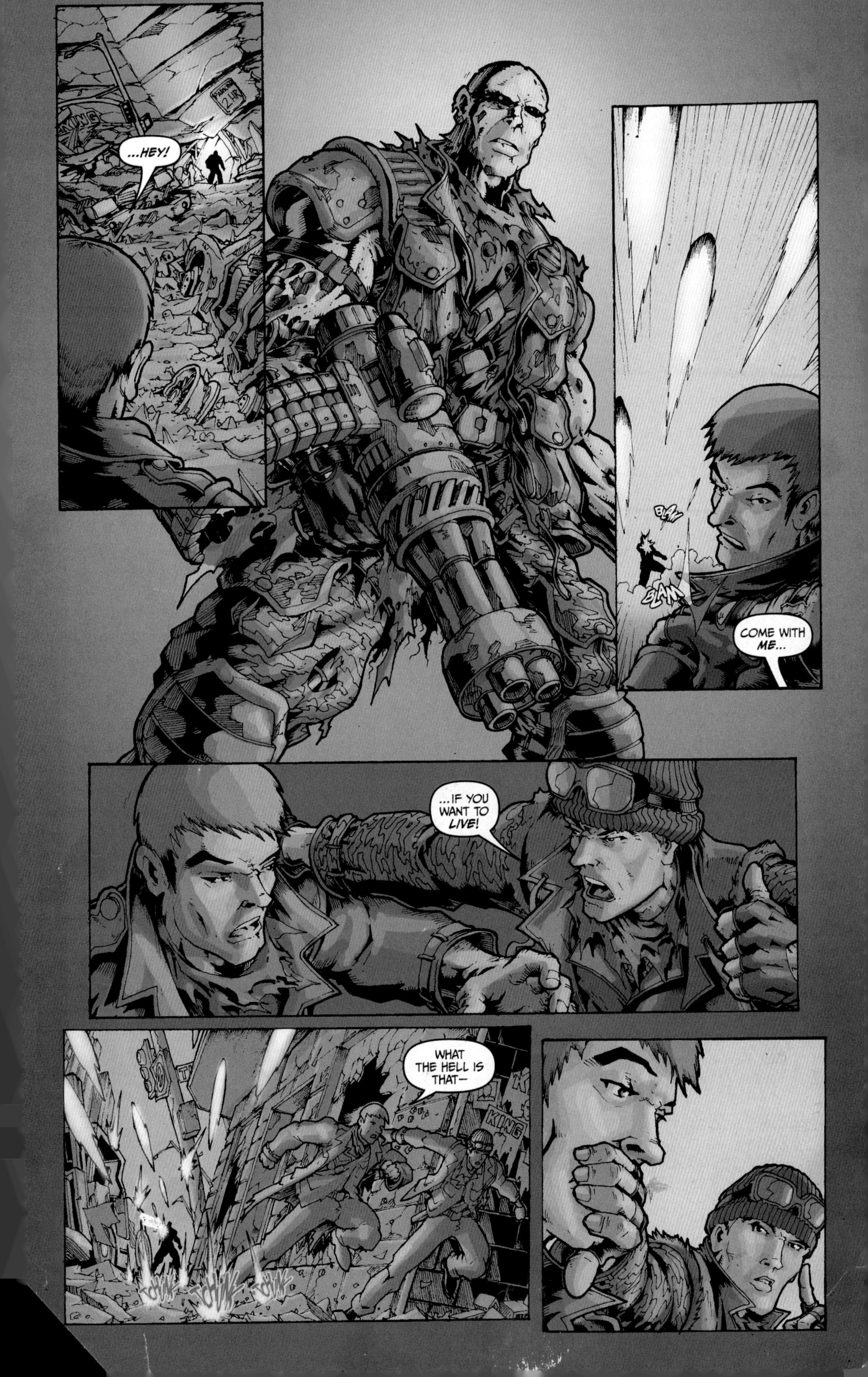
...HEY!
BLAM
BLAM
COME WITH ME...
...IF YOU WANT TO LIVE!
WHAT THE HELL IS THAT—

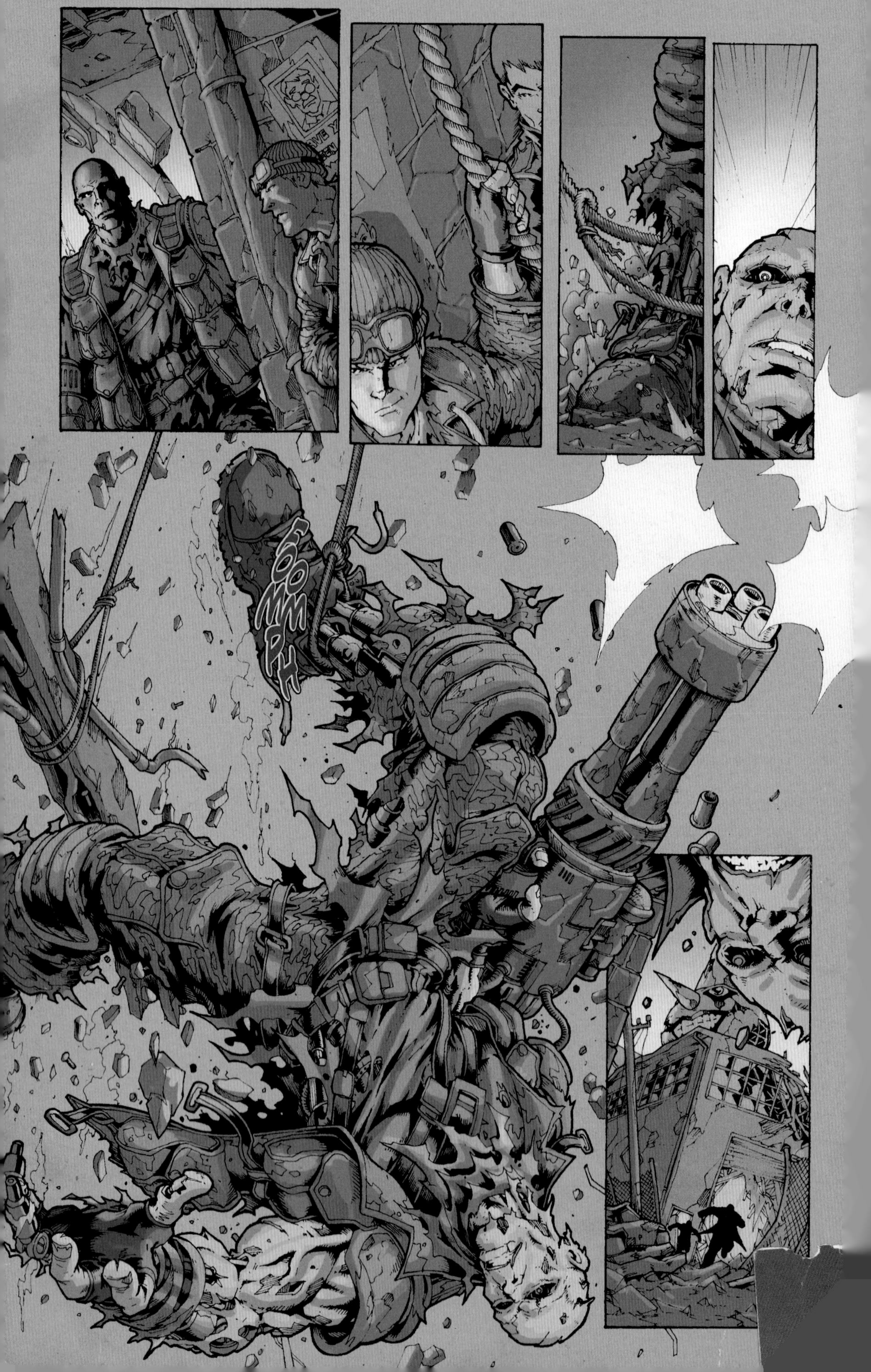
FOOMMPH

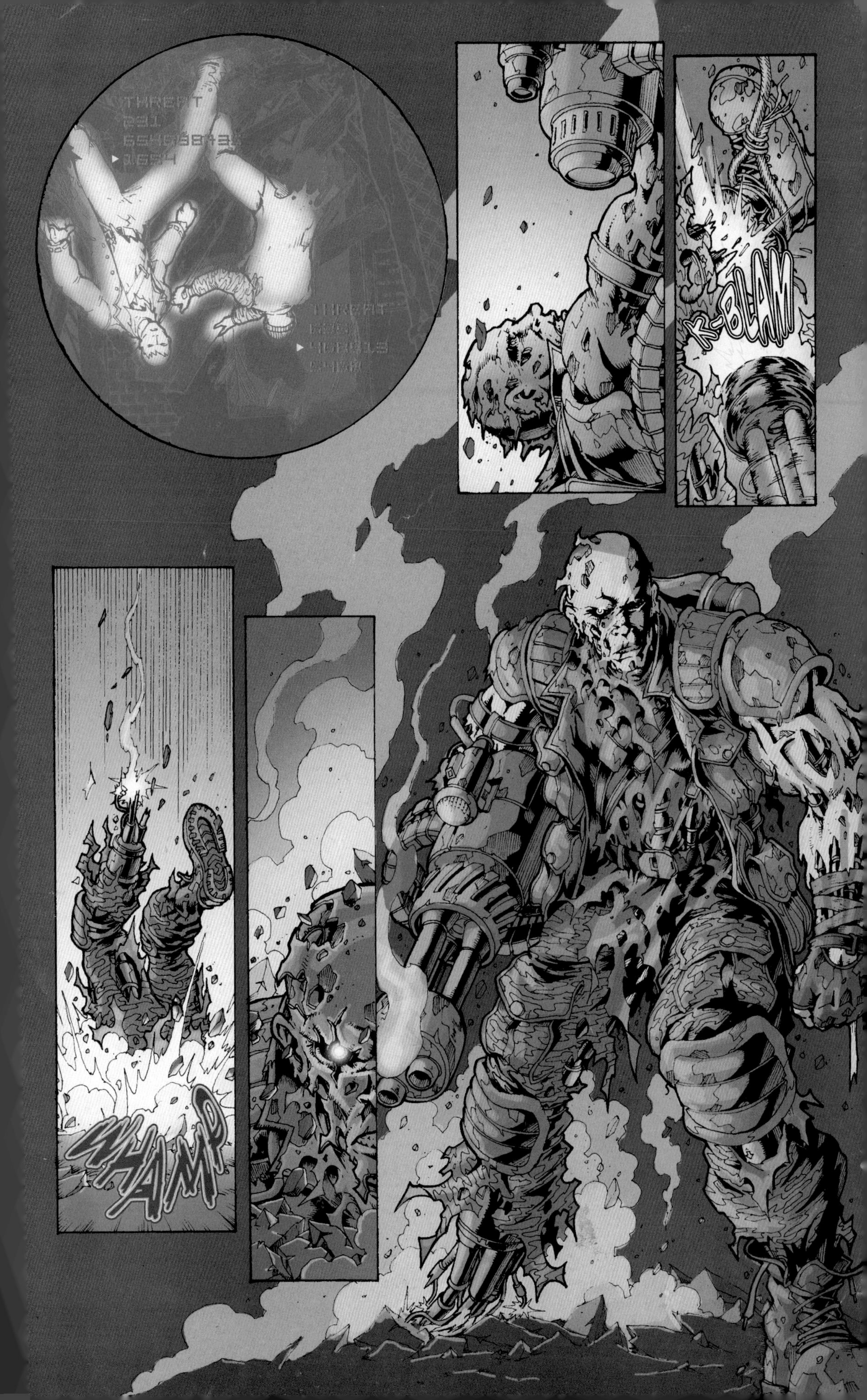
THREAT
THREAT
K-BLAM
WHAMP

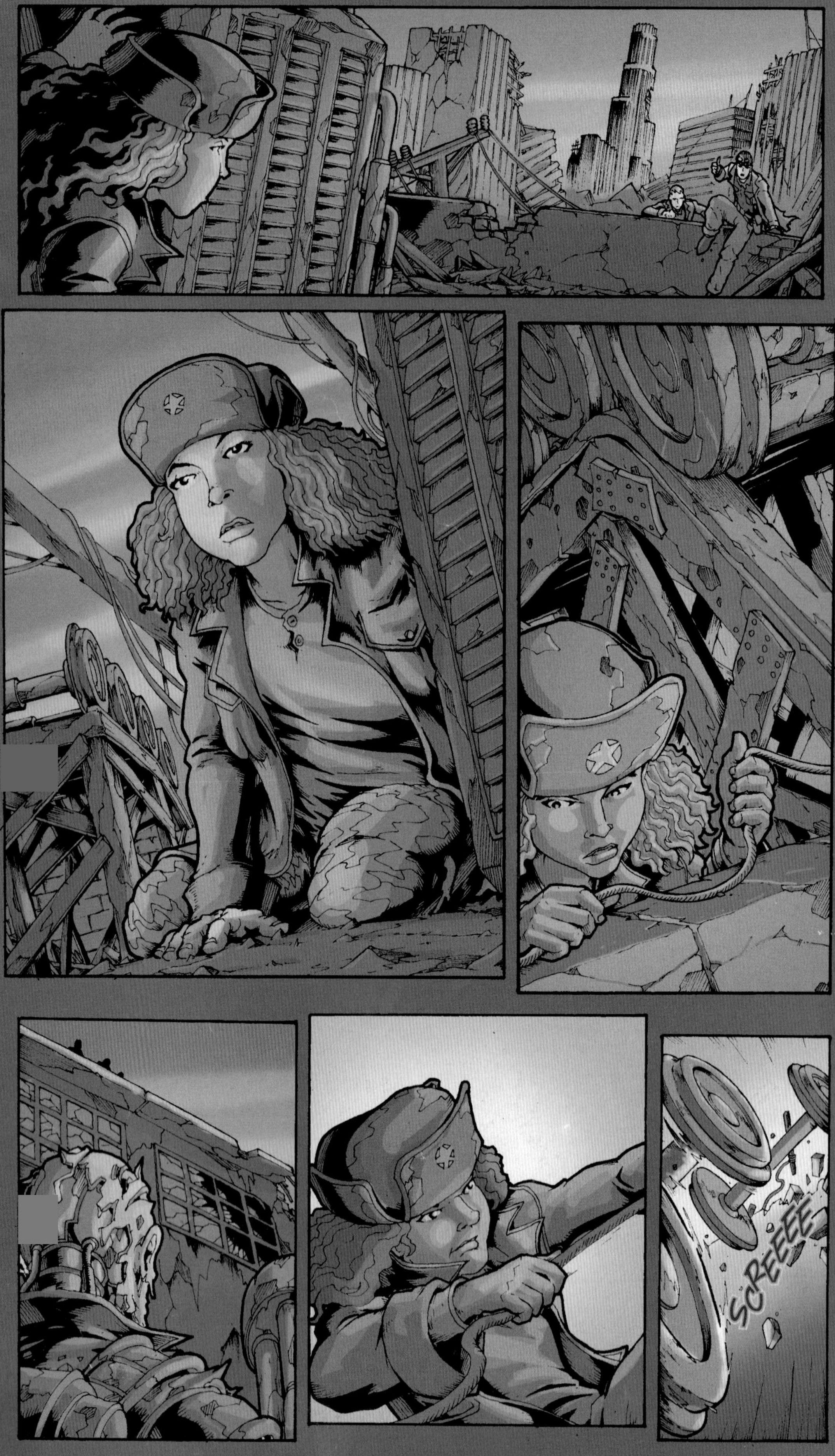
SCREEEE

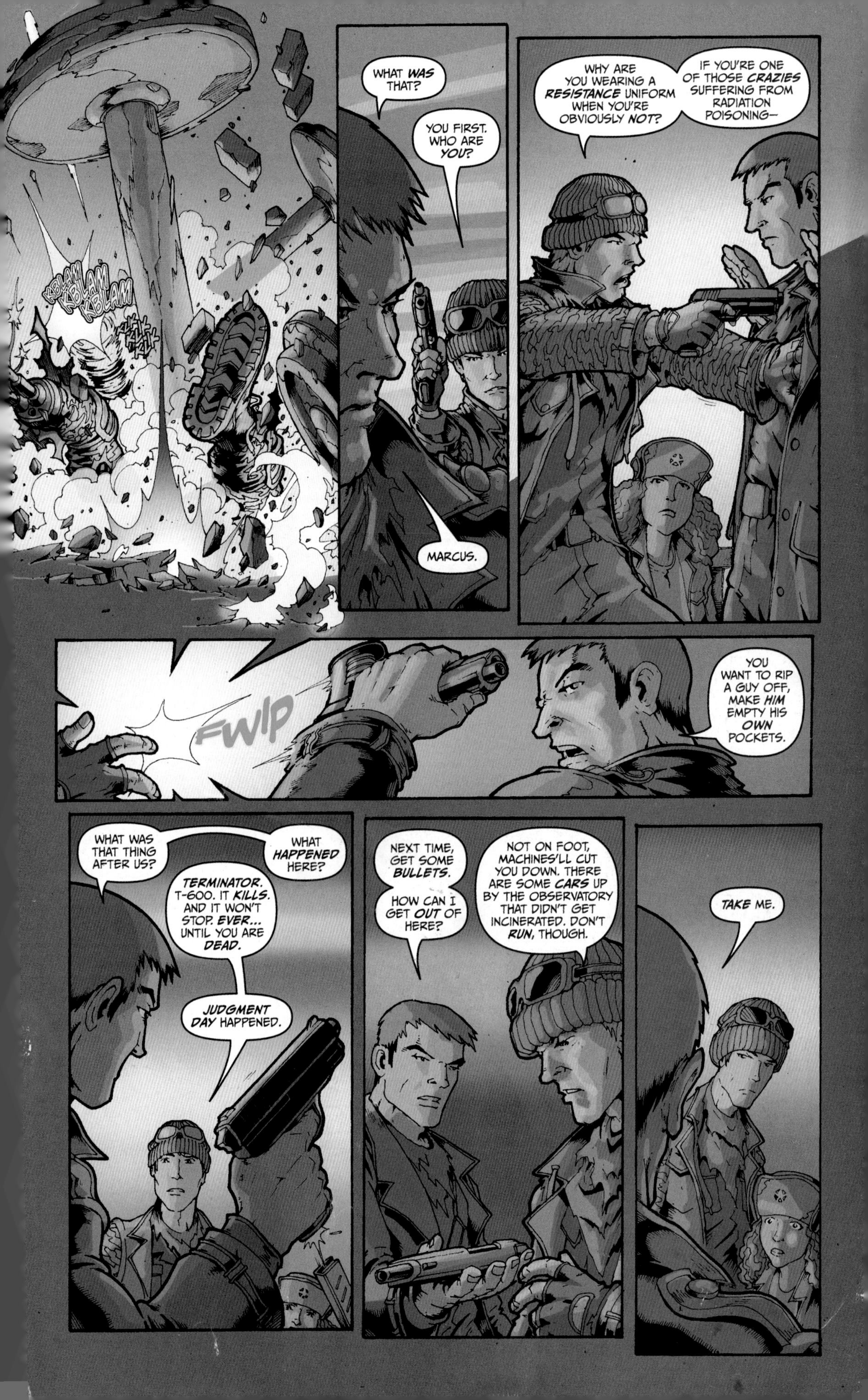

KBLAM KBLAM KBLAM
WHAT WAS THAT?
YOU FIRST. WHO ARE YOU?
MARCUS.
WHY ARE YOU WEARING A RESISTANCE UNIFORM WHEN YOU'RE OBVIOUSLY NOT?
IF YOU'RE ONE OF THOSE CRAZIES SUFFERING FROM RADIATION POISONING—
FWIP
YOU WANT TO RIP A GUY OFF, MAKE HIM EMPTY HIS OWN POCKETS.
WHAT WAS THAT THING AFTER US?
TERMINATOR. T-600. IT KILLS. AND IT WON'T STOP. EVER... UNTIL YOU ARE DEAD.
WHAT HAPPENED HERE?
JUDGMENT DAY HAPPENED.
NEXT TIME, GET SOME BULLETS.
HOW CAN I GET OUT OF HERE?
NOT ON FOOT, MACHINES'LL CUT YOU DOWN. THERE ARE SOME CARS UP BY THE OBSERVATORY THAT DIDN'T GET INCINERATED. DON'T RUN, THOUGH.
TAKE ME.

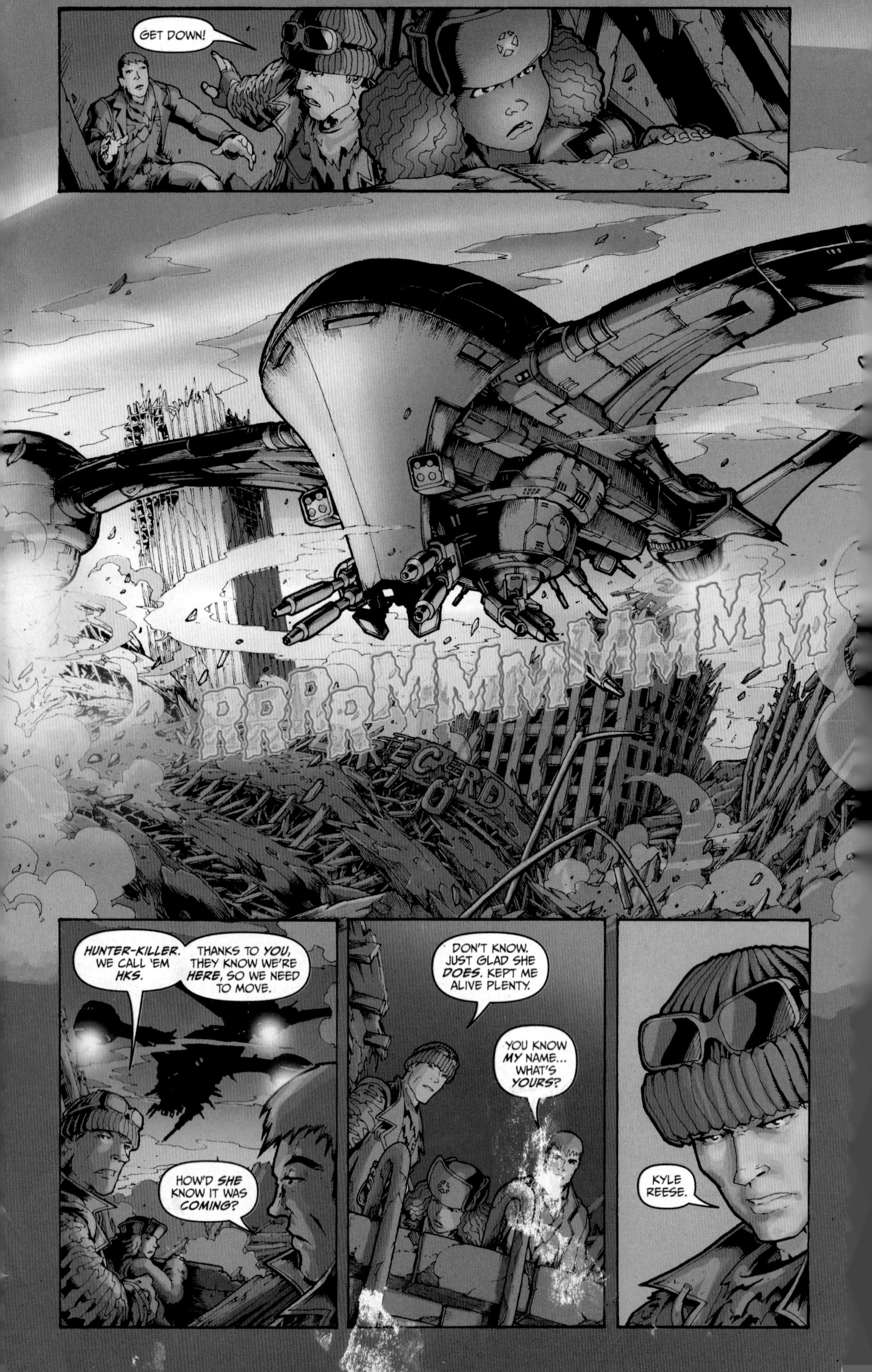
GET DOWN!
RRRRMMMMMMMMM
HUNTER-KILLER. WE CALL 'EM HKS.
THANKS TO YOU, THEY KNOW WE'RE HERE, SO WE NEED TO MOVE.
HOW'D SHE KNOW IT WAS COMING?
DON'T KNOW. JUST GLAD SHE DOES. KEPT ME ALIVE PLENTY.
YOU KNOW MY NAME... WHAT'S YOURS?
KYLE REESE.

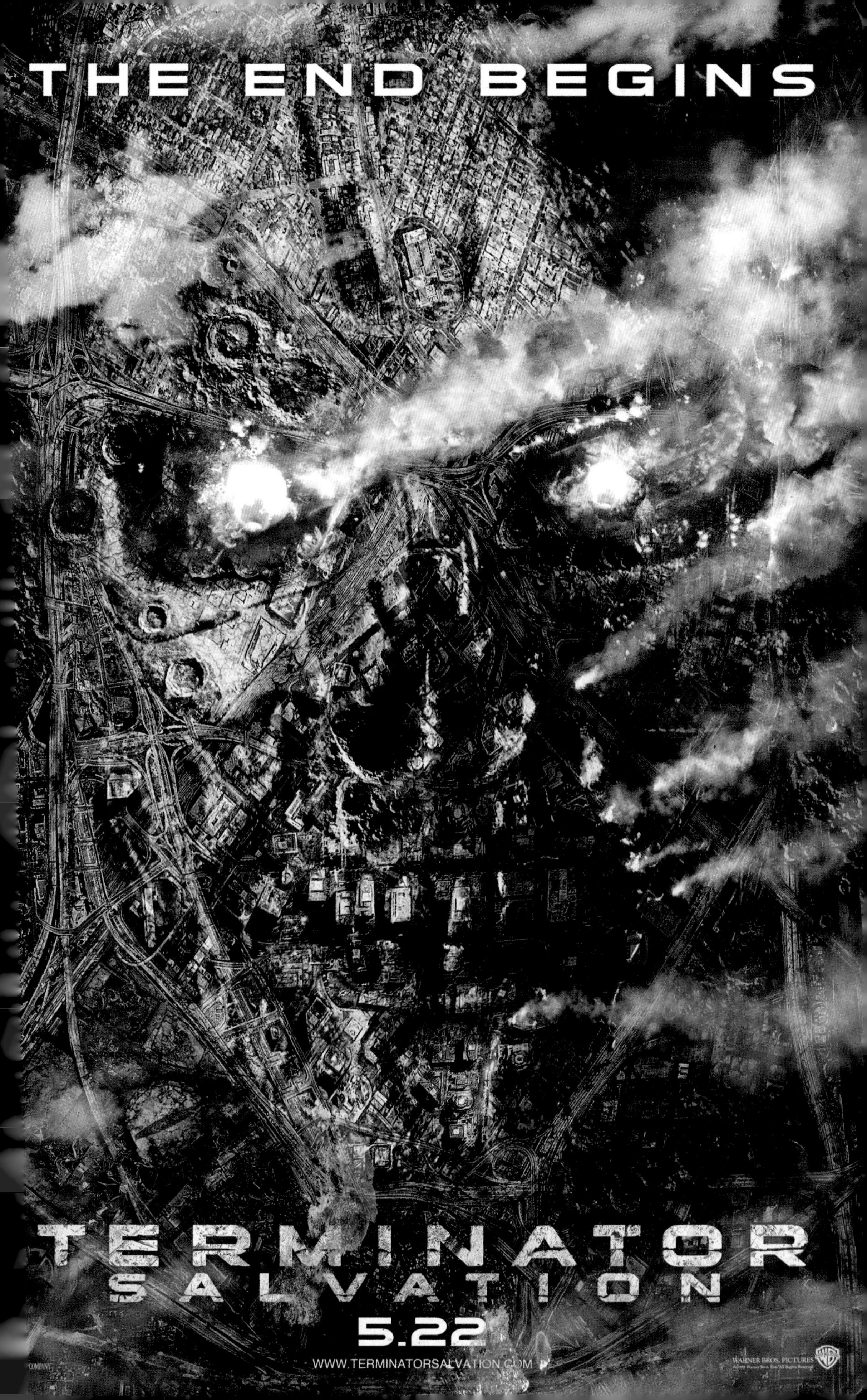
THE END BEGINS
TERMINATOR
SALVATION
5.22
WWW.TERMINATORSALVATION.COM
COMPANY
WARNER BROS. PICTURES

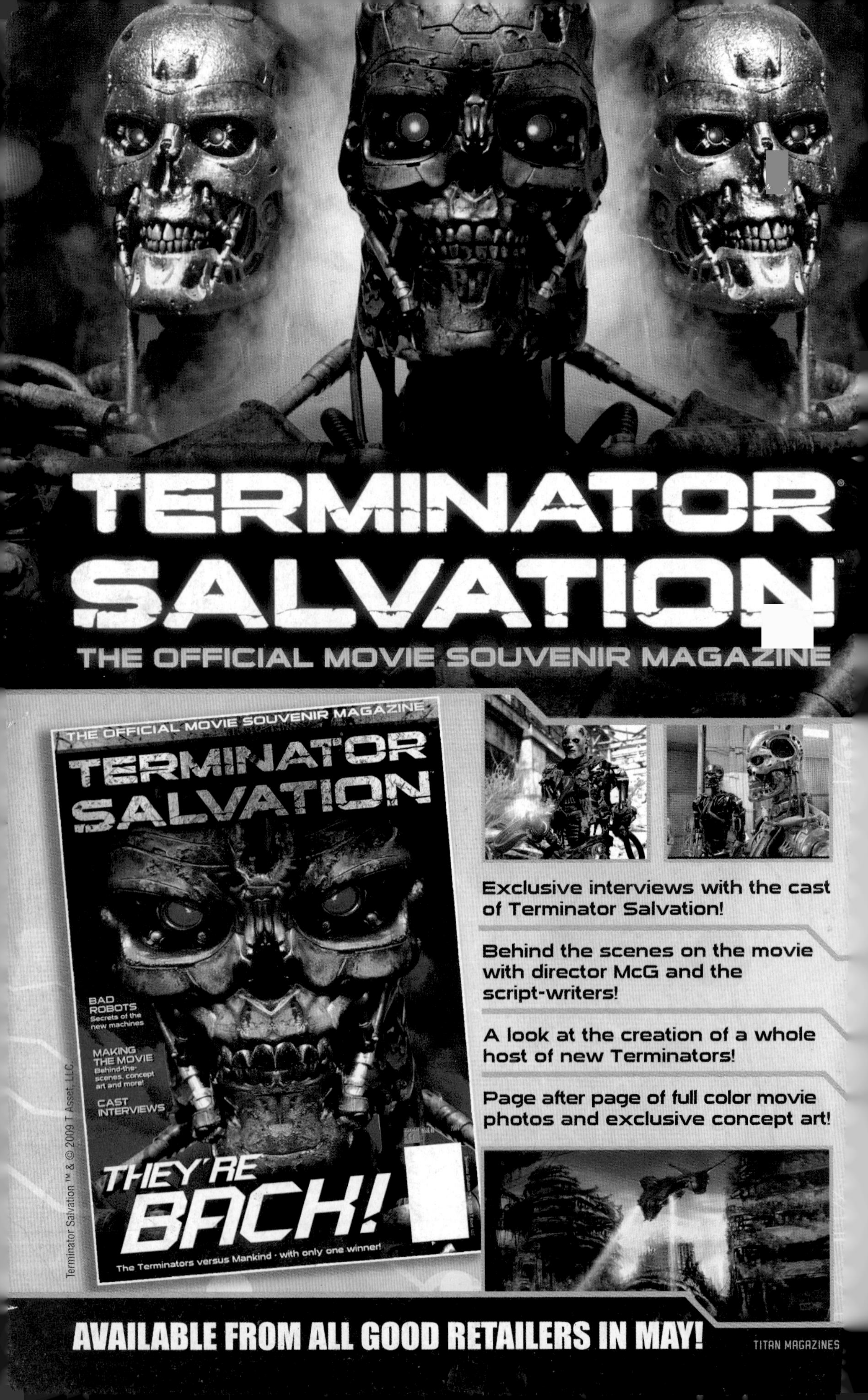
TERMINATOR SALVATION
THE OFFICIAL MOVIE SOUVENIR MAGAZINE
THE OFFICIAL MOVIE SOUVENIR MAGAZINE
TERMINATOR SALVATION
BAD ROBOTS Secrets of the new machines
MAKING THE MOVIE Behind-the-scenes, concept art and more!
CAST INTERVIEWS
THEY'RE BACK!
The Terminators versus Mankind · with only one winner!
Exclusive interviews with the cast of Terminator Salvation!
Behind the scenes on the movie with director McG and the script-writers!
A look at the creation of a whole host of new Terminators!
Page after page of full color movie photos and exclusive concept art!
Terminator Salvation ™ & © 2009 T Asset, LLC.
AVAILABLE FROM ALL GOOD RETAILERS IN MAY!
TITAN MAGAZINES

TERMINATOR SALVATION

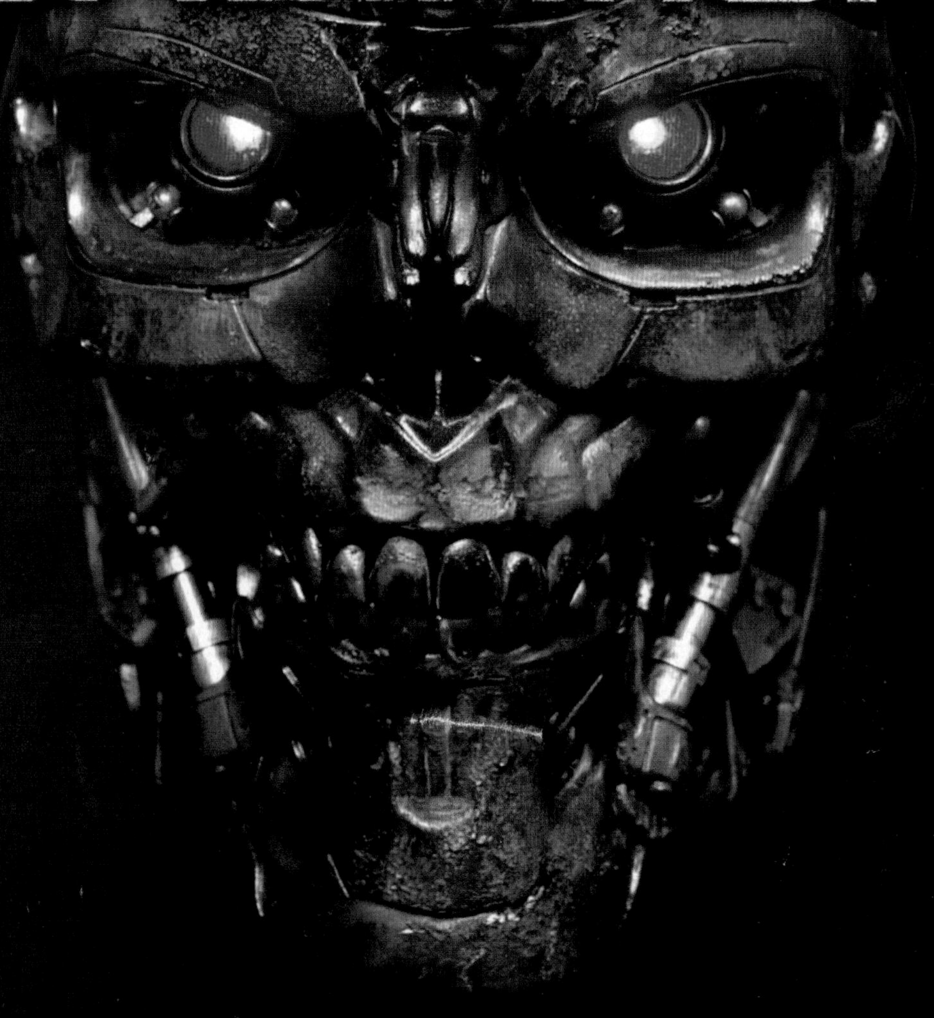

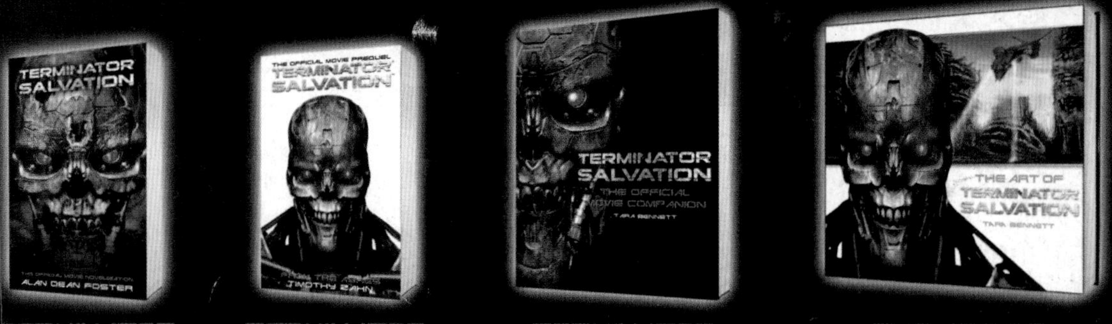
TERMINATOR SALVATION
ALAN DEAN FOSTER
THE OFFICIAL MOVIE PREQUEL
TERMINATOR SALVATION
TIMOTHY ZAHN
TERMINATOR SALVATION
THE OFFICIAL MOVIE COMPANION
TARA BENNETT
THE ART OF
TERMINATOR SALVATION
TARA BENNETT

TERMINATOR SALVATION:
The Official
Movie Novelization
By Alan Dean Foster

TERMINATOR SALVATION:
The Official Movie Prequel -
From The Ashes
By Timothy Zahn

TERMINATOR SALVATION:
The Official
Movie Companion
By Tara Bennett

THE ART OF
TERMINATOR SALVATION
By Tara Bennett

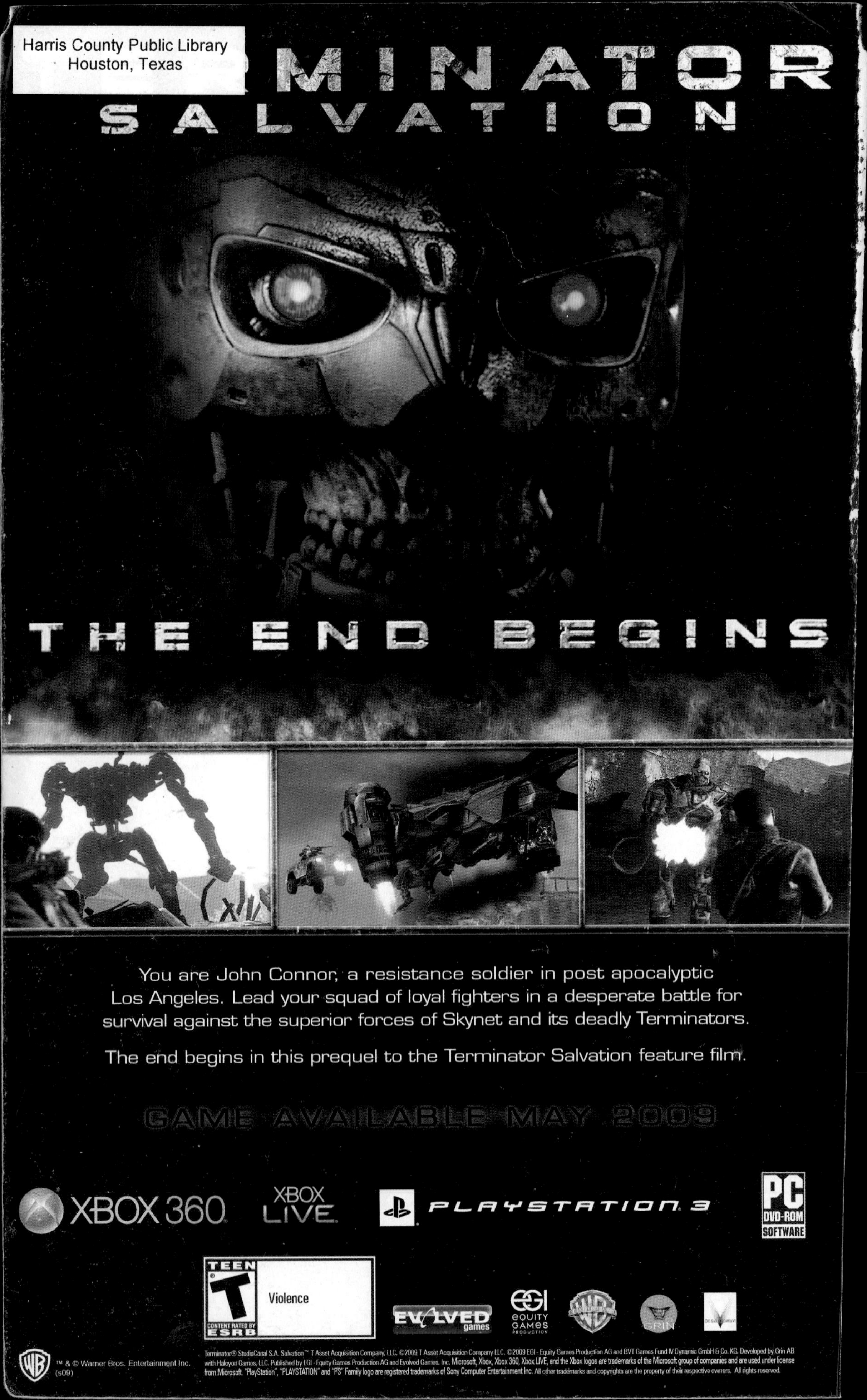
MINATOR
SALVATION
THE END BEGINS
You are John Connor, a resistance soldier in post apocalyptic Los Angeles. Lead your squad of loyal fighters in a desperate battle for survival against the superior forces of Skynet and its deadly Terminators.
The end begins in this prequel to the Terminator Salvation feature film.
GAME AVAILABLE MAY 2009
XBOX 360
XBOX LIVE
PLAYSTATION 3
PC DVD-ROM SOFTWARE
TEEN
T
CONTENT RATED BY ESRB
Violence
EVOLVED games
EGI equity games production
GRIN
TM & © Warner Bros. Entertainment Inc. (s09)
Terminator® StudioCanal S.A. Salvation™ T Asset Acquisition Company, LLC. ©2009 T Asset Acquisition Company LLC. ©2009 EGI - Equity Games Production AG and BVT Games Fund IV Dynamic GmbH & Co. KG. Developed by Grin AB with Halcyon Games, LLC. Published by EGI - Equity Games Production AG and Evolved Games, Inc. Microsoft, Xbox, Xbox 360, Xbox LIVE, and the Xbox logos are trademarks of the Microsoft group of companies and are used under license from Microsoft. "PlayStation", "PLAYSTATION" and "PS" Family logo are registered trademarks of Sony Computer Entertainment Inc. All other trademarks and copyrights are the property of their respective owners. All rights reserved.